A FOREST OF DREAMS

A FOREST OF DREAMS

Capitalism, Conservation, and Indigenous Rights in the Philippines

Noah Theriault

University of Hawaiʻi Press
Honolulu

Printed in the United States of America

First printed, 2025

Library of Congress Cataloging-in-Publication Data

Names: Theriault, Noah, author.
Title: A forest of dreams : capitalism, conservation, and indigenous rights in the Philippines / Noah Theriault.
Description: Honolulu : University of Hawaiʻi Press, 2025. | Includes bibliographical references and index.
Identifiers: LCCN 2024060722 (print) | LCCN 2024060723 (ebook) | ISBN 9780824899509 (hardback) | ISBN 9780824899530 (epub) | ISBN 9780824899547 (kindle edition) | ISBN 9780824899523 (pdf)
Subjects: LCSH: Indigenous peoples—Legal status, laws, etc.—Philippines—History. | Indigenous peoples—Philippines—Politics and government. | Marcos, Ferdinand E. (Ferdinand Edralin), 1917-1989. | Capitalism—Philippines—History.
Classification: LCC KPM519.I64 T44 2025 (print) | LCC KPM519.I64 (ebook) | DDC 342.59908/72—dc23/eng/20250111
LC record available at https://lccn.loc.gov/2024060722
LC ebook record available at https://lccn.loc.gov/2024060723

Cover art: Hypercolor view of forested mountainsides of the Mantalingahan range in southern Palawan, April 2011. Source: Noah Theriault.

University of Hawaiʻi Press books are printed on acid-free paper and meet the guidelines for permanence and durability of the Council on Library Resources.

To Danielle and Luna, my loves, my life.

Contents

Acknowledgments ix

Abbreviations xiii

Introduction 1

Chapter One
Colonial Sorcery 21

Chapter Two
Producing and Consuming the "Last Frontier" 44

Chapter Three
Civets, Saplings, and Sweating Rocks 79

Chapter Four
Forest Dreams, Conservation Fantasies 107

Chapter Five
Indigenous Rights in the Orbit of Capital 133

Conclusion 156

Notes 163

Bibliography 189

Index 211

Acknowledgments

The research leading to this book unfolded over the better part of two decades. Along the way, I accumulated many debts of gratitude. First and foremost come my hosts in southern Palawan, who were incredibly generous with their time and insight. I am eternally grateful to Ama Jimi, his immediate family, and the rest of their *rurungan*, who welcomed me into their homes, kept me safe, and vouched for me. I cannot use these individuals' real names, so it must suffice to say that this book owes its existence to their care and curiosity. *Sampulong selamat banar dimuyu ginsan.*

Elsewhere in Palawan, my elders and peers have humbled me time and again with their openness and hospitality. Despite being thousands of miles away, James Eder was a constant source of support during my early days on the island. His research inspired me to go there, and his local kindred were my first contacts. Among them, Oscar and Susan Evangelista were constant sources of guidance and friendship from the moment I arrived. Through the Evangelistas, I met three supportive colleagues who became lifelong *kabarkada*: Carinnes Alejandria, Rhodel Magrata, and Ralph Pulanco. I join them in loving memory of Doc Oca, whose legacy of kindness lives on in these pages.

Palawan's dedicated community of advocates, organizers, journalists, and activists opened their offices and even their homes to me. Some of them have returned to Manila or moved abroad, but all of them continue to inspire my work. *Maraming, maraming salamat po kila* Norlita Colili, Victor Colili, Mercedes Limsa, Dionesia Banwa, Cleofe Pablo, Elizabeth Maclang, Dayang Galit, Jayjay Pamfilo, Robert Chan, Lorie Cagatulla, Ofelia Lizardo, Cristina Guerrero, Grizelda Mayo-Anda, Redempto Anda, Edward Lorenzo, Yasmin Arquiza, and Jeanne Tabangay. I have also been grateful for help from personnel at the Southern Palawan Planning Council; mayors, barangay captains, and councilors throughout southern Palawan, especially Nelson Dupo in Punta Baja; and the Protected Area Management Board of the Mount Mantalingahan Protected Landscape, especially the former superintendent, Clarissa Pador. Palaweños Lourdes Bediores, Alvin Aurelio, and Eden Aurelio provided vital assistance with language training, transcription, and encoding.

Several Philippine universities hosted me at various times during the research for this book. My thanks go to the Cebuano Studies Center at San Carlos University, the Palawan Studies Center at Palawan State University, and the Institute of Philippine Culture at Ateneo de Manila University.

At Carnegie Mellon University, my colleagues in the History Department have patiently and generously supported my work. My heartfelt thanks go to Paul Eiss, Ema Grama, John Soluri, Benno Weiner, Chris Phillips, Judith Schachter, Nico Slate, Allyson Creasman, Lisa Tetrault, Scott Sandage, Abigail Owen, Arko Dasgupta, and Ezelle Sanford III. Colleagues from other CMU departments and other universities in Pittsburgh have also welcomed me into their intellectual community. Many thanks to John Walsh, Emily Wanderer, Tomas Matza, Nicole Heller, Paper Buck, Nida Rehman, Ruth Mostern, Michael Goodhart, Alexa Woloshyn, Molly Warsh, Philipp Stelzel, Esther Kang, Maddie Sides, Hajira Qazi, Sobia Ahmad, Kyla Fullenwider, Hillary Carey, Donna Maione, Erica Dorn, Jonathan Chapman, Terry Irwin, Gideon Kossof, and Sarah Fox.

Some of my dearest collaborators are spread around the world, but connected by a common commitment to supporting Indigenous resistance and resurgence. In 2016, Audra Mitchell invited me to participate in a workshop she was organizing. There and in several gatherings after, I got to know thinkers who have transformed how I approach my own lifework: June Rubis, Sarah Wright, Lara Daley, Zoe Todd, Sandie Suchet-Pearson, Kate Lloyd, Timothy Leduc, Aunty Shaa Smith, Uncle Bud Marshall, Paul Hodge, Lorene Sisquoc, Cindi Alvitre, Michelle Bishop, Lauren Tynan, Corina Norman, Jo Rey, Gena Edwards, and members of the Bawaka and Yandaarra collectives. Thank you, Audra, for the term "lifework" and for being such an amazing colleague, friend, and accomplice.

At the University of Oklahoma, I learned about exceptional collegiality from Erika Robb Larkins, Miriam Gross, Afshin Marashi, Kathleen Kelly, Andreana Prichard, Dan Mains, Manata Hashemi, Emily Rook-Koepsel, Eric Heinze, Sherri Irvin, Lupe Davidson, Michele Eodice, Zev Trachtenberg, and Jessica Pearson. Some of them read parts of this book; all of them helped sustain its writing.

During my doctoral training at the University of Wisconsin, Madison, Katherine Bowie and Paul Nadasdy were steadfast sources of intellectual guidance, moral support, and practical advice. For their mentorship, my thanks go to Kenneth George, Larry Nesper, Michael Cullinane, Maria Lepowsky, Ian Baird, Kirin Narayan, Claire Wendland, Maureen Justiniano, Sheila Zamar, and Alfred McCoy. Finally, I was blessed with amazing peer mentors, now colleagues and friends: Dolma Roder, Sambo Dul, Aloysius Cañete, Alberto Perez-Pereiro, Alex Nading, Sarah Besky, Jason Hopper, Hsiao-Ling Su, Prakirati Satasut, Boonlert

Visetpreecha, Supaluck Pornkulwat, Katie Lindstrom, Ruth de Llobet, Alison Carter, Chelsea Chapman, Zach Throckmorton, and Lisa Jackson.

Senior scholars in Palawan studies have always been remarkably supportive of my work. In addition to Jim Eder, I want to acknowledge Wolfram Dressler, Charles Macdonald, Rebecca Austin, Dario Novellino, Koki Seki, Eufemia Pinto, and Melanie McDermott, who have all been generous with their time and insight. Will Smith and Sarah Webb get special mention for the extraordinary moral support they offered during fieldwork. In the broader field of Philippine studies, I owe much of my intellectual growth to dialogue with Paul Michael Leonardo Atienza, Oona Paredes, Alyssa Paredes, Rosa Cordillera Castillo, Kristian Saguin, Kathleen Gutierrez, Thea Quiray Tagle, and Allan Lumba.

Major grants for my research came from the Social Science Research Council's International Dissertation Research Fellowship, with funds provided by the Andrew W. Mellon Foundation, and a Doctoral Dissertation Improvement Grant from the National Science Foundation (SES 1023901). I received funding from the University of Wisconsin's Center for Southeast Asian Studies, the Scott Kloeck-Jenson Fellowship, the University of Oklahoma, and Carnegie Mellon University. Parts of chapter 4 originally appeared in "A Forest of Dreams: Ontological Multiplicity and the Fantasies of Environmental Government in the Philippines," *Political Geography* 58 (2017): 114–127. Some material in chapter 5 is reprinted with permission from "Unravelling the Strings Attached: Philippine Indigeneity in Law and Practice," *Journal of Southeast Asian Studies* 50, no. 1 (2019): 107–128. At University of Hawai'i Press, Masako Ikeda and her team brought remarkable clarity and collegiality to their support of this project. I am eternally grateful for the opportunity to publish with them.

Last but certainly not least, I would be lost without the support of my kin, both given and chosen. Ehsan and Simi share my intellectual curiosity, yet keep me grounded. My parents have always encouraged me, even when my career choices surprised them; my sister, Liz, has been a lifeline more times than I can count; and my cousins, Margaux and DD, have shown me what true resilience looks like. Finally, Danielle and Luna, words cannot express how incredibly grateful I am for our life together. Thank you, Danielle, for supporting me every step of the way. Thank you, Luna, for bringing such joy to our family. I love you both so much.

Abbreviations

ADECOR	Aguinaldo Development Corporation
ALDAW	Ancestral Land/Domain Watch
CI	Conservation International
DENR	Department of Environment and Natural Resources
IPRA	Indigenous Peoples Rights Act (1997)
NATRIPAL	Nagkakaisang mga Tribu ng Palawan (United Tribes of Palawan)
NCIP	National Commission on Indigenous People
NGO	nongovernmental organization
NIPAS	National Integrated Protected Areas System
NTFP	non-timber forest product
PANAMIN	Office of the Presidential Assistant on National Minorities
PCSD	Palawan Council for Sustainable Development
SEP	Strategic Environmental Plan for Palawan (Republic Act 7611, 1992)
USAID	United States Agency for International Development
WesPal	Western Palawan Timber

Introduction

"Are there Palawan in America?" The first time a Palawan person asked me this question, I was not sure how seriously to take it. Not long before, an older man named Dison had asked me a different question about America:[1] "Where's the crossing to America?"[2] He was referring to the various crossroads along the highway in the lowland—in effect, which exit does one take to get to America? Before I could decide how to answer, other participants in our conversation snorted and then, unable to control themselves, erupted into raucous laughter. Dison smirked, never letting on whether he had been serious or kidding. Afterward, the question became an inside joke, with variations like "Which of these paths goes to America?" and "Which of those mountains is America?"

That's why, when I was asked about Palawan in America, I expected everyone to start laughing with (or at) the person who asked. But no one did. Everyone stayed quiet in the way they did when I was being "interviewed" by a curious group. I hesitated, unsure how to respond. No, I thought, there were no Palawan in America, at least none that I was aware of. But such a literal answer did not seem appropriate. Instead, I asked Palaya, the female head of the family I was living with, what exactly she meant with this question. She explained, in effect, "you know, Indigenous people like us—poor, belittled swiddeners who live in the mountains?"[3]

"Oh," I said, "well, yes, there are Indigenous people in America," and then tried to explain the European invasion and colonization of North America.[4] Palaya and her co-wife, Jiha, exchanged a knowing glance. Someone mumbled "*keingasi,*" a Palawan expression of sympathy or compassion. Then we all sat silently for a moment. "So," Palaya ruminated, "they're like us," now addressing others in the group. "But do they speak English?" someone asked. "They do?! Well, then they're civilized now [*sibilais ne*], also like us."[5]

This was not the only time I was asked about Palawan in America. Each time my response would prompt generative dialogue. "So they were treated like serfs [*alipin*]? We too are treated like serfs." "Are they allowed to farm and hunt, or is their land 'protected'?" I sat awkwardly with my position in these conversations—a white citizen of a settler-colonial empire that had once colonized the very land on which we stood. More than that, these conversations helped me understand how my Palawan hosts saw themselves in relation to others.[6] Unlike Indigenous activists in the provincial capital, the rural Palawan men and women who asked me such questions were not self-consciously invoking indigeneity as a transnational identity and movement. Their question was a hypothesis about their own position in world history. We must not, they posited, be the only people on earth who face the loss of our land and the transformation of our lifeways at the hands of foreign powers. Where wealth and power concentrate along ethnic or racial lines, there is bound to be a history of occupation and dispossession. This is an insight they have gained through many generations of dealing with the expansionary designs of "state-bearing peoples."[7]

Even if they were mostly unaware of the transnational Indigenous movement, Palaya and her neighbors were engaging critically with the concept of indigeneity. Indigeneity has long been an important distinction in colonial contexts, especially those that have been invaded and settled by large numbers of Europeans. Over the past four decades, Indigenous peoples and their advocates have formed a global movement for Indigenous rights.[8] They have challenged centuries of subjugation, demanding recognition of their territories, cosmologies, and sociopolitical institutions. Their efforts have had a profound effect. A growing number of states and the United Nations have enacted policies that explicitly attempt to redress the marginalization of Indigenous people. What's more, these developments have not been limited to settler-colonial societies like Canada or Australia, or even to the former Iberian colonies of Latin America. Indigenous movements in Europe, Asia, and Africa have also led this charge, none more so than those in the Philippines.[9]

The Paradox of Indigeneity

After the fall of Ferdinand Marcos's dictatorship in 1986, the Philippines became the first country in Asia to institutionalize Indigenous rights. This hard-fought reform aimed to protect the human rights and ancestral lands of the archipelago's remaining Indigenous groups. Since then, however, these groups have become increasingly embroiled in resource politics, and many have found that claiming their rights does as much to facilitate their dispossession as to prevent it.[10] As a result, Indigenous peoples in the contemporary Philippines face a dilemma. To assert their land rights, they must invite closer scrutiny from the institutions that have long marginalized them. In the process, they bring their lands and livelihoods further into the regulatory orbit not just of government officials but also of conservationists, investors, settlers, and others with an interest in exploiting their land and labor.

A Forest of Dreams examines how these developments have unfolded on Palawan, an island in the far southwestern Philippines. Recognized by UNESCO as a Biosphere Reserve, Palawan is the ancestral territory of three ethnolinguistically distinct Indigenous populations and the habitat for some of the highest concentrations of endemic species in the world. It's also where large tracts of old-growth forest survived intact through the latter part of the twentieth century, even as those in most of the rest of the country were degraded or cleared. Recent decades have seen Palawan's forests decline rapidly as settlers from other islands have arrived in large numbers, industrial monocrop plantations have spread, and loggers have pushed farther into the interior.[11] Meanwhile, countless Filipino and foreign conservationists have come aspiring to "save the last frontier" by establishing conservation enclosures and promoting "sustainable" livelihoods. All of these pressures are felt acutely by Palawan's Indigenous peoples, including those in the southern part of the island, whose experiences are the focus of this book. Numbering around 50,000, Palawan people share their demonym with the island itself—it is their ancestral land, its forests are a product of their way of life, and its transformation is the source of the profound dilemmas they face.[12]

Rather than theorizing these dilemmas as a hopeless double bind, I invite readers to join me in considering how a range of people navigate and contest them in their everyday lives.[13] We will hear from bureaucrats, investors, and conservationists who impose their own designs on Indigenous rights as they vie for land, labor, and legitimacy. But we will also see how those designs collide with the dreams—both figurative and literal—of Indigenous people themselves. This is a microhistory of socioecological change, in which humans, wildlife, and powerful forest beings complicate what often seems like an inevitable process of dispossession and assimilation.[14] Rather than an all-or-nothing force of domination or resistance, the recognition of Indigenous rights turns out to be a paradox—at once a tool of neocolonial rule and a catalyst for everyday encounters that challenge it.[15]

At the heart of this book is a particular Palawan community, which I call Tenga't Gebaq. Tenga't Gebaq was my home base for a series of visits between 2010 and 2018. I chose this community because of Jimi, whom I introduce below. But he wasn't the only reason. What made Tenga't Gebaq such an interesting place for me—and for Jimi—was its location in the overlapping boundaries of a recognized ancestral domain, a biodiversity protection area, and an encroaching hellscape of monocrop plantations. As Anna Tsing put it, "This is the salvage frontier, where making, saving, and destroying resources are utterly mixed up, where zones of conservation, production, and resource sacrifice overlap almost fully."[16] Although Tsing was referring to Kalimantan, her words speak to conditions in Palawan as well. *A Forest of Dreams* is my attempt to convey what I learned from engaging with residents of Tenga't Gebaq as they experienced, analyzed, and sometimes confronted these conditions in their everyday lives.

Scholars and activists have long highlighted the critical agency that Indigenous peoples bring to their encounters with states, corporations, and other powerful

Map 1. Palawan Island, showing the location of the Malambunga River watershed, the primary site of research.

actors.[17] Yet when it comes to the recognition of indigeneity in Asia, many academic accounts remain deeply skeptical and pessimistic.[18] Such assessments are entirely reasonable, but they risk dismissing Asian indigeneities as effects of governmentality and imperialism. What I propose is not optimism, which, as Lauren Berlant has argued, can be cruel and self-defeating.[19] Rather, it is close attention to the critical acumen of those who, for better and worse, face the paradox of indigeneity in their everyday lives. While it is true that a range of vested interests instrumentalize indigeneity in service to their agendas, let us also hold intellectual space for forms of Indigenous endurance that persist amid—and despite—the forces seeking to contain them.

The Global Context

At first glance, the Philippines' embrace of Indigenous rights may seem like something of an anomaly. Although the archipelago was a colony, first of Spain and then of the United States, for more than 350 years, it never became a destination for large numbers of settlers. There was no racialized settler/aboriginal dichotomy to serve as a basis for determining who was Indigenous and who was not. Nevertheless, Philippine indigeneity has its roots in colonial history—a legacy of how successive colonial authorities divided and ruled the native population.[20] *A Forest of Dreams* explores how this "transimperial" history laid the groundwork for the paradox of Indigenous rights as it exists today.[21] Throughout the book, I also aim to connect the intricacies of the Philippine case to historical and contemporary processes unfolding at the global scale. In particular, I call attention to the collision of three global trends.

Since the 1980s, the global winds of social solidarity have not favored movements conceived in terms of class struggle. Deindustrialization in the West, the decline of the Soviet bloc, and the rise of neoliberalism weakened the political valence of worker solidarity in favor of movements for recognition, self-determination, and sovereignty.[22] In this climate, long-standing struggles for the rights of minoritized groups, including Indigenous peoples, gained visibility and momentum.[23] Meanwhile, governments were increasingly inclined to recognize rights based on claims of cultural difference rather than shared socioeconomic interests.[24] In many countries, including the Philippines, this policy shift has sought partly to discourage the participation of peasants and Indigenous peoples in radical, class-based movements.[25] Those who are willing to forgo class-based organization are promised self-determination, whereas those accused of supporting radical leftist movements are collectively punished.[26]

Another important part of this global story is the financialization of capitalism. With the advent of postindustrialism and the consolidation of large multinational corporations, capitalist interests encountered a dilemma: "what to do with the vast surpluses at their disposal in the face of a dearth of investment opportunities."[27] The answer was to create "new financial instruments: futures, options, derivatives, hedge funds, etc."[28] These instruments do not simply move money around within financial institutions. Among other things, they have led to a frenzy of speculative investments in "frontiers" like Palawan. Betting on future demand for "rare earth" minerals, agricultural commodities, and environmental offsets, investors have flooded capital into financing for the expansion of mining, monocrop plantations, and conservation enclosures.[29] Including conservation on this list may seem counterintuitive. But remember that many conservation enclosures are established by international organizations, such as Conservation International, with funding from corporations and development agencies. In a financialized global economy, one way investors can generate shareholder value is by "reserving," "sequestering," or "securitizing" land in the name of biodiversity and carbon offsets.[30] That these projects often appear at odds with other extractive industries belies their common political-economic underpinnings. As a result, financialization has favored the co-optation of Indigenous rights as a means of legitimizing development and conservation projects on Indigenous peoples' lands.[31] By securing "free and prior informed consent" in the name of Indigenous rights, investors can present an extractive project as a mutually beneficial, even altruistic "partnership."[32]

Last but not least, we come to the global rise (and fall) of neoliberalism. Neoliberalism refers to an economic and political philosophy that calls for "rolling back" the state's governing capacities and "rolling out" those of the market.[33] Proponents of neoliberalism believe the latter to be more efficient and effective, especially when it comes to the use of labor and resources. Not coincidentally, the rollout of neoliberal reforms has favored the embrace of "participatory" approaches to development among financial institutions, governments, and nongovernmental organizations (NGOs).[34] The goal is to incentivize people to take responsibility for the outcome of projects in which they have a "stake." This approach has also taken root in the arena of environmental regulation and conservation, where local "stakeholders" are frequently called on to participate in project planning and implementation.[35] In the Philippines, post-1986 reforms have mandated participation by a range of sectors—students, women, farmers, fishers, Indigenous people—in all development or conservation activities that affect them.[36]

For example, when an Indigenous group seeks legal recognition of their ancestral territory, they must demonstrate their ability to manage its resources and maintain its "ecological balance."[37] In practice, this means agreeing to a vision of development and conservation that devalues their independent sources of livelihood, such as swidden farming, and encourages their reliance on market-oriented practices, such as ecotourism.[38] Without a commensurate transfer of resources or authority, the neoliberal approach to Indigenous rights becomes an extractive demand on labor, land, and knowledge rather than a guarantee of rights. This is what Wendy Brown calls the "alchemy" of neoliberal political culture, which transforms the promise of democratic rights into bureaucratic rituals of consultation and participation.[39] These rituals claim to engender empowerment, but instead augment capitalist systems of governance and production.

Together these global trends—multiculturalism, financialization, and neoliberalism—favor the co-optation of indigeneity while diminishing the radical potential of long-standing, intersectional struggles for Indigenous rights. Mark Goodale refers to this effect as "'dark matter': the ineluctable, constant, and veiled presence of trans-national (primarily extractive) capital working not against, but with, policies of indigenous rights."[40] This is a reality in Palawan, but it's not the whole story.

The Regional Context

Alongside the "dark matter" that co-opts indigeneity in service to capitalist interests, a host of other factors shape and complicate the implementation of Indigenous rights in the Philippines. Based on principles in the 1987 constitution, the Indigenous Peoples' Rights Act of 1997 (IPRA) defines Indigenous peoples as culturally distinctive and "homogenous."[41] It also assigns to them a number of "responsibilities" that can undermine the rights the law is meant to protect. As noted, Indigenous groups are expected to "maintain an ecological balance" in their ancestral domains "by protecting the flora and fauna, watershed areas, and other reserves." More specifically, in ancestral domains that the government deems "necessary for critical watersheds, mangroves, wildlife sanctuaries, wilderness, protected areas, forest cover, or reforestation," Indigenous people "shall be given the responsibility to maintain, develop, protect and conserve such areas with the full and effective assistance of government agencies." To reconcile these requirements with the right to self-determination and development, one must assume (as IPRA's authors evidently did) that Indigenous peoples are naturally inclined to do the work of ecological balance and environmental conservation. This "eco-indigenism" creates expectations that Indigenous people sometimes find very difficult to live up to—for example, when those who support or oppose particular conservation or development projects find their authenticity challenged.[42]

Despite such risks, Indigenous groups in Palawan and elsewhere have filed hundreds of applications for recognition of their ancestral domains. In turn, they have learned that the application process is laborious, expensive, and technically complex, requiring hundreds of pages of documentation.[43] Not only must applicants prove they meet the criteria for recognition—by producing maps, ethnographic narratives, kinship diagrams, and oral histories—they must also prepare an ancestral domain management plan that inventories local resources and establishes guidelines for their stewardship. In virtually all cases, this requires the technical assistance of NGOs and government experts and financial support from foreign or domestic funders. Even for groups who do manage to register their ancestral domains, the resulting documents are no panacea. They do not abrogate preexisting claims held by migrant settlers in the domain. Nor can any document simply undo the long-standing structural inequalities that drive dispossession and lead Indigenous groups to sell their lands or enter exploitative contracts.

For example, registering an ancestral domain is supposed to guarantee priority access to permits for non-timber forest products (NTFPs). Advocates have envisioned Indigenous control of local NTFP markets as a crucial step toward long-term tenurial security and sustainable development.[44] However, because few Indigenous people can afford permitting and other start-up costs, financiers have used capital advances and resulting cycles of debt to convert ancestral domains into de facto private concessions (see chapter 5). As Melanie Hughes McDermott foresaw more than twenty years ago, the rush to establish the discrete territorial boundaries of ancestral domains overlooks the "pathways" of patronage, debt, and exploitation that have the greatest consequences for Indigenous rights.[45]

Bureaucratic dysfunction is another factor. Because of its chronic underfunding and embroilment in resource politics, the agency charged with implementing IPRA—the National Commission on Indigenous People (NCIP)—has struggled to do so in an efficient and timely manner. It took nearly fifteen years to begin implementing the provision that requires Indigenous representation in all legislative bodies. As of April 2019, the NCIP has reportedly approved 243 Certificates of Ancestral Domain Title, covering some 5.7 million hectares and 1,314,419 Indigenous "rights holders."[46] Only a fraction of these titles has actually been registered, while an untold number of applications languish in the preapproval phase. In Palawan, some eleven ancestral domain titles have been approved since the passage of IPRA, but few of these have been officially registered. Meanwhile, uncertainty lingers around the legal status of Certificates of Ancestral Domain Claim, which were issued in the early 1990s before IPRA took effect. These claims are meant to be converted into titles, but most claim holders lack the resources to apply for conversion. Worse still, the NCIP has been widely criticized by Indigenous rights activists for helping mining companies secure "free and prior informed consent" for extractive projects and mishandling mining royalties that it manages on behalf of Indigenous groups.[47]

In short, what looked promising on paper has proven to be disappointing in practice. Very few applications for ancestral domain recognition have successfully made their way through the long, expensive, and technically complex bureaucratic process. Extractive industries have corrupted the enforcement of informed consent. The mandate for legislative representation has been severely delayed. Indigenous groups are increasingly involved in bureaucracy, litigation, and above all waiting—waiting for the provincial officer to come for a survey, waiting for an opening in the municipal court's docket, waiting for an international donor to fund the domain application, waiting for a mining company to pay royalties, and so on. Meanwhile, in many parts of the country, dispossession of Indigenous lands continues largely unabated.

Why has IPRA's implementation faltered? Part of the problem is that its full legal implications remain unclear. Not long after the law was passed, its constitutionality was challenged. The Philippines Supreme Court reached a split decision regarding which of two competing constitutional doctrines determined the scope of the law. One side favored the regalian doctrine, which is said to give ownership of all untitled land to the state regardless of any customary claims. The other side favored the Cariño doctrine, which derives from a 1909 US Supreme Court ruling and is interpreted as giving customary claims precedence over those of the state. As discussed in chapter 3, this jurisprudential ambiguity means that even successful assertions of Indigenous rights stand on a legally unstable foundation, and bureaucrats and lawyers can readily legitimate any number of contradictory positions with respect to what Indigenous rights entail in practice.

The Local Context

What if IPRA is doing precisely what it was designed to do? What if no amount of legal clarity or bureaucratic competence would change its paradoxical effects? Consider the following excerpt from a Survival International press release from 2010: "The Palawan tribe of the Philippines is celebrating after a local government panel refused to give the go-ahead to mining giant MacroAsia to mine on their traditional territory. . . . [The panel] heard evidence from a Palawan Indigenous leader and other experts about the Palawan communities' opposition to mining on their land, and how MacroAsia's explorations have been predominantly in highly protected areas of virgin forest."[48] This triumphant declaration contrasts starkly with the imagery of marginalization and exploitation found in the remarks of Palaya and others. Part of the explanation for this contrast is historical: Filipino policy makers only recently redefined indigeneity into a rights-bearing political identity. Indigenous activists and entrepreneurs may be familiar with this new signification, but many Palawan, like Palaya, are not. For the latter, the English words "Indigenous rights" are foreign.[49] Rather, to be *tribu, netibo, katutubo,* or simply Palawan is to be ruled, at least nominally, by state-bearing people from distant lands. In this context, the bureaucratization of Indigenous rights seems as if it were designed to codify rather than change the subordinate position of Indigenous peoples in Philippine society.

Ultimately, neither Palaya nor Survival International addressed what for me is the most important valence of indigeneity in the contemporary Philippines. For that, I turn again to Jimi. When we first met in 2008, I asked him about how certain Palawan individuals, usually men, come to recognized as leaders by the government and other institutions. He explained the situation to me: "In the past, the Muslims organized us. Now it's the NCIP and NGOs." We should remember, he suggests, that southern Palawan was once an important outpost for trading, raiding, and proselytizing by Muslim sultanates based in the Sulu Archipelago and Borneo.[50] Their domination of the area persisted through much of the Spanish colonial period and deeply affected Palawan communities, even leading to the ethnogenesis of the Penimusan as a distinct subgroup.[51] Today, in places where high-ranking Muslim settlers known as *datu* once embodied the authority of the sultan, the postcolonial Philippine state is represented by Christian settlers with ancestral ties to other parts of the Philippines. Because many of these settlers are from the Visayas region, my Palawan hosts referred to all Christian settlers—and even to the state itself—as Kabisayaan or Visayans. Jimi's remark called attention to a continuous history of being "organized" by imperious states, punctuated with interventions by even more far-flung empires (i.e., Spain, Japan, and the United States). Being Indigenous under Philippine law may be a novel experience for Jimi and his fellow Palawan, but dealing with world-making designs of powerful outsiders is certainly not.

As a government-recognized "chieftain," Jimi was keenly aware of how contemporary efforts to codify Indigenous rights constitute a form of regulation as much if not more than a source of empowerment. He was wary of NGO and government personnel coming to do interviews, take photos, and use them to pursue resources. He never saw any benefits from such representations, and he did not feel they were accurate. He wanted me to tell the truth, *kabanaran,* about Palawan people's complex realities. This is not to say he was offering unfettered access to his life or that of his community. Rather, he was advising me not to use his community to portray a patronizing, self-serving stereotype. It was up to me to stay and become *sibilais,* which is how Jimi and some other Palawan describe becoming civilized or accustomed to the ways of others. Palawan had no choice but to become *sibilais* to the language, values, and laws of the Spanish, Americans, Japanese, Sulus, and Visayans. Few outsiders have done the same in return, instead objectifying Palawan bodies and lifeways for their own interests.

Jimi invited me to stay with his family in Tenga't Gebaq, where he lived with about a dozen fellow Palawan households, almost all of whom were his and his wives' kin. When he first brought me there in 2008, he explained that the path we took was an old logging road, abandoned in the 1980s during the turmoil of the late Marcos years. During that period, he and many other Palawan took refuge higher in the mountains. During times of relative stability, Tenga't Gebaq was the place he considered home. It was a good place to live because it was in the foothills—far enough from the coast to be somewhat remote but close enough to be accessible by motorbike. It was also a strategic place to do business. For Jimi and his wives, this meant trading in almaciga resin and rattan, as we will see in chapters 4 and 5, and running a small *sari sari* store for mass-produced commodities, such as soap, rice, instant coffee, and canned food. Jimi was (and is) a resourceful, intelligent, and entrepreneurial man who commands a great deal of respect in Tenga't Gebaq and the surrounding area. But he also had (and has) rivals and enemies who sought to defuse his ambitions.

We will learn much more about Tenga't Gebaq in chapter 2. For now, it suffices to say that it was *du't tengaq*—in the middle. Palawan often identify themselves and fellow Palawan as either *taw't daja* (upstream people) or *taw't napan* (downstream people). Jimi considered himself *taw't daja* because of where his parents were from and where he grew up. But when I asked whether people from Tenga't Gebaq were *taw't daja* or *taw't napan,* he explained that until recently, his answer would have been *taw't daja,* but now they were more like *taw't tengaq.* This means "people of the middle" and is not an actual identifier. Jimi made it up to describe the "in-between" condition of the village as an economic, cultural, and ecological crossroads between the settler-dominated, intensively farmed lowlands and Palawan communities in the forested mountains. I came up with the pseudonym Tenga't Gebaq by combining Jimi's pun with *gebaq,* a Palawan word for forest. The village was surrounded on all sides by forested land and swidden fields. This position placed the residents of Tenga't Gebaq geographically and socially in the midst of a number of important transformations that were of interest to my research and to many of the residents. Fortunately for me, I wasn't the only one who wanted to think critically about the causes and effects of these transformations.

Ethnographic researchers like me can never disavow the colonial history and extractive institutions in which our work is embedded. Jimi was not naive to this reality and did not see my research as an act of altruism. But he did have a critical perspective that he wanted to share—and so did many of his neighbors. Once I showed my commitment to becoming *sibilais*—joining a Palawan household, learning the Palawan language, eating what everyone else ate, hiking long distances for the sake of my work, helping with chores, watching children for brief stints—I found that many Palawan men and women were curious about my observations and had critical insight to share.

My goal is to share some of the knowledge generated in these interactions. This is not an ethnography of the Palawan people or even of Tenga't Gebaq. It is an artifact of interpersonal knowledge creation that occurred between specific individuals in a specific place. The episodes I share are ones I have discussed at length with Jimi and others involved. Their analysis informs mine and vice versa. If ethnography has a redeeming quality, it's that it stages interpersonal spaces of knowledge creation that would not otherwise exist.[52] Jimi understood this and became one of my most formative intellectual mentors. Even though I occasionally disagreed with him, his perspective is present on every page of this book. He enabled me to see the paradox of indigeneity but also to unsee it—to join people in living their lives despite and at times athwart the dilemmas that the world thrusts upon them. By relating these experiences in an honest and respectful way, I hope to make good on the promise I made to Jimi and other residents of Tenga't Gebaq—to tell the truth that I learned as I became *sibilais*. By further translating this truth into a more-than-human analysis of Indigenous rights, capitalism, and conservation, I hope to bring the interpersonal knowledge we generated into intellectual conversations that Palawan are otherwise excluded from, regardless of their firsthand insights.

Intellectual Stakes

For decades, Southeast Asia's mountainous hinterlands have figured prominently in intellectual debates about environmental regulation, social change, and state formation. From Anna Tsing's classic work on marginality in Kalimantan to Michael Dove's decades of research on "dual" smallholder economies to Jonathan Padwe's study of Jarai memory-scapes in highland Cambodia, *A Forest of Dreams* is perched humbly on some very lofty shoulders.[53] What I offer is a fresh perspective on how indigeneity, capitalism, and conservation interact in Southeast Asia (and beyond). This means intervening in three current debates that crosscut anthropology, history, and Asian studies.

Highland Peoples as Agents and Analysts of World History

Even in precolonial times, Southeast Asia's highland peoples, including those in Palawan, participated in long-distance trade networks, especially as providers of valuable forest products like camphor, rattan, and gutta-percha.[54] For centuries, they provided labor, sometimes against their will, to elites backed by lowland states. Unlike their lowland counterparts, highland peoples generally did not establish hierarchical states based on controlling water, agriculture, or trade. Instead, like my Palawan hosts, they maintained relatively egalitarian social formations that complemented the practice of foraging and shifting agriculture in a forested, mountainous landscape. Particularly since the colonial period, these "nonstate spaces" in the mountains have animated (and often frustrated) lowland states' efforts to control them. As a result, today many of Southeast Asia's highland peoples are politically marginalized and ethnically minoritized within the geobodies of modern postcolonial nation-states.[55]

These fraught relations—between "stateless" highland peoples and lowland states—have inspired historians and anthropologists to ponder why, in James Scott's words, "civilizations can't climb hills."[56] Scott's influential answer to this question rests on the allegedly state-phobic character of the region he calls "Zomia," a term invented by Willem van Schendel to encompass the mountainous highlands of continental Southeast Asia (Myanmar, Laos, Thailand, Vietnam, Cambodia, and China's Yunnan Province).[57] The peoples of Zomia, Scott argues, have actively resisted and sought refuge from lowland states by maintaining "illegible" ecologies, livelihoods, languages, cosmologies, and social formations. This sweeping account has proven controversial, leading critics like Hjorleifur Jonsson to dismiss Zomia as "a vast playground for western libertarian distraction and delight."[58]

With all due respect to Scott, I agree with Jonsson that Zomia "offers no place for Asian highlanders on whatever have been their own terms."[59] It's not that Zomia and other general theories have no value. The problem is that they obscure the varied, sometimes conflicted, and always site-specific motives that highland people bring to their interactions with states and other powerful actors.[60] *A Forest of Dreams,* by contrast, aims to reflect how Palawan people themselves theorize the state, capitalism, and other forces of social and environmental change. Fortunately, I am not alone in this endeavor.

As Dove has revealed through decades of work in Borneo, highland smallholders have long been important actors in long-distance trade of forest products and commodity crops.[61] Their involvement in this trade, Dove argues, has not been merely responsive to external forces, nor has it inevitably led to their abandoning subsistence-oriented activities, such as swidden farming and hunting. Instead, their strategic participation in commodity production as part of diversified livelihoods has often enabled them to sustain subsistence activities amid pressures to intensify land use. Despite entrenched representations of highland smallholders as isolated and conservative, they are in fact historical agents who bring critical thought and action to their entanglement in the capitalist world system.[62]

Differently engaged with this historical dynamism is Tania Li's work on the "emergence of capitalist relations" among Indigenous highlanders in Sulawesi. Building on her earlier work on development and conservation schemes in the area, Li calls attention to the "mismatch" between highlanders' lived experiences and dominant narratives about "indigenous people living in harmony with nature and with each other, eager to pursue development 'alternatives.'"[63] In so-called frontiers like Palawan and Sulawesi, the experiences and aspirations of highland Indigenous people are varied and sometimes conflicting. Beyond facing the material consequences of capitalism's expansion, which often include landlessness and exploitation, these individuals must contend with rapidly changing cosmologies of value, time, and personhood. For example, as land in highland Sulawesi has been enclosed by capitalist interests, many highlanders have been left landless and jobless, "no longer [able to] meet their own standards for what it means to be a whole person—someone who sustains a family, builds relations of care, and works hard to secure improvements in their material conditions."[64] Li is not telling a story of proletarianization, where erstwhile smallholders become full-time wage laborers, but one of material and cosmological dislocation, where people find themselves abandoned to the vicissitudes of the "salvage frontier."[65]

In some parts of Palawan, conditions are similar to what Li observed in Sulawesi. In Tenga't Gebaq, things have not (yet?) gotten quite so dire. Nonetheless, capitalist expansion is at the heart of what I observed there—not just in the form of encroaching monocrop plantations but also in conservation and Indigenous rights. Rather than assuming that these "frontier dynamics" follow a predetermined script, Li sought a new framework for understanding them, one built from her observations and those of her interlocutors. Like Li, I have intentionally sought to combine my observations with Palawan understandings of and engagements with capitalism in all its forms. Proletarianization and landlessness are possible outcomes of the ongoing enclosure of Indigenous land in Palawan. But these are not the only possibilities, nor are they the ones that Jimi and other residents of Tenga't Gebaq imagined and strove for. What results isn't an "alternative" or Indigenous vision of development. Rather, it's an idiosyncratic, place-based, and interpersonal analysis that foregrounds the critical capacity of the professional researcher and those whose lives are being researched.[66]

Cosmological and Ontological Politics

This brings us to our second theoretical intervention: how to approach the cosmological and ontological dimensions of environmental politics in a neocolonial context like Palawan. Throughout the book, we will see how a range of other-than-human agents, such as wild animals and invisible forest beings, affect relations among Palawan communities, their environment, and the institutions vying to control them. It will become clear that the drivers of "modernization"—the state, NGOs, and capitalists—do not simply "disenchant," assimilate, or co-opt these complex relationships. Instead, the state-backed capitalist frenzy for Palawan land, resources, and labor can actually accentuate the agency of "supernatural" forces.

In this respect, Filomeno Aguilar's prescient work on the development of sugar plantations in the colonial Philippines is an important touchstone. In *Clash of Spirits,* Aguilar shows how Visayan peoples' syncretic onto-cosmological theories shaped their understandings of and engagements with their rapidly changing social, economic, and geophysical landscape.[67] These theories entailed contending with a range of other-than-human spirit beings, such as *anito* and *engkanto,* as well as efforts to harness the more-than-human power of merchant Freemasons. Instead of diminishing in the face of modernization and "disenchantment," the presence of these entities was, if anything, amplified by rapid change.[68] More recent scholarship tells a similar story about the onto-cosmological dimensions of capitalist expansion in Cambodia, Myanmar, Sarawak, West Papua, Mindanao, and elsewhere.[69]

These accounts anticipate what residents of Tenga't Gebaq were experiencing and debating as they sought to navigate their changing world. Inspired by their debates, *A Forest of Dreams* asks what happens to political ecology and social history when we acknowledge other-than-human beings, including animals, plants, and spirits, as important historical agents. In addition to my conversations with Palawan people, recent work in anthropology and Indigenous studies informs my approach to this question. In chapter 4, we will see how invisible forest beings influenced some of my Palawan hosts' land use decisions in ways that conflicted with the state's assumptions about Indigenous practices. Instead of interpreting this conflict as a result of cultural differences, I argue that it is a conflict between different world-making practices and the onto-cosmological theories that underlie them.

But what does that really mean? Let's consider the basic scientific principle that Earth is one of eight (or is it nine?) planets in our solar system, with all that this implies about our knowledge of outer space. This is not simply a "fact"—it is a cosmological theory deeply embedded in our cultural and political institutions. Nor can it exist independently of those institutions, their technologies of observation, and protocols of interpretation. Ditto for the ontological proposition that the universe is made of particles like protons, electrons, neutrinos, and so on, and for the ontological principle that animals and plants are alive but rocks and robots are not. These are theories because they provide frameworks for making sense of complex relationships, processes, and phenomena. But they are not just ideas—they are integral to the structure of our society, and in this sense they are political. This is why encounters between different cosmological and ontological theories—such as those unfolding in places like Palawan—are so politically significant. They aren't simply encounters between different beliefs; they are collisions between different social orders and world-making practices.

Chapter 4 details the theoretical and methodological foundations of my argument. For now, it suffices to say that I draw direct inspiration from anthropologists Paul Nadasdy, Arturo Escobar, Mario Blaser, Elizabeth Povinelli, and Marisol de la Cadena.[70] And through them, I am influenced by theorists Michael Jackson, Eduardo Viveiros de Castro, Isabelle Stengers, and Bruno Latour.[71] Like Nadasdy, though, I reject the notion that "different peoples inhabit different, incommensurable, and only partially connected realities, or worlds."[72] I agree with him (and Michael Cepek) that the conditions in question are "far more dynamic, complex, and heterogeneous than can be captured by the multiple-worlds thesis." Instead, then, of "[flattening] the ethnographic record so as to produce distinct, homogenous, and radically other worlds," I aim to embrace the onto-cosmological "indeterminacy" that characterizes environmental politics in Palawan.[73] As we will see, the work of Nuu-chah-nulth philosopher E. Richard Atleo, who posits a "unified but polarized reality," offers critical guidance to my effort.[74]

Indigeneity in Asia

The third and final debate in which I intervene concerns the concept of indigeneity in Asia. Recall that the Philippines was the first country in Asia to codify Indigenous rights. Consider, too, its distinctive history of colonization by Spain and the United States. This history is front of mind when I, following Oona Paredes, describe Philippine indigeneity as a paradox, at once a potential source of empowerment and an enduring form of (neo)colonial rule.[75] It is tempting to conclude that the Philippines simply has more in common with Latin America than the rest of Asia. In fact, Philippine indigeneity is one piece of a larger regional puzzle that was shaped, in part, by the US empire's transpacific designs. Japan and Taiwan clearly reflect this legacy in their selective attempts to codify indigeneity such that they can recognize (and regulate) certain minoritized peoples.[76] Elsewhere in southern Asia, globally connected movements for Indigenous rights have prompted controversial efforts to afford Indigenous status to specific "tribal" or "customary" communities, as seen clearly in recent moves (and reversals) by governments in India, Cambodia, and Indonesia.[77]

Nevertheless, a number of scholars have engaged more skeptically with the concept of indigeneity in Asia. Juno Parreñas has suggested that activists and academics are misappropriating the concept from the Americas and imposing it on Southeast Asia in an act of "cultural imperialism" that fosters "ethnonationalism."[78] Will Smith and Viola Schreer have argued that highland communities do not necessarily have specific critical insight into the transformations they are putatively experiencing as Indigenous people. Smith suggests that Palawan people attribute climate disruption, social marginalization, and material hardship to their own moral failings rather than to larger historical forces, such as capitalism or colonialism.[79] Schreer claims that Ngaju Dayak communities in Borneo do not have a cosmologically specific relationship with their surroundings and, instead, uncritically embrace state-sanctioned narratives of capitalist development.[80] These accounts cast doubt on ethnographers' attempts to "reconfigure unsettling cultural difference into metaphoric parables of uneven power relations strategically deployed by the marginalized."[81]

I respect these arguments and find many of them insightful. Yet based on my own research, I do not share their suspicion of bringing Southeast Asia into theoretical and methodological dialogue with Indigenous studies. To be sure, regional context and history matter. "Indigenous" is a loaded English word that translates awkwardly into Southeast Asian contexts. Humans are flawed and often irrational. Western researchers long embarrassingly for subaltern Indigenous wisdom. . . . All of this is true, and there are Indigenous people in Southeast Asia who have their own critical interpretations of history, society, and ecology. Multiple, seemingly contradictory ideas can be true at the same time. In fact, in Indigenous studies, this paradoxical condition is no revelation. Directly confronting what Povinelli calls "the cunning of recognition," Indigenous scholars have developed a range of theories—such as Glen Coulthard's "self-recognition," Audra Simpson's "refusal," and Gerald Vizenor's "survivance"—to account for how Indigenous persons negotiate their paradoxical condition.[82] How Palawan persons do so is a central question of this book.

For now, let's recall Jimi's invitation to become *sibilais*. This was, he said, the only way I could tell a "true" story, one that is necessarily full of contradictions, self-deception, and hardship but also of creativity, endurance, and critical consciousness. That *A Forest of Dreams* emphasizes the latter reflects what I learned with Jimi and other Palawan people as we gradually became *sibilais* and found ways to co-create knowledge that was of mutual interest.

Overview

This book is an invitation to join me, Jimi, and other interlocutors in an ongoing project of critical interpersonal analysis. The book itself may be a static representation of our work, but the dialogue that informs it continues in Tenga't Gebaq and throughout the world. My hope is that readers will come away with their own novel ideas about the intersection of indigeneity, capitalism, and conservation in Palawan and elsewhere. I remain deeply fascinated and troubled by what's happening in Palawan, and so does Jimi. With that in mind, each chapter centers the critical knowledge, shared experiences, and lingering questions that emerged from thinking together with Palawan people about our rapidly changing world.

Chapter 1 begins with a Palawan take on Ferdinand Magellan's fateful encounter with Visayan chief Lapu-Lapu. Unlike in textbook accounts, Magellan isn't killed in Mactan but in Palawan, after he colludes with Lapu-Lapu to render the island visible to the outside world and they proceed to fight over its wealth. More than a historical myth, this Palawan-centric account offers a critical analysis of colonial projects from the Spanish period to the present. Woven together with a history of indigeneity in the Philippines, this analysis suggests how the current Indigenous rights framework has served to sustain rather than disrupt or repair the colonial structures that underpin the state, conservation, and extractive industry.

Chapter 2 opens by recalling Charles Lindbergh's advocacy for conservation in the Philippines, which he saw as a "last frontier" for conserving "primitive wildness."[83] His fantasy, we learn, was as much a vestige of the colonial era as it was a harbinger of how conservationists and many others would imagine Palawan in the latter part of the twentieth century. For Palawan's Indigenous peoples, the island's emergence as the last frontier has flanked a frenzy of tourism, mining, logging, monocrop plantations, conservation, and disputes about all of the above. This chapter traces how these regional processes have unfolded in the lives of a specific Palawan community, Tenga't Gebaq, whose local history is introduced in the process.

In chapter 3, we remain in Tenga't Gebaq, where we meet Jimi, his rival, Bordo, a screeching civet, and an invasion of tree-planting college students. Three episodes in the community's recent history illustrate how residents engage critically with competing designs for their lives and lands. In one case, Jimi faces a large group of municipal officials and college students hoping to plant hardwood saplings on sacred land. Rather than guiding them to land that was spiritually significant, he quietly brings them to an area that is locally disputed and might as well be occupied by an external authority. Chapter 3 also shows what happens when other-than-human beings interrupt such strategies—as when the meows of a captive civet provoke a tense but humorous encounter with the forest patrol. Such encounters are by no means isolated or unique to Tenga't Gebaq. Some ten kilometers downstream, we find Bordo counseling youth who are accused of participating in the wildlife trade while at the same time questioning the tangle of laws that arbitrarily protect and criminalize various sources of Palawan livelihood. At stake in these moments is the uncertain future of Palawan swidden farming, hunting, and access to other forest resources. For residents of Tenga't Gebaq, the stakes could not be higher.

Chapter 4 delves deeper into the more-than-human nature of these struggles by engaging the people of the forest (*taw't talun*), invisible beings who inhabit the landscape around Tenga't Gebaq. Through a series of dream encounters with these beings, including one of my own, we see how they have sometimes complicated the spatial designs of bureaucrats and conservationists. While the state, NGOs, and investors debate where to place fixed boundaries around discrete land use zones, Palawan land use decisions involve place-based, intergenerational knowledge and social accountability to their visible and invisible neighbors, human and otherwise. When a young man named Oto dreams of angry forest people, he decides to abandon the practice of charcoal making. His neighbors, meanwhile, have received no such feedback and continue the practice. Such inconsistency puzzles and disappoints conservation officials, who believe that practices like charcoal making reflect a loss of traditional Palawan culture.

Conservation isn't the only domain in which Palawan people confront dominant (mis)conceptions of indigeneity. Chapter 5 tracks how the booming trade in forest commodities, especially a valuable tree resin called almaciga, has drawn Palawan communities deeper into the orbit of capitalism. Officials see the trade in forest commodities as a way for Indigenous communities to sustain their way of life while sustainably managing their resources. In practice, the insatiable demand for these products intensifies competition among wealthy merchants, government agencies, and NGOs, along with their competing demands for Indigenous people's land and labor. Jimi learns this the hard way when he embarks on a protracted and inconclusive legal struggle with Bordo. On the surface, their dispute is over permits required to sell forest products. We will see that it also raises fundamental questions about Indigenous personhood, rights, and self-determination.

Meanwhile, on the other side of the mountains, a different Palawan community manages to establish a direct relationship with an almaciga factory, thereby bypassing the merchants to whom Jimi, Bordo, and many other Palawan traders are beholden. These cases suggest how Palawan people navigate the dilemmas they face and find subtle ways to assert their interests, despite the resource frenzy that surrounds them.

CHAPTER ONE

Colonial Sorcery

In April 1521, nearly two years into his attempt to circumnavigate the earth, Ferdinand Magellan encountered what later became the Philippine islands. Six weeks later, he sailed to the island of Mactan in the central part of the archipelago. He meant to vanquish a native chief or *datu* named Lapu-Lapu, who had refused to recognize the king of Spain. But things did not go as planned. Coral reefs kept the Spanish fleet beyond cannon range, leaving its passengers to wade through the surf in their armor. Magellan and his forty-nine men were vastly outnumbered, their muskets rendered useless by distance and their opponents' wooden shields. After burning the village failed to secure the natives' surrender, the invaders fled under a barrage of arrows and spears, their retreat recounted vividly by the voyage's chronicler:

> We fought thus for more than one hour, refusing to retire farther. An Indian hurled a bamboo spear into the captain's face, but the latter immediately killed him with his lance, which he left in the Indian's body. Then, trying to lay hand on sword, he could draw it out but halfway, because he had been wounded in the arm with a bamboo spear. When the natives saw that, they all hurled themselves upon him. One of them wounded him on the left leg with a large scimitar . . . that caused the captain to fall face downward. Immediately they rushed upon him with iron and bamboo spears and with their cutlasses, until they killed our mirror, our light, our comfort, and our true guide.[1]

And thus, we are told, Magellan met his untimely demise. The surviving members of the expedition sailed west and took refuge on the island of Palawan before journeying onward.

For Lapu-Lapu's side of the story, we must look to Visayan oral histories. As summarized by Resil Mojares, these enthralling accounts involve the literal petrification of Lapu-Lapu's father, dramatic acts of divination, and a multispecies effort to repel the European invasion:

> When Magellan and his men waded to the shore, they were attacked by various marine creatures: crabs, clams, tabugok (young octopi), ba'at (trepang)—"as big as human pillows"—that encircled the feet of the Spaniards with their sticky saliva; seaweeds (lusay) that wound themselves around the intruders' legs, "thousands and thousands of sea-urchins sticking their thorns into the fallen bodies" of the enemies. Thus bedevilled, the Spaniards were left vulnerable to Lapulapu and his men, who rushed in to give the coup de grace.[2]

Centuries later, nationalist historians took up this fateful encounter as a foundational moment in Filipino nationhood, with Lapu-Lapu as the first hero to resist colonization.[3] These academic histories split the difference between the Spanish and Visayan versions. The "supernatural" elements were left aside, but the chain of events remained the same.

Now let's consider an entirely different version of the story, one that retains the sorcery but changes the plot. Many generations ago, the island of Palawan was invisible to outsiders. Its inhabitants lived without any fear that they would be taken as slaves or otherwise exploited by others. But one day a pair of powerful men named Magellan and Lapu-Lapu discovered the island and used some kind of sorcery to render it visible. Upon beholding Palawan's vast wealth, particularly its gold, the powerful men competed for control and eventually fought to the death. Since then, Palawan and its original inhabitants have faced a succession of outsiders with designs on the island's resources. Muslims, Spaniards, Americans, and now migrant Filipinos have all come to see—and seize—the wealth that Magellan and Lapu-Lapu unveiled.

This is the story that Palawan elders told me when I asked them about the origins of the world.[4] It's not an ancestral myth but a reworking of competing textbook and oral narratives of national history.[5] Palawan have encountered such narratives relatively recently through their contacts with Filipino settlers, missionaries, and schools. It is telling that Palawan use the term *Kabisayaan* (Visayans) to refer to all Christian Filipino settlers regardless of their place of origin. From their perspective, it makes perfect sense that a Visayan chief colluded and then fought with a Spanish conquistador. Magellan's chronicler conjured Palawan as a paradisiacal refuge, a "promised land" that offered salvation from hunger and hostile natives. By contrast, the Palawan account of the island's "discovery" centers on Spanish-Visayan collusion, greed, and violence. As a place and as a people, Palawan comes into a new state of being as an object of imperial desire—as a site of struggle rather than refuge.

De/constructing Palawan as the "Last Frontier"

If you encounter Palawan in advertising, documentaries, or other popular representations, chances are the island will be referred as the Philippines' "last frontier." Inspired by the Palawan account of how the island was rendered visible, this chapter unpacks the last frontier narrative as a form of liberal exceptionalism, which, unlike the Palawan account, obscures long term of processes of colonization. Palawan has become an international hot spot for struggles between extractive industries like logging and mining, on the one hand, and promoters of biodiversity conservation, Indigenous rights, and eco-tourism, on the other hand. Among the latter in particular, references to Palawan as the last frontier are all but universal. Consider the following passages:

> Palawan is the Philippines' last frontier. Its relative isolation from the rest of the archipelago spared many of its resources from the systematic exploitation practiced elsewhere. As the planning and development coordinator for the province phrases it to us, "Palawan has been thrown out to into the China Sea." Indeed, its closest neighbor is not even another Philippine island, but the Malaysian state of Sabah on the island of Borneo. . . . Until recent decades, the rest of the Philippines viewed Palawan simply in terms of its isolation. As transport costs fell, however, and as the other islands were increasingly overlogged and overfished, it became only a matter of time before Palawan was "discovered" by thousands of poor farmers and fishers from other islands—and by big commercial loggers.[6]

> Welcome to Rizal—the last frontier of Palawan, the country's last ecological frontier. Though the Municipality is one of the least known among the countless destinations in the Province, it boasts of truly unforgettable sights. Mt. Mantalingahan, Palawan's highest peak and a veritable paradise of lush virgin forests, home to rare flora and fauna, majestically towers over the Municipality. Spectacular white-sand beaches stretch along the entire coastal length. The Tau't Bato tribe, a unique group of Indigenous people, can be found in Singnapan Valley. . . . To those who have experienced its largely unspoilt natural and cultural treasures, Rizal is truly worth the visit, again and again. Its people, representing a diverse combination of different ethno-linguistic groups, have been a showcase of peace and unity. Working in harmony, they have been able to harness the untapped resources in them, and directing these into worthwhile courses of action geared towards the common goal of development.[7]

> The struggle to save Palawan (known as the Philippines' Last Frontier) is not only about saving trees and rare species. It is also about nourishing the Filipino cultural heritage, so powerfully represented by those Indigenous communities that—after escaping Spanish and American colonization (while resisting the new "mining imperialism" now)—continue to represent the "living roots" from which all Filipinos originate. Therefore, environmental plundering by mining companies is not only a crime against nature but it is also a crime against culture, a sort of genocide that annihilates the most profound roots of the Filipino's history and ultimately plunders the cultural heritage of the whole nation.[8]

The first passage is from *Plundering Paradise,* an award-winning account of Philippine environmental politics by Robin Broad. The second comes from a tourist pamphlet produced by the municipality in which I conducted much of my fieldwork. The final passage is from a video produced by ALDAW, an Indigenous rights organization then headed by a Palawan activist and an Italian anthropologist. The sources vary widely, but in referring to Palawan as the last frontier, all three passages make use of a common trope. They exemplify what has become the standard narrative of Palawan's history, and with a quick online search, one can easily find legions of similar examples in other published sources.

According to the last frontier narrative, Palawan existed in a state of obscurity and isolation until the mid-twentieth century, when migration, logging, and eventually environmentalism pushed it into the spotlight of history. Today, Palawan is the last vestige of an authentic, precolonial paradise that has been lost in other parts of the archipelago. Palawan is also unique—a land with "thousands of kilometers of unexplored forests and coastlines" whose "flora and fauna . . . display more affinities with certain islands in Indonesia, especially Borneo, than other islands in the Philippines."[9] Faced with threats from migrant settlers, wildlife poachers, loggers, and miners, Palawan must be saved—or, ironically, consumed—before it is lost to the ravages of development.

But let's not dwell on what the last frontier narrative says. Instead, consider what it does not say—what history does it obscure? Calling Palawan "the last frontier" implies that the history of colonialism in the Philippines before independence in 1946 is mostly irrelevant for understanding the challenges the Palawan region faces today.[10] My goal in this chapter is to build on the analysis that Palawan elders shared with me by showing that there is, in fact, significant continuity between dominant imaginings of Palawan in the colonial past and postcolonial present. Palawan has been an object of desire, fascination, and anxiety for imperial states across more than four centuries. Its status as such has been underpinned by its imagined exceptionality and by the exceptionalism of colonial self-imaginings. In the first case, Palawan was not ignored by Spanish or American colonial officials. Records kept by these regimes suggest that officials saw Palawan as exceptional and were fully inclined to incorporate it into the colonial system.

In the second case, both the Spanish and the Americans found moral justification for their own acts of dispossession and violence, being duty-bound to bring "civilization" to an abundant but "wild" frontier. This moral exceptionalism was, I argue, especially pronounced in the case of Palawan because of the island's interstitial placement between the center of colonial power in Luzon; the Muslim polities of Sulu, Mindanao, and Borneo; and the British trading interests in Sarawak. No state could honestly claim to exercise territorial sovereignty over Palawan until sometime in the first half of the twentieth century, and even then it was a porous sovereignty at best. The Spanish and Americans positioned their interventions as efforts to protect Palawan's exceptional features—particularly its forest and "simple, timid" Indigenous inhabitants—from marauding Muslims and other nefarious interests.

Palawan was and is an exceptional part of what came to be the Philippine archipelago. Because of its location, it is ecologically distinct from the rest of the country, and it emerged from the colonial period with more of its forest cover remaining than most of the rest of the country. But Palawan is decidedly not exceptional if "exceptional" means somehow untouched or unchanged by the first three centuries of colonial rule. Last frontier narratives obscure Palawan's history and make it more difficult to identify the antecedents of present-day conditions. Furthermore, these narratives reinforce the sense of liberal exceptionalism that exculpates contemporary efforts to "save" Palawan, its forests, and Indigenous inhabitants from their role in ongoing processes of colonization.[11]

This is not just a question of academic precision. My main concern is not with the frontier narrative's (in)accuracy but with how its effacement of history naturalizes the extractive relations and interventions that emerge in a contested "frontier" landscape. Following recent work in political ecology, I consider frontier narratives of Palawan's history to be environmental narratives. As defined by Forsyth and Walker, "environmental narratives are simplified explanations of environmental cause and effect that emerge in contexts where environmental knowledge and social order are mutually dependent."[12] Narratives depicting Palawan as the last frontier do more than promote a simplified understanding of environmental change in the region. They also prescribe identities for Indigenous people, whose fate is equated with that of the nation's precolonial heritage, and for non-Indigenous people who claim a stake in that fate.

As part of larger environmental narratives, last frontier narratives produce what Michel Foucault calls a heterotopia.[13] That is, in frontier narratives, Palawan is a real place that can be located on a map but is nonetheless "outside of all places." Heterotopias are hyperreal spaces onto which collective desires and anxieties are projected. They represent the inversion of places familiar to the beholder, and they define what is standard by embodying or containing what is exceptional or deviant. According to Foucault, colonies are heterotopic because they can contain deviants from the metropole and provide a tabula rasa on which to realize a utopic alternative. If the Philippines as a whole was a heterotopia for Spanish and American imperialists, Palawan was something of a heterotopia within a heterotopia—as, for example, when the island was chosen to host exiles and eventually a penal colony. Today, Palawan is reinscribed as a frontier heterotopia by narratives that obscure its place in colonial history. Such narratives reflect an elite longing for authenticity that often overshadows local visions of the region's past, present, and future. In the context of myriad efforts to "save" Palawan, identifying it as a heterotopia is another way of asking "what exactly is being saved and for whom?"

One of the main themes of this book is the complicated entanglement of environmental regulation with the regulation of minoritized people. This chapter places these complications in a deeper historical context. My hope is to temper the liberal exceptionalism of the present so that all of us who look to Palawan as a place worthy of being saved, protected, or understood will be more aware of the will to control that we share with our colonial predecessors. "In the end," writes Neil Smith, "the frontier discourse serves to rationalize and legitimize a process of conquest, whether in the eighteenth-or-nineteenth-century West, or in the late-twentieth-century inner city."[14] Or in the contemporary Philippines. If we better understand how Spanish and American colonial authorities imagined and intervened in Palawan, we can anticipate potential unintended consequences of current efforts to "save the last frontier."

Academics and the Last Frontier

Compared with other parts of the Philippines, and despite growing interest in the area, little has been written about Palawan's colonial history.[15] Even so, I am by no means the first scholar to cast doubt on frontier narratives of Palawan's history or trace the colonial antecedents of its present-day challenges.[16] Fabinyi takes a step in this direction when he invokes Tsing's treatment of frontiers as "scale-making projects" that render a region's "natural resources" available for "development" regardless of existing socioecological relations.[17] His analysis focused on how Palawan is today imagined and treated as a resource frontier by various groups, rather than the colonial precedents for their actions.

Nilo Ocampo is the only scholar to have undertaken anything approaching an exhaustive history of Palawan's colonial experience.[18] His deliberate efforts to challenge frontier amnesia highlight Palawan's interstitial positioning between colonial regimes based in Manila and Muslim polities in Sulu, Mindanao, and Borneo. Ocampo notes repeatedly that both Spanish and American officials "gushed" over the riches of Palawan and came to see the island as strategically vital in their effort to establish sovereignty in the archipelago. He writes:

> The "frontier" is there, to be sure, well represented in printed material and, therefore, a historical fact. But it should be pursued with a caveat. Frontier it was for the Spaniards and Americans and Filipinos from other provinces, but it was home for a congery of local peoples (Batak-Tagbanua-Palawan-Cuyunon-Agutaynen-Cagayanen) and a beachhead for a dominating Muslim presence. The notion of Palawan-as-frontier is a recurring one, but it is not the crux of the interfacial history that is in order.[19]

Much of what I relate in this chapter rests on Ocampo's account, but I also hope to take his argument further. Palawan's status as a frontier is not a potentially misleading fact but a political project that has its roots in the same colonial projects it obscures.

"Just as Good as That of Borney": Palawan's Natural History

A narrow, mountainous island, Palawan cleaves the South China Sea from the Sulu Sea as it traces a line between Mindoro to its northeast and Borneo to its southwest. Shattered into an array of outcroppings and satellite islands, Palawan's northern end abounds in sheltered inlets, while its sharp southern tip points toward Sabah as if to offer modern historians a clue about its precolonial past. Palawan is 425 kilometers long and barely 40 across at its widest point, yet it is the Philippines' fifth largest island and the mainland of its largest province.[20]

Palawan's location on the northeast extremity of the Sunda Shelf has been decisive in its natural and cultural history. Connected to Sundaland by a land bridge during Pleistocene glaciations, Palawan's flora and fauna are more similar to those of Borneo than to the rest of the Philippines. The peculiarity of the island's biota was not lost on the first Europeans to settle there—a monastic order known as the Augustinian Recollects—who noted in 1624 that its supply of forest products was, unlike most of the Philippines, "just as good as that of Borney."[21]

Palawan sits in the intertropical zone, which tends to have seasonal (as opposed to highly seasonal) rainfall patterns according to Bellwood's typology.[22] In this general pattern, geomorphic and other variables intervene so that the "extreme northern and southern parts of the island as well as the entire northwest coast have six dry months and six wet months, while the rest of the province has a short dry season and no pronounced wet season."[23] Palawan as a whole receives an average of 2,607 millimeters of rain a year, while the annual average of 1,600 millimeters on the island's east coast makes it among the driest areas in the Philippines.[24] The area's weather is highly sensitive to El Niño and La Niña—periodic oscillations in sea surface temperatures and wind patterns that affect rainfall. Still, its historically reliable dry seasons of at least three months "support more open monsoonal forests with a deciduous tendency during the driest periods."[25] Compared with the evergreen rainforests of the humid tropics, semi-deciduous monsoonal forests of the type found in Palawan "generally provide more plant food for human consumption."[26]

A spine of mountains bisects most of Palawan, dividing the flatter, drier east side from the steeper, wetter west. On the southern half of the island, Mount Mantalingahan peaks at 2,086 meters and is the centerpiece of an impressive forest landscape that constitutes one of the largest tracts of forest cover remaining in the Philippines.[27] Because Palawan is so narrow and mountainous, most of its rivers are not navigable for any significant distance inland. Its coastal plains are relatively small and prone to flooding, especially on the west coast. Despite their limited utility for transportation, Palawan's rivers are numerous and often separated by steep valley walls that make north–south travel difficult in places. Furthermore, because the island's mountains have not been volcanic in recent millennia, its soils are mostly alluvial or formed from underlying bedrock and tend to be nutrient poor.[28] Shallow waterways, steep gradients, and relatively poor soils combine to impose constraints on wet rice cultivation and timber production. In addition to extensive mangrove forests, Palawan's terrestrial forests are of a monsoonal, "molave" type, which include some key hardwood species, but historically have been of less commercial significance than the dipterocarp species found on islands like Luzon and Borneo.[29]

Palawan in the Sulu Zone

In part because of its geography, Palawan has never been at the center of a major polity. This does not mean that it was not involved in trade. The earliest evidence for external trade with the Philippines comes from ceramic evidence dating to sometime between the tenth and twelfth centuries CE.[30] By the thirteenth century, Chinese documents begin to indicate well-established trading networks between South China and the Philippines.[31] Although early Chinese records contain no unequivocal references to Palawan, Kress dates the region's involvement in Chinese trade to the tenth century or earlier.[32] The earliest unambiguous documentary evidence of Chinese trade with Palawan comes from the Recollect missionaries. In 1624, the Recollects reported that forest products, including rattan, beeswax, and edible bird's nests, were among the most common exports from the island, while Chinese porcelain and metalwork were the main imports.[33] Although Chinese demand for Palawan's forest products continues today, the Chinese themselves have had only a limited physical presence on the island, least of all in the south. Islamic civilization, on the other hand, has had a direct impact. Islam reached what would become the southern Philippines in the thirteenth century, connecting the islands to trade networks extending westward to South Asia and beyond. Until the later nineteenth century, seafaring Islamic sultanates in Borneo, Maguindanao, and Sulu prevented the Spanish from controlling most of the southern part of the archipelago. In Palawan, Spain was limited to little more than a tenuous foothold in northern Palawan. Even in the north, Spanish records indicate frequent conflict with Muslims coming from the south. It is difficult to say with any certainty which Muslim polity controlled southern Palawan at any particular point during this time. What we do know is that Palawan was ceded by different sultans at different times to both Spain and the East India Company, suggesting that no one state can be said to have "controlled" Palawan in the manner of a territorial sovereign. We also know that Palawan played an important role in the regional ascendancy of the sultanate of Sulu, which emerged in the latter part of the eighteenth century and lasted until 1915.

Long a trading corridor for seafaring polities, the Sulu Sea became a pivotal zone in the world system as a result of European demand for tea. To meet the insatiable demand for tea, European trading companies had to find commodities that the Chinese wanted. Among these, the most important and infamous was opium, but the Europeans also turned to the marine and forest products of Southeast Asia.[34] The sultanate of Sulu—dependent on trade for staple starches, prestige goods, and eventually opium—came to dominate the Sulu Zone in the first half of the nineteenth century. The Tausug people, who made up the ethnic core of the Sulu sultanate, obtained the goods for this trade in two ways: (1) through secondary trade with raiding groups like the Iranun and Balangingi, who captured people throughout the archipelago and traded them in Sulu, where they were enslaved in the production of goods for trade with the Europeans and Chinese; and (2) establishing settlements in outlying islands whence Tausug chiefs, known as *datu,* could collect tribute from native groups.

Both methods were used by Muslim traders in Palawan.[35] By the 1780s, there is evidence for Muslim settlements along the coasts of Palawan's southern cone, although their size and duration is uncertain. By 1857, a single Tausug *datu*, Alimuddin, had all but monopolized trade between Palawan and Britain's ascendant entrepôt in Labuan.[36] Indigenous Palawan people traded forest products like edible swallow's nests, rattans, resins, and beeswax for goods they did not manufacture locally, particularly salt, metal tools, and kiln-fired earthenware items like plates and bowls.

The Sulu sultanate's fortunes began to wane in 1848, when the Spanish started using steam-powered ships to patrol the Sulu Sea. In 1858, Spain managed to establish a permanent garrison on Balabac, an island located strategically in the strait between Palawan and Borneo. This was followed in 1872 by the founding of Puerto Princesa, Palawan's capital. By the late 1870s, Spain had succeeded in blockading most trade in the Sulu Zone, forcing the sultanate to submit to Spanish sovereignty.

We can place southern Palawan within this regional history thanks largely to Warren's pioneering work.[37] At the same time, we know little about what life was actually like for Palawan's Indigenous population during this period. What we do know comes from a handful of European intellectuals who included Palawan in their Philippine expeditions.[38] Only one of them—a British biologist named John Whitehead—wrote in detail about southern Palawan. In 1887, Whitehead spent nearly three months at a site he called Taguso (Tagusao) on the island's southeastern coast. In a brief report published in an ornithological journal, he offers a basic if partial sense of social relations between Palawan people and Muslim settlers:

> When we landed in Taguso there were no Spaniards there, and the natives were doing much as they liked. Palawan is notorious for the bad characters which have taken refuge there from the Sulu and other islands. . . . In the interior of Palawan is another race, nearly related to the Bornean Dusans and Muruts; these people are under the thumb of the coast Sulus. The Sulus will not allow a Dusan to sell any jungle-produce to the Chinese, but oblige the Chinese to buy from them, as middle men.[39]

In an elaborated version of his report, Whitehead mentioned the existence of two additional groups of people, whom he referred to as Orang Sungei ("half-cast Sulu Dusuns") and Orang-Utan ("wild interior tribes").[40] Whitehead mistakenly used the Bornean demonyms with which he was familiar, but I agree with Macdonald, who interprets the distinctions as follows:

(1) "Sulus" referred to Tausugs and other Muslim settlers who lived along the coast, made a living from fishing and trading, and were organized under hereditary *datu* chiefs;
(2) "Orang Sungei" referred to Indigenous Palawan who had converted at least nominally to Islam, settled along the coast, and were analogous to second-class citizens within the *datu* system;[41]
(3) "Dusuns" referred to Indigenous Palawan who practiced foraging and shifting agriculture, were influenced by the Muslims but remained largely independent of them, and spent most of their time in the interior; and
(4) "Orang-Utan" referred to the most remote and least extroverted Palawan persons, who lived in the mountains and avoided contact with non-Palawan.[42]

Whitehead provides most detail about the Dusun (i.e., Palawan), whom he describes as engaging in agriculture on the mountain slopes; living in small, single-family houses; hunting with decorated blow guns and poison-tip darts; and treasuring "common earthenware plates and bowls" that were used only as bride wealth. As Macdonald points out, this four-part ethnic typology may lack nuance, but it provides a plausible description of the distinctive socio-politico-ethnic landscape that existed in southern Palawan until the early twentieth century and remains perceptible there today.

"The Promised Land": Palawan during Spanish Rule (1565–1898)

As we know, representatives of the Spanish empire first encountered the archipelago we know as the Philippines in April 1521 when Magellan's fleet landed at Cebu.[43] After losing their captain and abandoning a ship, the surviving members of the fleet followed a circuitous route to the islands of Bohol and Cagayan de Sulu before eventually anchoring off the west coast of Palawan.[44] According to the record of the voyage kept by Antonio Pigafetta, the crew was practically starving by the time they reached Palawan. Finding the island abundant in food, the chronicler wrote that "we could well call that land 'the promised land' because we suffered great hunger before we found it."[45] Still eager to find the Spice Islands, the two remaining ships soon left "the promised land" in their wake. Although the ships eventually reached Maluku, they were a decade late. The Portuguese were already well established there and went on to hold a monopoly on the spice trade for the next century.[46] Despite this fateful setback, Spain pursued colonization of the Philippines, establishing their first permanent settlement at Cebu in 1565. In addition to the allure of gold, spices, and trade with China, Spain envisioned an Asian "arsenal and warehouse of the Faith."[47]

Despite initial hopes that the Philippines would develop along the lines of Spain's American colonies, the archipelago never became a popular destination for European settlers.[48] Instead, the islands were administered as a subcolony of New Spain. As such, they lacked prestige and had an air of danger and backwardness that kept most Europeans away. This was especially true in the rural areas beyond the walls of Manila, where only representatives of the Church and politico-military establishment had a sustained presence.[49] Colonizing remote areas like Palawan was a collaborative but often acrimonious project of the various religious orders and the military.[50] Once an area had been "pacified" and the locals forcibly resettled into permanent villages, a resident friar would train native priests to evangelize in their own languages. Meanwhile, politico-military officials would select loyal native leaders, called *principales,* to serve as local administrators and landlords. This process, known as *reducción* (reduction), created a rigid social hierarchy with a small class of landed elite at the top and a large mass of dependent peasants at the bottom.

In 1624, the Recollects were sent to "reduce" the Calamianes and Palawan. At Taytay in northern Palawan, they managed to establish a large village and fort, but only after considerable difficulty: "The people were opposed to living congregated in one settlement, and that was the greatest hindrance; but fathers were able to attain in part, by dint of patience and constancy. The greatest annoyance arose from the Moros, who infested those coasts, and the natives were unwilling to expose themselves to their injuries by establishing themselves on the beach."[51] With Taytay secured, the Recollects and their military escorts proceeded south, claiming success in establishing a handful of villages in the northern part of Palawan and its satellite islands.

In their report on these activities, the Recollects refer to Palawan as "the famous one . . . a rich and fertile island."[52] This description is strikingly reminiscent of Pigafetta's, and it suggests that the Recollects either saw significant economic potential in Palawan or were hoping to attract more resources from authorities in Cebu and Manila. In any event, Spain's interest in Palawan was evidently strong enough to warrant this effort, making it difficult to sustain the claim that Palawan remained isolated from the Spanish colonial polity. Still, unparalleled challenges presented themselves in Palawan, and Spain's subsequent efforts to gain a stronger foothold there mostly ended in failure.[53]

Colonial Designs, Indigenous Forests

Throughout its first three hundred years in the Philippines, the Spanish colonial regime made no systematic attempt to study or manage the archipelago's forests. This does not mean that they did not take an interest in them. As early as 1569, the first governor general of the Philippines, Miguel de Legazpi, revealed this interest when he wrote to King Philip II describing the great "abundance of timber" observed on many of the islands. When Legazpi and his contemporaries saw these forests, they envisioned building excellent ships for transpacific trade and sturdy homes for Spanish settlers.[54] Although most of these visions never materialized, some areas experienced significant forest clearance during the first three centuries of Spanish rule.[55] By the late seventeenth century, travelers were already reporting lumber shortages in Manila, and reports of sylvan abundance increasingly refer to places farther from the main centers of Spanish settlement.[56] Forest clearance in this era owed largely to expanding settlements and agriculture, as the archipelago's population grew from fewer than 1 million in the mid-sixteenth century to around 7 million by the end of the nineteenth century (see figure 1.1).[57]

In 1821, the Mexican Revolution forced Madrid to assume direct administration of the colony. Because the Philippines had never been self-sufficient, Spain was faced with a major fiscal problem. Its solution was to push for more intensive commercialization of forest products and other natural resources. By establishing the Inspección General de Montes (Forest Inspection) in 1863, colonial authorities sought to determine which state-owned lands were best left forested for reasons of health, hydrology, and climate, and which could be sold for cultivation.[58] By law, the Forest Inspection controlled all forested lands except for those under communal village tenure. In practice, the unregulated timber industry was growing so rapidly in the later nineteenth century that the Forest Inspection met with staunch resistance from local timber fellers and traders. For its part, the Inspection placed the blame for deforestation on swidden agriculture. Forest inspector Sebastian Vidal y Soler lamented the changes he observed in popular attitudes toward the forests, writing, "It is a common enough opinion that the climatic conditions of the Archipelago improve at the same rate as the forest diminishes, and there is no lack of those [here] who see the tree as the enemy of man."[59]

The need to liquidate state lands and the push to regulate forest extraction made securing control of Palawan and other outlying islands increasingly urgent for the Spanish. These were not the only factors in play. In 1762, the British laid siege to Manila and held the city ransom for two years. This defeat so disrupted colonial administration that it limited Spanish activities in Palawan to a bare minimum for some seventy years.[60] Hoping to prevent a repeat of this humiliating experience, Spain sought to fortify Palawan as a first line of defense against the British in Borneo. A fortuitous technological development finally made this possible. In 1848, colonial authorities acquired "steam vessels with maneuverability, speed, and armament . . . able to combat effectively the swift sailing craft of the Moros."[61] Armed with this new technology, Manila was able to establish a garrison on the island of Balabac in 1858 and founded Puerto Princesa, the site of Palawan's present-day capital, in 1872.

Far from a neglected backwater, Palawan and its forests were the objects of palpable desire and considerable effort on the part of the Spanish. It was not indifference that kept them at bay—it was a struggle for control shaped by the same sorts of geographic, political, and technological factors that shaped Spain's experience in Luzon, Cebu, and elsewhere. Palawan may have been a frontier in the sense that it marked the constantly shifting edge of Spain's territorial power in the Philippines, but it was more integral to metropolitan affairs than is often assumed.

Spain's Legacy

Barely twenty years after Spanish ships took tenuous control of the Sulu Sea, Filipino revolutionaries declared their independence, Spain lost a war with the United States, and American forces occupied the archipelago. As a result, Spain never managed to gain a durable foothold in southern Palawan outside of Balabac Island, which was a military garrison and "agricultural reform colony" (*colonia agrícola de refora*) rather than a *reducción*. Even Puerto Princesa was more of a penal colony than a colonial settlement.[62] Still, Spanish colonial policies have had profound consequences for Palawan's Indigenous peoples.

From the start, Spanish officials had an extremely difficult time deciphering the ethnolinguistic heterogeneity they encountered in the Philippines. In 1682, after encountering mass resistance to its attempt to ban certain native practices of debt bondage and slavery, the Royal Audience in Manila wrote this to King Charles II:

> For the fact that these islands should not be considered the same as the other kingdoms and provinces of America, where all the slaves are either negroes or mulattos or they are pure indios. Out here, such a diversity of nations is found that it is not easy to comprehend it and impossible to name them, and only by giving the races in general is it possible to form any concept of the many different kinds of slaves that are found in these parts.[63]

What emerged from Spain's confusion was a tripartite division of the native population into *Indios, Paganos,* and *Moros*—Hispanized Indians, uncivilized pagans, and unconquered Muslims. Among the indios, Spain had a policy of indirect rule that sought to co-opt the authority of precolonial chiefs, often known as *datu* as a result of prior sultanic influence. Chiefs who acquiesced to Spanish rule were appointed to a hereditary noble class known as the *principalía.* Members of the *principalía* were exempt from paying tribute or contributing *polos y servicios* (corvée labor) but were expected to extract the same from their subordinates.[64] This system laid the groundwork for the emergence of the so-called caciques—a numerically small but politically dominant class of landowners, businesspeople, political bosses, and warlords who assumed control of the state during the American period and continue to control it today.[65]

The second Spanish category, pagans, was a stigmatized one encompassing many of the groups who are today recognized as Indigenous people. Then as now, the connotations of this designation were ambivalent. Some pagans, such as the Igorot groups in northern Luzon, were seen as a belligerent threat to the realm and were targeted for pacification by the military. Others, like the Tagbanua and Palawan, were seen as hapless victims of Moro exploitation in need of friary protection. Pagan groups that persisted in the hinterlands of Hispanized settlements were largely exempt from Spanish laws prohibiting bondage.[66]

Spain's attempt to establish a forestry bureaucracy in the late nineteenth century had no direct effect on southern Palawan. The same cannot be said for Spain's ambivalent treatment of native land tenure. According to Lynch, King Philip II hoped to avoid repeating the brutal dispossession that accompanied colonization in the Americas. He issued decrees intended to ensure some measure of property rights for all Philippine natives regardless of whether they converted to Catholicism.[67] This policy stood (at least on paper) for more than three hundred years. In 1894, colonial authorities enacted the Maura Law, which effectively vested the state with ownership of all untitled lands. This law, along with what Lynch refers to as the "mythical Regalian Doctrine," established a precedent of state ownership of forests that has had profound implications up to the present.[68]

Although Spanish officials never managed to implement the *principalía* system in most of Palawan, Spain's trifurcation of the archipelago's population has had profound effects on the imagination and legislation of the island's Indigenous peoples up to the present. Likewise, although Spain never realized its plans for Palawan's forests, it laid the groundwork for future processes of dispossession during the American and postcolonial periods. Both legacies should be clear in later parts of this chapter and those to follow.

Palawan under American Rule (1898–1946)

In 1892, a coalition of Filipino landholders, *ilustrados,* middle-class urbanites, workers, and peasants formed an underground revolutionary movement known as the Katipunan.[69] Six years later, amid the Spanish-American War, the Katipunan declared Philippine independence from Spain and established a revolutionary government at Malolos. The Malolos Republic assisted the United States in defeating Spain and in return was promised support for its independence. Yet when the Americans claimed victory, they reneged on their promise and took possession of the Philippines, Guam, Cuba, and Puerto Rico. President William McKinley ordered a brutal invasion of the archipelago that resulted in hundreds of thousands of Filipino civilian deaths.[70] Even as this "counterinsurgency" campaign raged on, US officials established a commission to gather information about the new colony and make recommendations for its administration.

The first Philippine Commission issued a comprehensive four-volume report to the president summarizing its interviews, archival research, and firsthand observations. Besides justifying the US occupation as an act of "tutelage," the commission devoted much attention to determining the extent and location of the new colony's best forests, which were seen as the main source of economic potential. Eager to exploit this potential and concerned about rates of clearance due to shifting agriculture, the commissioners stressed the urgency of completing a forest assessment and taking measures to prevent "trespassing" on state-owned forest lands.[71] Two years later, the commission established the Bureau of Forestry and, in 1910, founded a Forestry School at Los Baños.[72] Meanwhile, the bureau was actively involved in importing mechanized logging technology and began to grant large logging concessions to American logging companies.[73]

Even in its initial reports, the Philippine Commission deemed it urgent to gain a more refined knowledge and control of Philippine forests. On the one hand, simple economic logic provided an obvious motive for this urgency. The sooner they controlled the forests, the sooner they could profit from them.[74] On the other hand, the Americans' will to control also drew strength from their belief that native land use was economically wasteful and environmentally destructive.

In its reports, the commission described all regions with extensive forest cover as "either peopled by wild tribes or . . . uninhabited." "In many instances," they observed, "these regions are covered with magnificent timber; in some cases mineral deposits of great wealth lie within their limits, and as a rule their soil is extremely fertile."[75] Such arguments on the behalf of state control combined political expedience with a white supremacist worldview. The Americans willfully ignored the possibility that heavily forested areas, such as Palawan, were semi-anthropogenic landscapes shaped by human societies with territorial claims to them.

Although forests covered as much as 70 percent of the archipelago in 1900, the commission's report repeatedly highlights those of Palawan and a handful of other areas for their exceptional wealth. Echoing earlier Spanish impressions, the commission wrote that "the island of Paragua is second to none in the wealth of its vegetable kingdom."[76] This evaluation was prefigured by Dean Worcester's scientific expeditions to Palawan before the American takeover. In 1887–1888 and 1890–1893, Worcester participated in unofficial scientific expeditions to the Philippines that made him a leading expert on the islands, a member of the Philippine Commission, and eventually the Insular Government's secretary of Interior. In December 1893, Worcester's team, guided by a group of local Tagbanua men, hiked to the top of Mount Pulgar in central Palawan, whence they hoped to survey the landscape.[77] In his report on the expedition, he wrote the following about their arrival at the mountain's peak:

> We had been shut in by dense clouds, but suddenly they broke away, and it was worth all the fatigue of the trip to see the astonishment of those savages. They now realized for the first time that they were *in* the clouds, and we could hardly make out which surprised them most, that fact, or the wonderful view which spread out before them. They had never dreamed of anything like it, nor, for that matter, had we. To the north and south lay absolutely unbroken forest, as far as the eye could reach. To the east we looked over the Mindoro Sea to distant mountain peaks beyond it, and to the west we searched the China Sea in vain for any sign of land; *but our eyes ever came back to that vast expanse of splendid forest, which seemed to stand as it was in the beginning, with never a trace of the marring hand of man.*[78]

The sense of awe Worcester felt upon seeing Palawan's forests made its way into the commission's reports and into the Insular Government's efforts to establish control over the island.

Logging proceeded sluggishly in Palawan at first, primarily because of the island's lack of infrastructure and shortage of wage-dependent laborers. For this reason, the Insular Government's first priority was to build roads. By 1920, forestry officials reported that loggers on the island had begun operating two sawmills and using tractors to harvest large ipil (*Leucana leococephala*) and kalantas (*Cedrela calantastrees*). Most of this activity was concentrated in the northern part of the island, where foresters reported shortages of kalantas as early as 1924.[79] Although Palawan's forests were becoming an increasingly important source of timber and other products, they only supplied a fraction of total timber extracted in the prewar era. In the 1910s and 1920s, for example, forestry records indicate that they provided 4–5 percent of all lumber extracted from state-owned land.[80]

If American officials shared their predecessors' impression that Palawan's forests were the best in the archipelago, they also shared an abhorrence for the practice of swidden agriculture (*kaingin* in Tagalog). Whereas the Spanish typically couched their discussions of *kaingin* in terms of religion or law, the Americans saw it as an absence of civilization and rationality. In either case, colonial officials believed that the practice of swidden demanded their salvational intervention. "There has been," cautioned the commission, "much needless destruction of valuable timber in the past." This "needless" destruction, they reasoned, had occurred at the hands of the colony's native inhabitants whose "plantations . . . are speedily invaded by 'cogon' and other strong-growing grasses, which they are powerless to combat with the crude agricultural instruments at present in use, so they simply clear more forest land from time to time, and often burn the felled trees where they lie."[81]

To combat the "caiñgin evil," the Bureau of Forestry launched a campaign to suppress it in 1921. Suppression involved more intensive enforcement efforts and the granting of *kaingin* permits on land that was then supposed to be converted to permanent agriculture. In Palawan, there were two different types of *kaingin* being practiced: that of Christianized migrants and that of the island's Indigenous groups. Compared with the former, the latter was less destructive to the forests because it involved smaller clearances, longer fallows, and integration with a belief system adapted to the local environment. Although all *kaingin* was illegal unless permitted by the state on noncommercial forest land, colonial authorities acknowledged the difference and stipulated that non-Christians caught making illegal swiddens should be warned and not arrested on their first offense. This leniency had two primary causes.[82] On the one hand, officials saw their relationship with Palawan's Indigenous groups in paternalistic terms. On the other hand, the Americans sought Indigenous cooperation in winning control of southern Palawan from the Muslims.

For their part, forestry officials expressed frustration at this policy, which, they argued, was easily subverted by the natives. As one exasperated forester wrote, "The destruction of the forest by non-Christians is becoming a serious problem, due to the law requiring that they be warned at the first offense, as these people can rarely be caught a second time, since they are smart enough, should a forest official detect a caiñgin made by a man who has already received his warning, to claim that it is being made by his father or some other relative or friend."[83] The state should, foresters concluded, "put [non-Christians] on an equal footing among their Christian brothers." Despite its perceived ineffectiveness, the campaign against the "caiñgin menace" led to a dramatic increase in *kaingin* warnings and arrests, up from 6 in 1915 to 156 in 1924.

The American "Civilizing" Mission

In their calls for equally strict policing of Christian and non-Christian swiddeners, American foresters were critiquing one of the very basic principles of US government in the Philippines: the exceptional treatment of non-Christian tribes. In

1901, the Philippine Commission established a Bureau of Non Christian Tribes under the Insular Department of the Interior.[84] Its mission, as stated in its founding circular, included "the investigation of the little known pagans and Mohammedan tribes of the Archipelago, the conduct of systematic work in the anthropology of the Philippines, and the recommendation of legislation in behalf of these uncivilized peoples."[85] As parts its civilizing mission known as "benevolent assimilation" or "benevolent tutelage," American colonial officials saw themselves as saving the Philippines from the morass of exploitative Spanish misrule, even as they reinscribed the same social categories and moral impulses with which Spain had legitimated its colonial enterprise.

Regions populated primarily by non-Christian tribes—including Palawan, Mountain Province in northern Luzon, Moro Province in Mindanao, and Mindoro—were considered "special provinces" and placed under the jurisdiction of the Bureau of Non-Christians Tribes.[86] Unlike regular provinces, where most day-to-day administrative functions were handled by Filipinos at the municipal or barrio level, the American governors of non-Christian provinces had special authority to administer non-Christian populations directly. In Moro Province and Mountain Province, these arrangements essentially constituted personal fiefdoms for US officials seeking unfettered access to new resource frontiers.[87] In Palawan, this policy manifested itself in three primary ways, all of which dovetailed with their desire to control the island's forests: (1) a program to promote sedentary agriculture among "wild" tribes, (2) a campaign to concentrate and pacify the Muslim Moros in the south, and (3) the classification of forested lands as public domain.

Although American foresters came to protest the exceptional treatment of non-Christian tribes, the Insular Government's civilizing mission nonetheless went hand in hand with its effort to eradicate shifting agriculture and gain control of the forests. Palawan played an important role as a proving ground for these related efforts. In 1905, Palawan's governor established a "reservation" and school for the Tagbanua at Aborlan, intended to teach them superior agriculture methods, give them access to markets for their products, and protect them from the Moros. This reservation was cited as a model for civilizing tribal people in other parts of the colony.[88] In the Bureau of Forestry's annual report for fiscal year 1913–1914, it noted its experience that criminalizing swidden alone would not effectively suppress this "deep-seated" custom. Instead, citing the results of the Aborlan reservation, the report argued that natives should be taught the virtues of conservation and intensive agriculture while also being "induced or required" to resettle into "permanent homesteads."[89]

No such reservations were established in southern Palawan, where the greater concern was establishing control over the Moros and their trade in forest products. Beginning in 1910, successive governors of Palawan attempted to persuade and, failing that, coerce all Moros to relocate to the jurisdiction of a cooperative Moro leader, Datu Batarasa, on the southeast flank of the island. The administration also established "government exchanges" at which Palawan could sell forest products: "The opening of so-called Government exchanges where the Tagbanuas [Palawan?] can sell their products and can purchase what they need at reasonable prices has greatly pleased them and is bringing about helpful contact between provincial officials and wild men from the most inaccessible regions."[90] Although these policies sometimes involved armed encounters with uncooperative *datu* and their followers, they were justified as necessary to protect Palawan and Tagbanua from the Moros and their exploitative trade practices. The Moros of Palawan, one governor wrote, were known even by fellow Moros in Mindanao to be "renegades" of an "especially treacherous and dangerous" nature.[91]

A third and final way American treatment of non-Christians dovetailed with its forestry policy was through the classification of lands deemed to be in the public domain. Despite a 1909 US Supreme Court ruling (*Cariño v. Insular Government*) recognizing native land title, the Insular Government effectively treated all untitled land as public land. Resource zones, particularly commercially viable forests, were reserved for the public domain, with remaining land eligible for individual title. To that end, the Insular Government instituted a total of eleven forest reserves and national parks throughout the archipelago, while enacting a series of laws predicated on the Torrens title system.[92]

Developed by British colonists in Australia, the Torrens system enabled people to gain private title to cultivated parcels of the public domain if they could demonstrate that they were using the land consistently and productively.[93] In forested areas that were deemed alienable and disposable, individuals could apply for free homestead titles of up to twenty-four hectares if they agreed to occupy and develop the land. Combined with the continued disamortization of friary lands, this system helped entrench the existing elite and favored Hispanized sedentary agriculturalists. It greatly disadvantaged groups like the Tagbanua and Palawan, whose ancestral lands often included commercially valuable forests, whose system of usufruct tenure was incompatible with individual titles, and whose land uses were seen as the antithesis of efficient productivity.

The Beginnings of Mass Migration and Settlement

Alongside their efforts to control the colony's forests, US authorities pushed poor farmers, fishers, and laborers to migrate, resettle, and develop its "uninhabited" hinterlands. In their reports to the Philippine Commission, successive American governors in Palawan complained of chronic labor shortages and suggested the island's settlement by Filipinos from other islands. Although they worried that "simple" and "timid" groups like the Tagbanua and Palawan would be exploited by their Filipino counterparts, bringing sedentary agriculturalists to "wild frontiers" would serve the civilizational mission.[94] Granting free homestead patents encouraged migrants to claim and develop "unreserved" public lands regardless of whether Indigenous peoples lived on them.

Rapid population growth in Hispanized areas was the other key driver of migration. In 1903, the Philippines had approximately 7 million residents. Since then, the national population has grown exponentially by an average rate of well over 2 percent a year. By 1948, there were some 19 million people in the archipelago; by 1975, 42 million; and in 2020, just over 110 million (see table 1.1). Because of a vastly unequal distribution of wealth and power, this demographic expansion strained resources and stoked unrest in Luzon and the Visayas, accelerating the state's effort to resettle people in less densely populated regions like Palawan and Mindanao.

Table 1.1. National, provincial, and municipal population change in the Philippines, Palawan, and Rizal, 1903–2020

Year	*Philippines*	*Palawan*	*Rizal*
1903	7,635,426	35,369	
1918	10,314,310	69,053	
1939	16,000,303	93,673	
1948	19,234,182	106,269	
1960	27,087,685	162,669	
1970	36,684,486	236,635	
1980	48,098,460	317,782	12,950
1990	60,703,206	528,287	16,819
2000	76,504,077	755,412	31,745
2010	92,337,852	994,340	42,759
2020	109,033,245	1,246,673	56,162

Source: National Statistics Office.

In the early twentieth century, most migrants to Palawan were from Cuyo, a small, Hispanized island about midway between the northern tip of Palawan and Panay. "At midcentury," Eder notes, "immigration was by national standards comparatively limited, and Palawan was not the demographically important settler destination that [various parts of Mindanao] were. The decades following World War II, however, brought a large surge in immigration to Palawan that has continued down to the present."[95] In other words, after effectively filling the frontier in Mindanao, migrants from Luzon and the Visayas turned to Palawan, eventually outnumbering their counterparts from Cuyo. Muslims from impoverished, politically unstable parts of Mindanao and the Sulu archipelago have also migrated in significant numbers, particularly to the southern part of Palawan. Though only Balabac today has a Muslim majority, all of the municipalities in southern Palawan, including Rizal, have sizable and growing Muslim minorities.[96]

Although most of this migration was unregulated, if tacitly encouraged, some was part of an explicit government policy. In 1954, Congress authorized the National Resettlement and Rehabilitation Administration, a relocation program for landless families and those who had joined the anti-Japanese insurgency (which had since evolved into the armed wing of the Communist Party of the Philippines). Through this program, thousands of families were given homesteads in Mindanao and Palawan. Like its colonial predecessor, the independent Philippine government has continued to encourage migration to Palawan, using the region as a "politically convenient safety valve to relieve some of the pressures caused by government inability or unwillingness to control population growth or to resolve agrarian problems in the more densely populated lowlands."[97] Perhaps more than any other single factor, this influx of settlers has had transformative effects on Palawan's Indigenous people and their environments, as will become clear in chapter 2.

In light of this history, it is clear that the Palawan account of Magellan's encounter with Lapu-Lapu is more than an example of creative storytelling or self-fashioning. Rather, their account of how the island was "rendered visible" critically theorizes the epistemological and ontological transformations that accompany colonization in the past and present. Rendering visible is both a metaphorical and a literal step in the process of colonization. Their account offers visibility as a complementary notion to other common tropes of state incorporation, particularly Scott's "abstraction" and Li's "rendering technical."[98] To render people, places, and things abstract, technical, and therefore governable, they must first be rendered ontologically accessible to the imperial power.[99] Magellan and Lapu-Lapu accomplished this through techniques of sorcery. Colonial governments and their flanking institutions did so through coercion, missions, surveys, enclosures, resettlement, and other techniques. This process continues to the present.

This analysis will come full circle as we encounter more prosaic accounts of social and environmental change that people shared with me. For example, as I explain in chapters 2 and 3, virtually all Palawan elders I knew told me that both their environment and their way of life had declined since the time of their ancestors. Most of them attributed these changes to the mass arrival of Kabisayaan and the imposition of their laws.[100] In southwestern Palawan, mass Christian settlement is a relatively recent process, one that elders locate within living memory. The Lapu-Lapu/Magellan story, by contrast, pushes the historical origins of this process deep into the past, serving as a genre of social critique and social memory.[101] On the one hand, it interprets ongoing transformations as the latest and most intense phase in a long-term history of foreign encroachment. On the other hand, it places Palawan at the center of this history rather than at its periphery. In both respects, the story challenges dominant narratives of Palawan's history, which ignore the island's place in a broader history of colonialism.

In a first step toward challenging the last frontier narrative, this chapter has drawn on a Palawan theory of history to trace the region's involvement in centuries of contact, trade, and struggles for control. We saw particularly how Spanish and American depictions of Palawan as "a promised land" with "never a trace of the marring hand of man" coincided with their efforts to control the region's Indigenous inhabitants and profit from its forests. Suggesting that Palawan was peripheral to or somehow "escaped" colonial designs ignores their very real continuities with the processes of dispossession and degradation that are occurring today. In chapter 2, I follow the trajectory of these processes in the postcolonial period.

CHAPTER TWO

Producing and Consuming the "Last Frontier"

In 1969, famed American aviator Charles Lindbergh made the first of several expeditions to the Philippines, where he sought to galvanize support for environmental conservation and the protection of endangered species. Despite his tarnished reputation as a Nazi sympathizer and antisemite, Lindbergh had refashioned himself as a conservationist through high-level roles with the World Wildlife Fund, International Union for the Conservation of Nature, the Nature Conservancy, and the Oceanic Foundation. During his first Philippine tour, he visited several "remote" parts of the country, including Palawan, where he "acquired an intimate knowledge" of one of the island's Indigenous groups. The *New York Times* covered Lindbergh's tour in a front-page profile that quoted him at length explaining his beliefs about conservation.

"I don't believe," Lindbergh opined, "[that] our civilization can continue very long out of contact with *the primitive*. . . . I believe that many of the social troubles we face today result from our being already too far removed from our ancestral environment. . . . That is one of the reasons I like to visit the wilderness and sometimes its isolated tribes." For him, preventing the destruction of "primitive" environments and cultures in the Philippines was part of preventing the decline of "civilization" in the West. "The Philippines," he declared, "are one of the last frontiers of conservation."[1]

Lindbergh's commentary makes for an interesting comparison against the American colonial imagery we encountered in chapter 1. On the one hand, he maintains the distinction between civilized people and tribal primitives. On the other hand, he romanticizes "the primitive" and identifies it with "the wilderness," which he wants to protect. Lindbergh again: "We can learn a great deal from [tribal people], for they are much closer to the primitive man than we. They can help us retain contact with the roots of life, to understand the values as well as the hazards of instinct."[2] Although far from new in the West, Lindbergh's romanticism portended a broader shift in metropolitan imaginings of Indigenous people and their role in environmental regulation. One outcome of this shift, a quarter century later, was the Philippine government's attachment of Indigenous rights to conservation.

This chapter picks up where the first left off, situating Palawan's history in the co-evolution of minority–state relations and environmental regulation beginning with the end of American rule, through the authoritarian years that followed Lindbergh's visit, to the post-1986 reforms and their unfolding. In particular, we will see how events at the national and regional scales play out in the lives of Indigenous people in southwestern Palawan. As in the colonial period, the past six decades have seen intensifying efforts to incorporate Palawan's forests and Indigenous peoples into wider networks of regulation and capital. These efforts, as we saw with Lindbergh, are animated by imaginings of Palawan as "the last frontier," a land that was spared from colonization and now must be saved from destruction by environmental government. The irony is that Palawan's ongoing portrayal as an exceptional, heterotopic space obscures how present-day interventions have carried colonial projects into the twenty-first century.

Let's begin by introducing the people known as Palawan, as well as the specific Palawan community that hosted me during my research.

"The" Palawan

With their present numbers estimated at somewhere between 40,000 and 50,000, Palawan-speaking people represent a sizable minority in the five southernmost municipalities of Palawan Island.[3] Given this relatively large population and the rapid but uneven processes of differentiation they are experiencing, one cannot speak about Palawan people as single group with defining characteristics. Nonetheless, I outline some of the patterns that, according to my research and that of other scholars, distinguish their "traditional" ways of life—what they call the "ways of the ancestors" (*keedatan et keguranggurangan*).

The demonym "Palawan"—occasionally spelled Palaqwan, Pala'wan, or Pälawan—refers to a common, self-ascribed ethnolinguistic identity.[4] But it also overlooks a lot of variation, not all of which can be attributed to recent changes. This demonym is more meaningful as a boundary between Palawan and non-Palawan, while Palawan subgroups identify one another with terms that mark association with particular places or ecological orientations. Southern Palawan is drained by dozens of small rivers, which serve as reference points for subgroup identification—for example, *taw't Ransang* for people of the Ransang River, *taw't Malambunga* for people of the Malambunga River. Likewise, Palawan refer to one another as *taw't daya* (upstream people) or *taw't napan* (downstream people) depending on place of birth or residence and on cultural orientations.

Historically, Palawan have relied on swidden agriculture, hunting, fishing, and collecting other wild foods for their subsistence. Their list of cultigens was long, including most importantly rice, cassava, banana, taro, yam, corn, sweet potato, and variety of other tubers, cereals, and medicinal plants.[5] They hunted a wide variety of game, including such animals as jungle fowl, fruit bats, squirrels, pangolins, civets, and wild pigs. Depending on the size and behavior of the prey, hunting methods included blowguns, trained dogs and spears, various kinds of traps and snares, and the more recent addition of air guns and "pig bombs." River fish and crustaceans provided an important source of protein, as did marine and mangrove species for Palawan near the coast. Other wild food sources included honey, various parts of the sago palm, wild tubers, and a long list of other plants and fungi. Beyond subsistence, Palawan were long engaged in the trade of forest products for goods they did not produce locally, especially salt, kiln-fired ceramics, and metals.[6] Their long-term contact with Muslim traders seems to have been especially influential in terms of shaping marriage practices and other aspects of customary law.[7]

Palawan's relatively pronounced monsoonal pattern results in a dry season of January to May and a rainy season of June to December. The swidden cycle was attuned to this seasonality, as was the corresponding ritual calendar, and the swidden rice spirit (*Empuq et Parey*) was one among many invisible beings of various demeanors with which Palawan people maintained social relations. A more detailed discussion of Palawan cosmology will come in chapter 4. Here it suffices to say that despite their increasing participation in organized religions and the marginalization of their ritual practices, many Palawan continue to have cosmological orientations different from those of their Christian and Muslim neighbors.

According to Macdonald, everyday life in Palawan communities reflected not just an egalitarian ethos but a radically anticoercive form of "fellowship" that defied classification according to conventional concepts of social organization, such as tribe or chiefdom.[8] This anticoercive ethos was possible because each intergenerational household produced its own food, could relocate with relative ease, and was not obligated to perform labor for anyone else. This does not mean that Palawan did not share or cooperate. To the contrary, they were (and are) constantly giving food to one another, and they have long engaged in reciprocal labor exchange when they need to clear a large swidden. Most of the time, they met their basic needs without depending on a patron or employer. Under these conditions, Macdonald suggests, the lack of an enduring social hierarchy went hand in hand with an avoidance of interpersonal conflict and violence.[9]

So far, I have been speaking about Palawan practices mainly in the past tense because many have undergone dramatic changes in recent years. For example, although it seems safe to say that the majority of Palawan still practice swidden farming, yields have declined as communities have lost access to land and started to invest more of their time in other activities. Hunting is much less common than it used to be, especially in lower-lying areas that have been deforested or otherwise overexploited. Instead, Palawan increasingly depend on cash-generating activities—particularly marketing forest products and wage labor—to purchase food, medicine, and other mass-produced goods.

Macdonald provides a comprehensive (if somewhat formulaic) view of this variation. Based on his decades of fieldwork in southern Palawan, he describes what he calls an "inland-coastal gradient" along which Palawan communities vary in terms of their ecological and economic orientation and in terms of their "beliefs and representations, [and] practices relating to the supernatural."[10] This gradient downplays many past and present complexities, including the movement of Palawan people from the coast to the mountains (and vice versa), as well as the blurring of boundaries between Palawan and other ethnolinguistic groups. Still, certain patterns remain evident.

Palawan who live at higher elevations are characterized by a nearly universal involvement in swidden and are more likely to hunt, with a few still employing traditional methods like the blow gun. Despite their distance from lowland markets, cash-oriented trade in forest products, especially rattan and almaciga, has become increasingly important. Those who live nearer the coast, often still involved in swidden and hunting, are more likely to be involved in intensive agriculture (as smallholders and/or seasonal laborers) and other cash-oriented livelihood activities (such as charcoal production). Across the inland-coastal gradient, bilateral kinship ties remain most people's primary consideration in household location and everyday social interactions. Uxorilocality—where newly married couples live with the bride's parents—remains in wide practice; however, settlements vary in structure and size, with larger, more diverse settlements more common near the coast, and smaller, more uniform clusters more common in the mountains.[11] Monogamy remains the dominant pattern across the population, with polygamy anecdotally more common high in the mountains and among Muslim Palawan.[12]

Palawan ritual practices vary along the gradient; however, with their ancestral ritual practices increasingly marginalized, it is difficult to generalize in this manner. Near the coast, many Palawan have converted to Christianity, and a long-term process of ethnogenesis continues as Palawan join the Islamized population known as Penimusan.[13] Among residents of the lower elevations who have not converted to Christianity or Islam, traditional ritual practices tended to favor large gatherings, music, dance, and other forms of performance, while including men and women as ritual specialists and healers (*belyan*). Meanwhile, Palawan communities in the mountains were more inclined toward introspective "shamanic" rituals led exclusively by male healers. In either case, the figure of the *belyan* has remained important, although diminished from what it once was.[14]

One arena of Palawan tradition that remains relatively robust is customary law (*adat*). Contact with hierarchical, state-based societies has had profound effects in this area, as have new forms of social differentiation associated with money and property accumulation (see chapter 5). Nevertheless, many Palawan groups maintain *adat* practices that are largely independent from those of the state, and many remain strongly egalitarian in their practices and values. To the extent that Palawan have leaders of any kind, they are elders (*pegibuten,* "the one who is followed") whose opinions are respected and often heeded but are rarely backed by a threat of coercion. Those who develop expertise in *adat* and the oratory skill to participate in public discussions (*bitsara*) can command respect as negotiators or arbitrators (*memimitsara, menunukum, panglima*). Their authority to negotiate marriages and settle disputes depends entirely on their efficacy in building consensus among the parties to the negotiation, not on any coercive authority.[15] The law they practice is basically advisory and conciliatory rather than punitive.[16]

In all cases, the respect afforded to a trusted elder, healer, or mediator is not reckoned in terms of mutually exclusive territory but through kindred networks that depend on mutual trust and assent.[17] Since the 1970s, some Palawan have gained state or nongovernmental organization (NGO) recognition as the leaders of particular territories (often under the title chieftain, *kapitan,* or *panglima*). Being recognized by the state as a chieftain may add to one's credibility as an arbiter of customary law (and vice versa), but it does not simply entitle one to respect and authority among fellow Palawan. That respect must be earned. Likewise, although some chieftains and other titleholders leverage their recognition in the pursuit of greater wealth and power, the titles themselves are significant almost exclusively when dealing with the government, NGOs, and other outsiders. Bureaucratic recognition of Palawan leaders has led to no end of frustration on both sides because the state often expects a recognized leader to exercise authority on a jurisdictional basis and make binding commitments on behalf of a territorially defined community (see chapter 5).

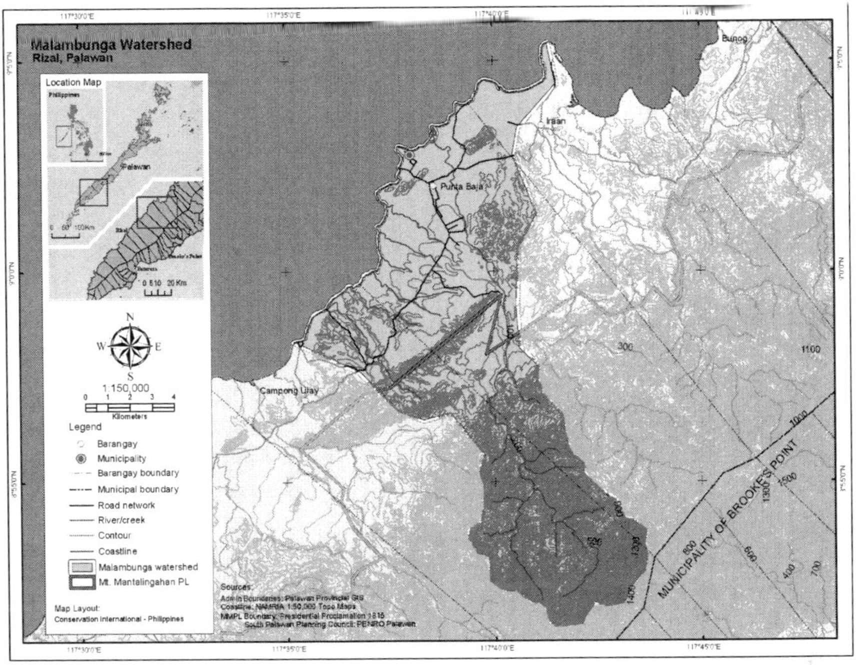

Map 2. Malambunga River watershed. Source: Conservation International—Philippines.

Tenga't Gebaq

Tenga't Gebaq is a village in the western foothills of the mountains that bisect southern Palawan.[18] It was home during most of my fieldwork in 2010–2012 and during visits in 2014, 2015, 2016, and 2018. I have struggled with whether to write about Tenga't Gebaq in the past or present tense. As of this writing (February 2024), the village is still there, and according to updates on social media, it has not changed dramatically since my last visit. For this reason, I have decided to describe its enduring features in the present tense and relate circumstances specific to my research in the past tense.

Although I was never able to find Tenga't Gebaq on a government map, it was usually listed as a *sitio* of *barangay* Punta Baja in the municipality of José Rizal.[19] Some believed that it was, in fact, in the neighboring *barangay*, Campung Ulay, and this was the subject of some controversy. Whatever the jurisdiction, Tenga't Gebaq emerged as a settlement because a number of pathways intersect there. It sits atop a hill just west of the Malambunga River, which provides a steady source of fish, eels, and other riverine foods year-round, as well as easier hiking into the interior during the dry season (January–May). It sits at the end of a rough, long-neglected logging road that follows the river up from the lowlands. This road enables skilled (and brave) motorbike drivers to travel from the village to the municipal seat of Rizal in less than an hour. Tenga't Gebaq is at the base of the mountains, making forest products like rattan and almaciga resin more accessible. This strategic positioning has made the village a locally important site for selling products collected in the interior and buying consumer goods from town.

With two exceptions, everyone living in Tenga't Gebaq was of Palawan descent. The exceptions were two Christian men—one a Batangueño, the other a Bisaya—who had settled in Rizal and married Palawan women. These men were among a handful of non-Palawan people who owned land in and around Tenga't Gebaq. Most Palawan in the village identified not just as Palawan but also as upstream people (*taw't daya*). Most women and many men identified as people of Malambunga (*taw't Malambunga*), but more men than women identified with other areas because of women's tendency to stay with their natal kin.[20] All of the households were related through blood or marriage, except for one Palawan family who moved to the village to distance themselves from a dispute in Ransang.

Estimating the population of Tenga't Gebaq was difficult for several reasons. Though I call it a village, it did not resemble a dense lowland village centered on a church or other public space. It was a series of clusters of related households. All were built by hand from local materials, though a few had corrugated iron roofs, and a couple were large enough to include a small *sari-sari* storefront and host gatherings. During my time there, the number of households in residence varied from around fifteen to about two dozen (including the two small clusters of houses within a half kilometer downstream). Some households varied their residence seasonally, preferring to stay by their swiddens during the weeding, guarding, and harvesting months (May–September). Others preferred to build their swiddens nearby and stay in the village year-round. Still others moved around for any number of other reasons, such as finding employment on a plantation downstream, wanting to live closer to one's almaciga trees, starting or ending a marriage, getting into a dispute with the in-laws, or needing help with a new baby. Some houses in the village sat vacant, waiting for their owners to return; others were taken apart and moved elsewhere; and one was referred to as a *kelang benwa* (big house) for hosting nuptials and other gatherings (see figure 2.1).

Figure 2.1. A Palawan "big house" (*kelang benwa*) used to host gatherings. Source: Noah Theriault.

During my initial stays in 2010–2012, the only structures in the village that were not houses included a small cockfighting ring and a vending stall with an aluminum roof. These were used for the weekly *tabuqan*—a gathering, attributed to Muslim influence, where people from the village and neighboring settlements gathered to play cards, catch up, and sell food items. Though the cockfighting ring was used as a shelter for playing cards and preparing food for wedding ceremonies, never once was an actual cockfight held during my time there. In 2016, with funds from a mining company operating in a neighboring municipality, a "satellite" elementary school was built alongside a new waiting shed for the *tabuqan*. An accredited teacher was assigned to the school, but as of 2019, she was not Palawan, lived in the lowland town, and was only able to come when weather and transportation permitted.

Palawan in Tenga't Gebaq described the village to me as an example of how they had become *sibilais* (civilized). It was only within the last generation, they said, that upstream people like them had begun living in such large settlements. The ancestral pattern had been to live in smaller, more spatially dispersed clusters or neighborhoods (*rurungan*) and move semiannually to be near active swidden fields. Newly formed households often lived near trusted elders (*pinemikitan*, "the one to whom one sticks," or *pegibutan,* "the one whom one follows"), usually the wife's parents or parents' siblings, for several years before eventually becoming an anchor for their own household cluster. These "traditional" patterns factored into many of the comings and goings in Tenga't Gebaq. We can conclude, therefore, that long-standing patterns of residential mobility remained evident in Tenga't Gebaq even as people spoke of the village as a symbol of their modernity.

Though they continued to engage in swidden and other "traditional" activities, people in Tenga't Gebaq had increasingly diversified livelihood strategies. Like Palawan elsewhere, men in particular were increasingly drawn to wage labor opportunities in the lowlands and sometimes in the provincial capital or other provinces. I noted several examples of men from the village leaving for weeks or months at a time to earn money through farm labor. Some of them returned with harrowing stories of being smuggled into Malaysia or ordered to do illegal work. Most wage earners stayed in the village but walked downstream on a regular basis to work in farms along the road, in some cases clearing and planting land they had sold to settlers or investors. Despite the increasing emphasis on waged work, the forest remained the most important source of their food, shelter, and income. A majority of households in and around Tenga't Gebaq relied on collecting almaciga and rattan as their main source of cash income. Some women made baskets, brooms, and other handicrafts to supplement their income, with one couple specializing in elaborate rattan furniture. Almost everyone in the vicinity of Tenga't Gebaq continued to make annual swiddens, though they were widely said to be smaller, less diverse, and less productive than in the past.

If we scale up beyond the village, we find the surrounding hills and mountains dotted with a mosaic of forests, swiddens, the occasional paddy field, and a few areas overtaken by cogon grass. Smaller settlements, often no more than two or three households, were scattered in the heavily forested mountains upstream. Many of those living upstream had kin in Tenga't Gebaq and came there periodically to visit, gossip, buy consumer goods, and sell forest products.

Immediately downstream, the landscape was less densely forested, with large areas cleared for plantations, charcoal making, and other purposes. Though most non-Palawan settlers lived in the lowlands—and none lived upstream of Tenga't Gebaq—several settler households had farms along the Malambunga River just downstream of the village. One such couple, who settled there in the early 1990s, also established an Adventist church and mission. Some twenty years later, the small church sat amid a cluster of Palawan households along the old logging road about a half-hour walk downstream from Tenga't Gebaq. During my research, the church had two resident missionaries, both Filipinos from other provinces, and around twenty fairly regular Palawan attendees. Similar "tribal missions" of various denominations dotted the foothills and even the mountains of southern Palawan, some established as early as the 1970s.

As one proceeds farther downstream from the church, one encounters large areas that were in the process of being cleared for rubber, pineapple, cassava, and coconut plantations. These were controlled by Christian or Muslim settlers, often in the name of absentee investors. An increasing number of Palawan from Tenga't Gebaq and environs performed wage labor on these lands. After about an hour's walk downstream, the old logging road meets a larger road that leads to the coastal "highway" and is maintained by the municipality. At the intersection of these road sits the Area Servicing Unit of the local ancestral domain (see figure 2.2). For people in Tenga't Gebaq, this crossroads marks an important boundary. Upstream is a world where one rarely crosses paths with an unfamiliar person and is likely to be related in some way to most people one encounters. Downstream is a much more diverse world, dominated by settlers and their descendants. Many Palawan live downstream of this tacit boundary, and many Palawan from upstream traverse it on a daily basis on their way to the market, school, health center, government offices, relatives' houses, and so on. It nonetheless marks a significant, if porous, social boundary.

Figure 2.2. A structure built for the ancestral domain, with sacks of almaciga piled high. Source: Noah Theriault.

During my time in Tenga't Gebaq, I stayed with a family headed by a man named Jimi and his wife, Palaya. Their three children lived in the house with us, and their eldest daughter and her Christian husband lived next door. Jimi's second wife, Jiha, lived in a separate house nearby. Incidentally, theirs was the only polygamous marriage in the immediate vicinity, though there were several others farther upstream. They had a motorbike and the village's only gasoline-powered generator and TV set, around which everyone would gather several times a week to watch an hour or two of a Korean soap opera or Filipino action flick. These possessions marked them as relatively well-off by village standards but not at all by those of the lowland majority.

Together, Palaya and Jiha ran the only store in Tenga't Gebaq—a tiny operation attached to the side of Palaya's house.[21] Their wares included tobacco, instant coffee, packaged snack foods, instant noodles, canned sardines, dried fish, and sometimes government-subsidized rice. Virtually every household in the vicinity bought consumer goods from this store when they had money to do so (some would save up and make trips to town where the markup was lower). Jimi served as a middleman in the almaciga trade. Frequently, people would sell almaciga resin to Jimi and then use the money to buy goods from his wives' store. Unlike many similar operations in the lowlands, they did not allow fellow Palawan to rack up debts that would lock them into patron–client relations. Keep in mind that virtually everyone involved in these transactions were related in some way by blood or marriage.

How and why, one might wonder, did I end up living with this particular family? I first met Jimi in 2008 when I came to Rizal for preliminary research. He was the government-recognized chieftain in the area, so it was customary that I began my queries with him. He was affable and talkative but also openly skeptical. When I first called at his house, he turned me away, explaining politely that he was too busy to "entertain" me at that moment, and I should return the following day. It was a perfectly reasonable and honest response to an unexpected visitor but also one that I had almost never encountered in the rural Philippines.

What really struck me about Jimi was the incisiveness of his commentary on Palawan relations with NGOs and the state. As a chieftain, he held a title conferred by the government, but he maintained a critical view of it all, one that I return to frequently in this book. Our initial conversations about the ancestral domain, the protected area, and environmental government in general shaped my decision to return to this area for fieldwork in 2011. As explained in the introduction, I did not expect that I would end up living with his family for as long as I did. I found that holding my promise to become *sibilais*—that is, conversant in Palawan and familiar with everyday life in the village—took a long time. Jimi was considered by many in the area to be a highly skilled executor of customary law and someone who knew how to deal with outsiders. Earning his trust did not automatically make me trustworthy to others, but it helped.

For example, Jimi's support helped me disprove rumors that I was there in search of "gold"—a common and historically informed suspicion that people in rural Palawan attach to foreigners who are not missionaries (and even to some who are).[22] People were kind to me from the very beginning, but some definitely had their suspicions. Thanks in no small measure to Jimi, most eventually seemed convinced that I did not have any ulterior motives. My commitment to learning the language and my constant, publicly visible labor on my research helped in that regard. Whatever the reasons, over time many came to treat me with a genuine sense of familiarity and trust. I cannot claim that everyone was convinced of the value of a job that involves "loitering around and asking questions," as one man teased me. But thanks to Jimi, I was able to build mutual trusting relationships with most residents.

My association with Jimi also had trade-offs. There was some jealousy in the community about his government recognition, his family's relative wealth, and his American guest. At first, I found that some people were hesitant to engage in frank conversations about matters of controversy. To address this issue, I simply invested time getting to know them and did what I could to demonstrate my independence from my hosts without betraying anyone's confidence. Although one can never know what people are withholding, this strategy seemed effective as I heard "I don't know" or "just ask Jimi" less and less frequently. My initial conversations about the recognition of chieftains suggested wide agreement that the government should use heredity in awarding the title. Jimi's father had been a chieftain and therefore Jimi was his rightful successor. Later on, I learned that people did not agree universally with this practice. Isu, a deeply respected elder, healer, and expert in customary law, explained it thus: Jimi had a plausible claim to the title because many in the community respected and "followed" him, as they had his father before. But there was no reason why it had to be Jimi. Other respected elders also deserved consideration by the state.[23]

Another way my association with Jimi limited my research was in my relations with his rival and his rival's associates. The topic of chapter 5 is a bitter dispute between Jimi and a fellow Palawan man named Bordo. In 1997, Bordo was appointed by an NGO to serve as the "president" of the ancestral domain, which Jimi had refused to sign on to. By the time of my fieldwork, their rivalry had culminated in a protracted lawsuit over almaciga permits. I took time to build rapport with Bordo, and he was extremely accommodating, but I know that he never fully trusted me. His associates were a mixed bag. One of them expressed in confidence that they agreed with Jimi's position. Another was hostile, even to the point of helping spread those rumors about my search for gold. In the end, I gained some valuable insights from my conversations with Bordo and his associates, but I was never able to become a part of that community. It was too far from Tenga't Gebaq for me to visit more often than every few weeks, and spending extended amounts of time living there would have risked alienating Jimi. Instead, I did everything I could to gain multiple perspectives on anything to do with their dispute, and then I accepted my position as one of perceived bias. I valued my rapport with Jimi too much to sacrifice it for the sake of balance.

Part of what made Jimi such a compelling interlocutor was his candor. Recall his criticism of government and NGO personnel who claim to support Indigenous rights but only "use" Palawan to leverage resources for themselves. Jimi was by no means the only Palawan person I met who felt this way. He was the only one who would say so without hesitation, euphemism, or qualification. In his mind, this was not a controversial opinion but a simple fact of history—just the latest chapter in a long history of demands from distant elites. With that in mind, I now situate my Palawan hosts in a regional history of neocolonial state formation—a history of which they are acutely aware but which is often made invisible by efforts to "save the last frontier."

1946–1986: Integration and Authoritarianism

Although the Insular Government underwent "Filipinization" beginning in 1913 and was replaced by a semi-independent republic in 1935, the Philippines did not officially gain independence until 1946. For the next twenty-seven years, the Philippine government continued to operate under the 1935 constitution, which contained no specific provisions for recognizing or administrating non-Christian tribes. Although the Bureau of Non-Christian Tribes was closed in 1936, its assimilationist mission reemerged in 1957 with the creation of a Commission on National Integration, intended to "effectuate in a more rapid and complete manner the economic, social, moral and political advancement of the non-Christian Filipinos or national cultural minorities and to render real, complete, and permanent the integration of all said national cultural minorities into the body politic."[24] Despite this ambitious mandate, the commission was chronically underfunded and thus remained "moribund."[25]

This changed under the authoritarian administration of Ferdinand Marcos, who served as president from 1965 until his ouster in 1986. Although the policy remained one of "integration," Marcos sidelined the commission and instead appointed Manuel Elizalde, one of his wealthy allies, to head the Office of the

Presidential Assistant on National Minorities (PANAMIN).[26] Founded in 1968 as a private foundation, PANAMIN became a government agency when the commission was shuttered in 1975.[27] If taken at the word of policy alone, the Marcos administration appears to be the first to legislate special rights for "cultural minorities" as such. Article XV, Section 11 of the 1973 constitution stipulates that "the State shall consider the customs, traditions, beliefs, and interests of national cultural communities in the formulation and implementation of State policies." Presidential Decree 410 of 1974 explicitly mentioned the right of "national cultural communities" to gain legal recognition of their customary claims to "ancestral lands" then in the public domain. For its part, PANAMIN was chartered to "integrate into the mainstream of Philippine society certain ethnic groups who seek full integration into the larger community, and at the same time protect the rights of those who wish to preserve their original lifeways beside that larger community."[28]

In reality, the Marcos administration had a dismal record of dispossessing and oppressing tribal people, with PANAMIN amounting to little more than a fig leaf for Marcos-backed development projects.[29] Rather than any meaningful notion of Indigenous rights, Marcos-era policies reflected an authoritarian and nationalist paternalism wherein tribal groups were either to be assimilated or preserved as a sort of living museum of Filipino heritage. PANAMIN gained international notoriety in 1971 when Elizalde claimed to have discovered the Tasaday, an isolated, "stone age" tribe in western Mindanao. More than a decade later, it was revealed that although the Tasaday were real, much of what Elizalde had said about them was fabricated.[30] In the interim, Elizalde's "protection" of the Tasaday, who by law could not be contacted without PANAMIN's permission, gave symbolic legitimacy to the Marcos administration at the same time as logging, ranching, hydropower, mining projects, and counterinsurgency campaigns were devastating Indigenous groups in Luzon and Mindanao. Worse still, some of PANAMIN's activities involved not just propaganda but direct participation in counterinsurgency.[31] As I will explain, PANAMIN had a presence in Palawan, including in Rizal.

Marcos also attempted to position himself as an environmentalist. Twenty-one national parks were established during his tenure, including the Puerto Princesa Subterranean River National Park in central Palawan. In 1967, his administration declared all of Palawan a game refuge and bird sanctuary, in which all unauthorized killing of wildlife was prohibited.[32] This proclamation could have had dire implications for Palawan livelihood, which relied heavily on hunting, but like so many such policies, it was never really enforced. Eight years later, Marcos issued a Revised Forestry Code, which remains in effect and largely unreformed.[33] Presidential Decree 705 was meant to gain control over an unbridled postwar logging rush. Its more lasting effect has been to legitimate state dispossession of upland Indigenous people: The law makes all lands above 600 meters or with greater than 18 percent slope public domain, and it singles out swiddeners, squatters, and cultural minorities for monitoring and possible expulsion.

A final policy worth noting was the establishment in 1982 of an Integrated Social Forestry Program, which Marcos approved as a condition of development loans from lenders like the United States Agency for International Development (USAID) and the Asian Development Bank.[34] In practice this policy amounted to "nothing more than a glorified lease contract" for loggers, but the legal framework it established provided a legal framework for more meaningful reforms under later administrations.[35]

The Postwar and Marcos Years in Rizal: Logging, Settlement, and Monetization

As I learned during my research, the postwar years still loomed large in the memories of Palawan elders in Tenga't Gebaq but not because of the Marcos regime's conservation efforts. In 1945, the US Coast Guard established a LORAN radio navigation station at Tarumpitao Point near the mouth of the Malambunga River. Tenga't Gebaq is some ten kilometers upstream of Tarumpitao. Even though the dozen or so Americans stationed there never had administrative authority over the Indigenous population, their presence had a definite effect. One elder said her mother was among several Palawan women who lived as the companions of American servicemen during their tours there. Several elders reported that the Americans "taught" them to wear modern clothing (as opposed to the traditional *baqag* loincloth for men and *tapis* skirt for women). Jimi's father, who passed away in 1996, was said to be among those who first started wearing such clothing while working for the Americans in exchange for tobacco, clothing, and salt. His father, Jimi said, loved attending weekly movie screenings at the station and had a particular affinity for a film about a man who lived in the jungle and wore a loincloth (presumably Tarzan). The LORAN station was handed over to the Philippine Coast Guard in 1971 and closed six years later. Even so, it came up frequently in my conversations with people. Perhaps its greatest significance was as a point of cultural contact. The American presence was among the key turning points in local narratives of how Palawan people in the area became *sibilais*.[36]

For the people of Malambunga, another significant development of the postwar years was the advent of commercial logging in Rizal. Before the war,

American, Filipino, and Japanese companies logged most of the accessible areas along Palawan's coast, particularly in the northern half of the island.[37] After the war, Filipino companies backed by domestic and foreign capital set their sights on more remote areas. In the north, Pagdanan Timber Products made a fortune for its owner, Jose "Pepito" Alvarez, who remains a key player in Palawan politics today. The first logging company to receive a timber license agreement in Rizal, then still part of the municipality of Quezon, was the Aguinaldo Development Corporation (ADECOR). Its operation began around 1965 but ended in 1968, when the Marcos administration canceled its timber license agreement. In 1974, Western Palawan Timber (WesPal)—a company financed by the Philippines Veterans Development Corporation, a tax-exempt investment fund created by Marcos for military officers—took over ADECOR's concession. I never found any government documents related to these companies' activities, but I learned from former employees that they had timber license agreements to cut select species within five kilometers of the coast. They built a network of dirt roads going from loading docks at the coast into the foothills. Today most are little more than rocky footpaths, but they remain an important part of the local geography. As mentioned, Tenga't Gebaq is located at the interior terminus of one of these paths, affording residents somewhat easier access to lowland markets and services.

Although some Palawan obtained occasional wage work in the logging companies' reforestation projects, all Palawan who remembered the logging companies considered them a menace. I was told repeatedly that the companies had taken tree species that they were not permitted to log, including large hardwoods that many Palawan say are home to potentially dangerous spirits (see chapter 4). Worst of all was the threat the companies posed to the almaciga trees, whose commercially valuable resin Palawan relied on for access to trade goods. In some Palawan accounts of this time, WesPal's encroachment on the almaciga trees was the company's downfall. WesPal's operations in Rizal coincided with the nationwide spread of armed resistance to the faltering Marcos regime, and southern Palawan was no exception. Armed rebel groups, including those affiliated with the New People's Army (a Maoist guerrilla movement) and the Moro National Liberation Front (a Muslim separatist group), set up camps in the foothills and mountains of Rizal, including one just downstream of Tenga't Gebaq. This was a frightening time for residents, who say they were caught between the rebels and military. In recounting this history, some Palawan expressed gratitude to the rebels for driving out WesPal. By the early 1980s, the company's loggers had worked their way into the mountains and were starting to cut almaciga trees. But then, purportedly in an act of solidarity with Palawan communities, rebels attacked one of WesPal's camps and forced the company to cease its operations.[38]

During this turbulent period, the quasi-governmental agency PANAMIN was active in Rizal and in other parts of Palawan. PANAMIN's field officer in Rizal was a former employee of ADECOR. When I interviewed him in August 2011, he told me about how he and his colleagues had established "reservations" for Palawan in Iraan and Ransang (which are, respectively, north and south of Malambunga). Describing these settlements as an effort to teach Palawan basic literacy and sedentary farming, he denied that they had any relation to logging activities or insurgency. Around that same time, though, a local government official proposed her own version of a PANAMIN reservation in the Malambunga area, and she openly admitted that it was an effort to protect Palawan from clashes between the rebels and the military. Whatever its motives, PANAMIN was active at a number of other conflict-ridden logging sites in Palawan, and given what we know about the organization's operations in other provinces, it seems reasonable to speculate that the mounting insurgency in Rizal prompted its entry there. By the time of my fieldwork, the land that had been used for its reservations had largely been taken over by Christian settlers.

For the Palawan communities of Malambunga, the logging years were crucial for three additional reasons. The first has to do with the arrival of settlers. Although mass settlement had been under way in more accessible parts of Palawan since immediately after World War II, it was not until the 1970s and 1980s that large numbers of settlers began arriving in Rizal. In fact, before April 1983, Rizal did not even exist as an independent municipality but was instead part of Quezon to the north.[39] Between 1980 and 2010, Rizal's population grew from an estimated 12,950 in 1980 and to 42,759 in 2010—an astounding 7.67 percent average annual growth rate. For this same period, Palawan's overall growth rate of 4.76 percent was significantly lower, though still extremely high in absolute terms. In Rizal, logging operations helped fuel this process in two ways. First, they brought most of their employees with them from other areas. Second, in Rizal as in many other "frontiers," settlers followed on the heels of ADECOR and WesPal because of the infrastructure they built and commerce they generated. Logging has also been an inducement to pioneering agriculture because logged-over areas are easier to clear, burn, and plant.[40]

As in other parts of Palawan, migrant settlement has led to a radical transformation of the lowlands into a landscape dominated by intensive agriculture, particularly paddy rice and coconut plantations, that increasingly resembles other parts of the Philippines.[41] Although some Palawan have always lived in the mountainous interior, many lived and cut swiddens in forests closer to the shore, where they could rely on marine food sources seasonally. As the lowland population of Rizal has grown, many Palawan have sold their land near the coast (and, in some cases, in irrigable spots along rivers) and retreated to the foothills, where they can continue to engage in swidden and traditional subsistence activities. Others have stayed put but abandoned swidden in favor of intensive agriculture, with varying degrees of success. This process of land privatization and dispossession is dramatically changing how many Palawan conceive of the land and make a living from it, most notably by undermining their long-standing, cosmologically significant sources of livelihood and making them increasingly dependent on forest commodities, wage labor, and debt. It has also dramatically changed the landscape. In Rizal, following a pattern begun earlier in the rest of Palawan, much of the coastal plain was cleared of forest and converted to intensive agriculture during this period. Relative to logging, migrant settlement has been the greater cause of deforestation and thus the greater force in undermining Palawan subsistence.[42]

This leads me to the second momentous change that my hosts said accompanied the logging companies: money. Money was certainly in circulation in Rizal before the 1970s, as were commodity products like tobacco and salt. The influx of wage workers and settlers made monetized transactions increasingly common and unavoidable, particularly in the case of land sales. With an expansion of transport infrastructure, the almaciga trade started to pick up in Rizal during this time. Palawan use almaciga as a fire accelerant and incense, but its industrial applications produce varnish and other products. Along with rattan, almaciga had been big business in the northern parts of Palawan for some time. We know that the settler-controlled trade in almaciga and rattan had already become a major source of livelihood (and indebtedness) among Tagbanua in central Palawan.[43] In Rizal, Palawan elders consistently told me that their ancestors had long traded almaciga with settlers in exchange for salt and other goods, but it was typically small quantities and rarely resulted in debt. Selling almaciga, they said, had only become the centerpiece of their livelihood in the last generation. This development owed partly to the overall intensification of commodity flows as settlers brought Rizal more deeply into the regional economy. It also owes to a Marcos administration policy that encouraged the commodification of "minor forest products" by rewarding allies with exclusive territorial concessions. By the 1980s, concessionaires were firmly established in Rizal. In a pattern similar to what Fox described among the Tagbanua as early as 1950, almaciga was becoming the key source of Indigenous income—and debt—among Palawan.[44]

Finally, the third major change of the postwar years concerned the authority of the Muslim *datu*, a hereditary title indicating a relation to the sultan and conferring the authority to organize tribute and resolve disputes. Historically, no Palawan man ever became a *datu*, though Islamized Palawan women sometimes married *datu* and bore heirs to the title. Instead, *datu* appointed Palawan to positions with titles like *panglima, satya,* and *maradya,* some of which are etymologically of Sanskrit origin but are traced by Palawan to the Moros. These people served as intermediaries between the *datu* and fellow Palawan and would bring disputes to the *datu* when Palawan dispute mediators could not resolve them. Although the Sulu sultanate was dismantled beginning in the late 1870s, *datu* continued to hold a certain degree of moral authority over Palawan communities, particularly but not exclusively over those who lived near the coast and were Islamized to varying degrees.[45] Present-day Palawan elders told me that through most of the twentieth century, *datu* continued to serve as an external form of jural authority for certain segments of the Palawan population.

The number of Islamized Palawan or "Penimusan," has grown in recent decades, continuing a process that was foreshadowed in Whitehead's journal and that Macdonald characterizes as a long-term process of ethnogenesis.[46] Nevertheless, over this same period, the mass arrival of Christian settlers and the establishment of Philippine government institutions, particularly at the local or *barangay* level, has largely superseded the role of the *datu*. The result is that my Palawan hosts no longer associated external authority with Muslim *datu* or sultans. Instead, I found that Palawan elders associated the *gubyerno* (government) almost exclusively with the Kabisayaan (Christian settlers).[47] When I asked one respected elder what exactly the government was, he replied that I should be asking the Kabisayaan because they are the ones who introduced and control it. To the extent that claimants to the hereditary *datu* title held political authority, it was primarily a result of their having taken positions in local government. In the Malambunga area, for example, the descendants of Datu Lamba Kakoy Narrazid remained locally prominent as elected officials and businesspeople, even though none of them claimed to be a *datu* as such. In this respect, their relations with Palawan communities largely took the same forms as those of long-settled Christian migrants. Even so, my Palawan interlocutors did not generally equate the present-day government of the Kabisayaan with the authority of the Muslim *datu*. To the contrary, they saw the former as more capacious and transformative. For better or worse, I was told, the Kabisayaan state regulated Palawan affairs much more intensively than the sultanates ever did.

1986–Present: Indigenous Rights and Biodiversity

After Marcos's ouster in 1986, a new constitution was enacted and a process of liberal reforms undertaken. Two of these reforms, also connected to broader global trends, have had far-reaching consequences for Indigenous people and their environments. I am referring to the legal recognition of Indigenous rights and the institutionalization of biodiversity conservation. These reforms represented hard-fought victories for Filipino reformers and inspired hope around the world that the Philippines was finally transcending its colonial "plunder economy."[48] Fulfilling this hope has since proven extremely challenging.

Indigenous Recognition and Rights in the Philippines

The use of the word "Indigenous" in post-1986 reforms was a conscious repudiation of earlier categories (pagans, non-Christian tribes, national minorities) and the ethnocentric, assimilationist policies they underpinned.[49] Though actual beliefs about Indigenous people have retained older prejudices, it was no longer politically correct to treat Indigenous people as "uncivilized" or "wild."[50] Indigeneity was more inclusive. Whatever connotations it might carry, being Indigenous did not denote the presence or absence of tribal organization or religious affiliation. More concretely, the turn to indigeneity was driven by connections forged between minority groups' resistance to Marcos-era development aggression and an emerging transnational Indigenous rights movement. The struggle against the Chico Dam was arguably the most consequential. In the 1970s and 1980s, various Igorot groups in northern Luzon partnered with both communist rebels and international human rights activists to protest the World Bank–funded dam project. Dorothea Hilhorst writes that mainstream leaders of the movement ended up embracing notions of Indigenous self-determination and autonomy as a result of their collaboration with the United Nations and other proponents of the transnational Indigenous movement.[51] Their success in garnering support among Filipino intellectuals and activists played an important role in the constitutional embrace of Indigenous rights.

Although Indigenous rights had a foothold in the 1987 constitution, the language used was ambiguous. On the one hand, the constitution reinscribes the regalian doctrine, declaring all nonagricultural land as "public domain" under the ownership of the state.[52] On the other hand, the constitution provides for the creation of two autonomous regions (in the Cordillera and Mindanao) and enjoins the state to protect Indigenous rights and well-being elsewhere. Article XII, Section 5 stipulates, "The State, subject to the provisions of this Constitution and national development policies and programs, shall protect the rights of Indigenous cultural communities to their ancestral lands to ensure their economic, social, and cultural well-being. The Congress may provide for the applicability of customary laws governing property rights or relations in determining the ownership and extent of ancestral domain." With these potentially contradictory constitutional directives, it was left to the bureaucracy and legislature to define indigeneity and the rights it entails. What has ensued has been convoluted, to say the least. Initially, the Corazon Aquino administration created three subcabinet agencies charged with implementing the Indigenous rights provisions of the constitution: the Office of Southern Cultural Communities, the Office of Northern Cultural Communities, and the Office of Muslim Affairs. While waiting for Congress to pass enabling legislation, they began laying the groundwork for recognizing ancestral land claims. In Palawan, this involved appointing chieftains and establishing tribal councils in each *barangay* with Indigenous residents (more on this later). Beyond this, little progress was made. Eder and McKenna observe that "the local offices of these . . . agencies were lightly staffed and received little regular funding, [leaving] members of ethnic minority groups in need of material, legal, or other forms of assistance . . . to turn to a variety of better-staffed and better-funded NGOs."[53]

Meanwhile, the enabling legislation was stalled in Congress. This left implementation in the hands of the Department of Environment and Natural Resources (DENR), which had jurisdiction over all public lands eligible for recognition as ancestral lands. Although some in the DENR opposed recognizing customary claims to public lands, the Indigenous Community Affairs Division managed to push a series of policies through the approval process.[54] Their efforts culminated with the 1993 issuance of a Department Administrative Order, which spelled out guidelines for issuing Certificates of Ancestral Domain Claim. Some Indigenous rights groups opposed the order's guidelines for a number of reasons.[55] First, because these ancestral domains were recognized only on the basis of a departmental order, they could be overridden by other laws, such as the Mining Act of 1995, under which such a claim would "provide no impediment to the granting of mining exploration leases."[56] Second, these certificates only provided for ancestral domain claims and not titles, thus perpetuating state ownership of Indigenous land. Third, the DENR's guidelines included numerous clauses that could compel Indigenous groups to cooperate with conservation and other government interventions. I revisit these and other important features of the guidelines later.[57] For now, it suffices to say that whatever their limitations, these guidelines enabled the DENR to recognize more than 100 ancestral domain claims, covering some 2.546 million hectares in different parts of the country.[58]

One salient and arguably more salutary feature of the guidelines was the use of the term "ancestral domain" in addition to "ancestral land."[59] The constitution used both terms, but proponents of Indigenous rights reforms had favored ancestral domain as a more socioculturally inclusive and legally robust concept of territory. Filipino jurist Marvic Leonen, who has been a leading advocate for Indigenous rights, traces the use of "ancestral domain" to a 1985 conference of the

Anthropological Association of the Philippines. "Advocates," he recalled, "wanted a common slogan."[60] Unlike ancestral land or its Tagalog equivalent (*lupang ninuno*), "ancestral domain" encompasses the wide range of Indigenous conceptions of territory. Gus Gatmaytan, a Filipino anthropologist and attorney who has figured centrally in Indigenous rights advocacy, adds that the term "domain" signifies not just land but all of the dimensions of an Indigenous territory, including marine, lacustrine, subterranean, and spiritual spaces and resources.[61]

Never intended to be a permanent arrangement, the DENR's framework for ancestral domain recognition lasted only five years. In 1997, Congress finally passed the Indigenous People's Rights Act (IPRA), which provided a comprehensive legal framework for the protection of Indigenous rights, including an upgraded tenure mechanism called the Certificate of Ancestral Domain Title. A new government agency—the National Commission on Indigenous People (NCIP)—was created to oversee IPRA's implementation. As with the ancestral domain claim guidelines, policy makers again faced the politically fraught task of defining indigeneity. The Philippines was never a settler colony, making the question of who is Indigenous even more vexing than it already is in countries like the United States, Australia, or Mexico. After all, aren't all Philippine ethnic groups Indigenous to the archipelago?

In practice, indigeneity does not refer simply to place of origin but to historical processes of colonization and marginalization. Faced with this complexity, IPRA's authors arrived at the following definition:

> Indigenous Cultural Communities/Indigenous Peoples . . . refer to a group of people or homogenous societies identified by self-ascription and ascription by others, who have continuously lived as *organized community* on *communally bounded and defined territory,* and who have, under claims of ownership since *time immemorial,* occupied, possessed and utilized such territories, sharing common bonds of language, customs, traditions and other distinctive cultural traits, or who have, through resistance to political, social and cultural inroads of colonization, non-Indigenous religions and cultures, became *historically differentiated from the majority of Filipinos.* ICCs/IPs shall likewise include peoples who are regarded as Indigenous on account of their descent from the populations which inhabited the country, at the time of conquest or colonization, or at the time of inroads of non-Indigenous religions and cultures, or the establishment of present state boundaries, who *retain some or all of their own social, economic, cultural and political institutions,* but who may have been displaced from their traditional domains or who may have resettled outside their ancestral domains.[62]

Under IPRA, minoritized groups who meet these criteria are entitled to specific economic, social, political, and cultural rights, which are further divided into four general classes: rights to (1) ancestral domains, (2) self-governance and empowerment, (3) social justice and human rights, and (4) cultural integrity.[63] To protect these rights, IPRA requires "free and prior informed consent" be obtained under the NCIP's supervision by anyone hoping to engage Indigenous people in business contracts, research activities, or development projects.[64]

IPRA's passage made the Philippines the first country in Asia to adopt international standards for Indigenous rights and was hailed around the world as one of the most progressive pieces of legislation of its kind. Immediately, though, several aspects of the law raised concerns. To say nothing of the pitfalls of expecting Indigenous people to be culturally distinctive and "homogenous," IPRA stipulates a handful of responsibilities that could, under certain circumstances, undermine the very rights the law is meant to protect.[65] These responsibilities center on the expectation that Indigenous groups will "maintain an ecological balance" in their ancestral domains "by protecting the flora and fauna, watershed areas, and other reserves." Specifically, in ancestral domains that the government deems "necessary for critical watersheds, mangroves, wildlife sanctuaries, wilderness, protected areas, forest cover, or reforestation," Indigenous people "shall be given the responsibility to maintain, develop, protect and conserve such areas with the full and effective assistance of government agencies." To square these expectations with the right to self-determination and development, one must assume (as the authors of IPRA evidently did) that Indigenous people's self-determination by default will lead to ecological balance and environmental conservation. This "eco-indigenism" sets up expectations that Indigenous people sometimes find very difficult to live up to—as when Indigenous groups who support or propose particular conservation or development projects find their authenticity challenged.[66]

Notwithstanding these weaknesses, Indigenous groups in Palawan and elsewhere have filed hundreds of applications for recognition of their ancestral domains. The process is a laborious, expensive, technically complex, and it requires hundreds of pages of documentation. Not only do applicants have to prove they meet the criteria of indigeneity—by producing maps, ethnographic narratives, kinship diagrams, and oral histories—they have to prepare a management plan that inventories local resources and establishes guidelines for their stewardship. In virtually all cases, this requires the technical assistance of NGO and government experts and financial support from foreign or domestic funders. Hirtz has aptly described this paradoxical situation as a form of "bureaucratic Orientalism," wherein Indigenous groups must use the tools of modern government and science to demonstrate that they remain outside of modernity.[67]

Even for groups that do manage to obtain an ancestral domain claim or title, recognition is no panacea. Neither a claim nor a title can abrogate valid, preexisting claims held by non-Indigenous people in an ancestral domain. Nor can these documents simply undo the long-standing structural inequalities that drive dispossession and lead Indigenous groups to sell their land or enter exploitative contracts. For example, one of the main benefits of ancestral domain recognition is priority access to permits for the sale of non-timber forest products, such as almaciga, rattan, and honey. Indigenous rights advocates have envisioned Indigenous control of these permits as a crucial step toward long-term tenurial security and sustainable development. However, because the permits are costly to secure and marketing operations require capital, financiers have used capital advances and resulting cycles of debt to convert ancestral domains into de facto private concessions.[68] This is precisely what happened with the ancestral domain where I conducted my fieldwork.

For its part, the NCIP has done little to address these concerns. Part of its problem is a lack of funding and technical capacity. The agency took nearly fifteen years just to begin implementing the IPRA provision that requires Indigenous representation in all legislative bodies. It has refused to recognize ancestral domain claims issued by the DENR, instead subjecting claim holders to an intensive—and expensive—redocumentation and validation process. Meanwhile, ancestral domain title applicants must pay not just for the technical expertise needed to document land claims but also for the travel and per diem costs of government personnel when their presence is required in the field for documentation and validation. This practice means that title applications often stall when the organizations supporting them run out of funding. It puts deep-pocketed proponents of mining and other extractive projects at a systematic advantage over those who oppose them. What results is a conflict of interest such that the NCIP cannot operate independently of the companies and organizations that have resources to pay for its services. The agency is embroiled in the very resource politics that it is supposed to regulate on behalf of Indigenous peoples.[69]

Simply put, IPRA and the bureaucracy it created are fraught with ambivalences and contradictions. The law grants Indigenous people rights to greater self-determination and autonomy but then makes those rights contingent on more intensive coordination with the central government. Nevertheless, I think it would be a mistake to dismiss the ancestral domain system as little more than a project of bureaucratization and subjection. Minoritized people may come to see themselves as Indigenous subjects whose rights begin and end with the Philippine state. But they may also use those rights to challenge the state.[70] In chapter 5,

I detail a case where ancestral domain rights have been successfully invoked in a way that complicates the expectations of "bureaucratic Orientalism."

Protected Areas and Biodiversity

Reforms after 1986 also had profound implications for environmental regulation. Between 1950 and 1987, national forest cover declined from 55 to 22 percent, and the country's fisheries and coral reefs also experienced severe rates of decline.[71] Bolstered by growing international concern, Filipino reformers were eager to set the nation on a course to sustainable development and protect what was left of its "natural heritage." Among the first measures taken by the Aquino administration was a ban on the export of logs in 1986 and then of all timber in 1989. These restrictions have been eased somewhat by later administrations, but nonetheless they have had a real effect. Log harvests declined from 6.4 million cubic meters in 1980 to 0.8 million in 1995.[72] Since then, production has continued apace, but according to the DENR, only 2 percent of logs in 2011 were from wild sources, with the remainder harvested from forest plantations. Also in 2011, in the wake of devastating floods, President Benigno Aquino III placed a moratorium on logging natural forests on public land, ordered a comprehensive review of timber licensing policy, and created a special task force to combat illegal logging. Logging interests have charged that the ban favors illegal loggers and corrupt enforcers, the likes of which remain rampant in some areas. Yet with national forest cover stalled at around 25 percent, the disastrous effects of deforestation increasingly evident, and growing incentives to protect forests as carbon sinks, the ban was maintained by Rodrigo Duterte's administration and, as of March 2023, has yet to be overturned by Ferdinand Marcos Jr.[73] Even so, the rate of deforestation increased under Duterte and has remained at around 8,000 hectares a year since peaking in 2017.[74]

Although Philippine law still allows for industrial-scale timber operations, mining, plantations, and other drivers of deforestation, recent reforms have favored the "devolution" and "decentralization" of forest management, part of a global shift in thinking on forest regulation. I have already discussed one outcome of these reforms—ancestral domain policies—which reflect a convergence of decentralized approaches to forest management and the Indigenous rights movement. Another outcome was the 1995 establishment of a community-based forest management program.[75] As of its 2022 annual report, the DENR recognized 1,958 community-based forestry contracts covering some 1.633 million hectares, including renewals of analogous "social forestry" contracts issued during the Marcos administration.[76] Perhaps not surprisingly, the results of this reform have been mixed.[77] Some areas have been similarly co-opted by capitalist interests. As with ancestral domains, lax regulation of extractive activities means that forest products like rattan and almaciga are rapidly being depleted in areas covered by these agreements.

A related priority of post-Marcos reformers was conserving biodiversity.[78] Their efforts culminated in the formation of the National Integrated Protected Areas System (NIPAS), through which the DENR was to "secure for the Filipino people of present and future generations the perpetual existence of all native plants and animals through the establishment of a comprehensive system of integrated protected areas within the classification of national park" as provided for in the constitution.[79] Internationally, this was a time when US and European conservation NGOs, such as the World Wildlife Fund and Conservation International, were learning to tap into global financial markets and emerging as powerful multinational organizations.[80] In the Philippines too, NGOs of all types were enjoying unprecedented influence as a result of liberalization.[81] Impetus for NIPAS came largely from the lobbying efforts of two NGOs: the World Wildlife Fund and a Filipino environmentalist organization called Haribon. In collaboration with the DENR, they underwrote the first two "phases" of NIPAS's implementation with a $2 million "debt-for-nature swap" and a $16 million grant from the World Bank's Global Environment Facility.[82]

Like IPRA, NIPAS is an ambivalent policy. On the one hand, it aims to unify what had been a chaotic landscape of conservation instruments under the aegis of the DENR and then expand that unified system over new territories. On the other hand, NIPAS is intended to decentralize and democratize protected area management. Under NIPAS, there are seven different types of protected areas and an eighth category allowing for the creation of new types. These vary in the extent to which human activity is permitted—from "strict nature preserves" at one extreme to "protected landscapes" at the other—but each requires the creation of a representative protected area management board. Any such board, the law states, should consist of representatives from all levels of government (including all *barangay* that overlap with the protected area), from civil society, and from any affected Indigenous communities. In practice, these boards are composed of a mix of politicians, bureaucrats, and ordinary citizens, who bring very different skills and experiences to the table. Although each member technically has the same authority, relations among them are shaped by broader structural inequalities that make certain forms of knowledge more authoritative than others. As a result, the "expert" board members are legally instructed to assemble its management plan for submission to fellow members. In practice if not in policy, decisions on protected area policy are dominated by those with the technical knowledge and political acumen to make their voices heard (more on this later).[83]

Another salient but ambivalent feature of NIPAS is its inclusion of "protected landscapes" along with more conventional types of protected areas like wildlife sanctuaries and resource reserves. By definition, a landscape acknowledges the presence and ecological importance of human communities: "Protected landscapes and seascapes are areas of national significance which are characterized by the harmonious interaction of man and land."[84] Furthermore, NIPAS also contains provisions forbidding the eviction of Indigenous people and "tenured migrant communities." These provisions are a clear attempt to protect the tenurial rights of rural communities, particularly Indigenous ones. But here too we encounter ambivalence. Consider this question: Do the provisions of IPRA, which protect self-determination, give Indigenous people the right to refuse conservation?

The legal answer to that question is, simply, "no." NIPAS stipulates that Indigenous communities must be included in protected area planning and management, but the DENR has ultimate and unilateral authority to establish conservation enclosures on public lands regardless of whether the land is also an ancestral domain. As we saw already, ancestral domain policies, including IPRA, reconcile with NIPAS by stipulating that Indigenous groups "shall be given the responsibility" to manage the protected area. This reflects the assumption, also built into IPRA, that Indigenous communities "maintain an ecological balance" in their ancestral domains. A speciously simple narrative is thus constructed: Because Indigenous people live in harmony with nature, they will cooperate harmoniously with conservation, as will the various government agencies that supervise them. This narrative effaces tensions between the recognition of Indigenous territorial rights and the government's authority to create conservation enclosures, but it cannot make those tensions disappear entirely.[85]

Indigeneity and Biodiversity in Palawan

Since 1986, Palawan has become a key symbol—and a proving ground of sorts—for postauthoritarian policies like IPRA, community-based forestry, and NIPAS. With the global rise of biodiversity conservation, Palawan's high concentration of endemic species—and the relative health of its marine and terrestrial ecosystems—has attracted a deluge of international attention. In 1991, the province was declared a UNESCO Biosphere Reserve, and over the next decade two of its protected areas (the Puerto Princesa Subterranean River and the Tubbataha Reef) were listed as UNESCO World Heritage Sites. Filipino environmentalists have taken the lead in Palawan's rise as a biodiversity hot spot, but more often their initiatives have been backed by internationally funded

NGOs rather than by the Philippine state. As a result, the past quarter century has seen a proliferation of conservation and development projects sponsored by international development agencies (UN Development Programme, USAID, Danish International Development Agency, European Union, etc.) and transnational NGOs (World Wildlife Fund, Helvetas, Conservation International, World Vision, etc.). Palawan has also become home to an influential community of national and regional NGOs, which often receive foreign funding but have nonetheless demonstrated a significant degree of independence and durability.[86] In 1992, they successfully lobbied for a commercial logging ban that has remained in place ever since.

The first centralized, internationally funded effort to coordinate development and conservation in Palawan dates to 1981, when the European Economic Community sponsored the Palawan Integrated Area Development Project.[87] The first phase of the project (1981–1990) culminated in the passage of a national law, the Strategic Environmental Plan (SEP) for Palawan, and the creation of a government agency, the Palawan Council for Sustainable Development (PCSD), charged with the plan's implementation. The strategic plan and PCSD are unique—no other province in the country has a special bureaucracy mandated to oversee "sustainable development."[88] The PCSD is staffed by civil servants, but its governing board is composed mainly of politicians and their appointees, with a couple of seats reserved for civil society representatives.

Beyond serving as a permitting body and providing legal services, the PCSD's chief mandate is to oversee an exhaustive zoning scheme for the province's terrestrial and marine territory. This scheme, known as the Environmentally Critical Areas Network, aims to specify which (if any) human activities are acceptable in every square centimeter of the province. The network's zoning maps are meant to be integrated with planning and regulatory activities by all levels of government. This ambitious scheme calls for ongoing research, negotiation, and monitoring, which the PCSD has partially devolved to resource-strapped municipal governments. It has been politicized and manipulated by vested interests. In fact, among many Filipino environmentalists, the PCSD has lost much of its credibility because of its perceived bias in favor of the mining industry. Whether credible or not, the PCSD adds to a highly fragmented regulatory environment—one that sends government officials and Indigenous people conflicting signals about Indigenous rights and obligations.

In addition to serving as a laboratory of sorts for novel forms of environmental governance, Palawan has also been a pivotal site for ancestral domain recognition. In 1989, Indigenous leaders in Palawan founded an NGO known in Tagalog as the Nakakaisang mga Tribu ng Palawan (NATRIPAL; United Tribes of Palawan), which has since remained the only durable Indigenous-run NGO in the province. NATRIPAL was (and is) a federation of Indigenous people's organizations scattered throughout mainland Palawan, with its staff and board of directors drawn from its constituent organizations. In the early 1990s, as the DENR began issuing guidelines for ancestral domain recognition, NATRIPAL received international funding to assist its member organizations with applications for ancestral domain claims and forest product permits.[89] Claims were designed not to be awarded to whole ethnolinguistic populations (e.g., the Tagbanua or Palawan) but to legally registered people's organizations representing spatially contiguous "communities" in the larger population. Thus, for each member organization that applied for a claim, NATRIPAL organized a tribal council with a president and other officers bearing titles drawn from the Indigenous language. These organizations were essentially constituted as nonprofit businesses for buying and selling non-timber forest products, which were envisioned as a culturally appropriate form of sustainable development. Efforts to make these operations self-sustaining in the long run accounted for much of the technical support and funding provided by NATRIPAL and its partners.[90]

Dozens of ancestral domain claim applications were initiated, but only seven were ever awarded. (Keep in mind that this number does not include ancestral domain title applications that were initiated after 1998 under the aegis of IPRA.) Recall that the ancestral domain application process, whether for a claim or a title, requires a great deal of time, effort, and technical expertise. Application materials include detailed maps, censuses, ethnographic narratives, genealogies, forest product inventories, resource management plans, evidence of consultation with non-Indigenous residents, and more. All of this must be validated in situ by government agencies that charge a per diem and transportation costs to the applicant organization. Simply put, without the technical and financial assistance of NGOs, it was (and is) impossible for Indigenous groups in Palawan to apply for ancestral domain recognition.

In Rizal, NATRIPAL's original plan was to apply for contiguous ancestral domain claims on behalf of Palawan people in all of the municipality's eleven *barangays*. This ultimately proved unrealistic, so a combined claim was secured on behalf of Palawan communities in two neighboring *barangays*—Punta Baja and Campung Ulay—which had been chosen as pilot sites for the enterprise development support.[91] Tenga't Gebaq was within the resulting ancestral domain.

At the same time that NATRIPAL was working to establish ancestral domains in Rizal and other parts of Palawan, the European Union launched a conservation and ancestral domain initiative known as the Palawan Tropical Forest Protection Program. Their goal was to create an integrated watershed management system for all of southern Palawan. It sponsored the construction of "tribal education centers" in several ancestral domains, but by the time of my fieldwork, most of these were being used for other purposes. The main outcome was a set of watershed management plans and the creation of another specialized government agency, the Southern Palawan Planning Council, to execute them. This new agency had limited resources, so, in 2002, Conservation International (CI) picked up the initiative and shifted the agenda to establishing a protected area. In 2009, this became the Mount Mantalingahan Protected Landscape, a 120,457-hectare national park that straddles southern Palawan's mountainous spine, spanning thirty-four watersheds in five different municipalities.[92] In 2010, the European Union awarded another major grant to aid in Mantalingahan's establishment.[93] In 2020, CI partnered with megacorporation Procter & Gamble for a five-year project to strengthen the park as a "natural climate solution." Their main priorities were to intensify enforcement and expand CI's practice of forging "conservation agreements" with Palawan communities inside the park's boundaries. From the beginning, proponents have promised to make the park self-sustaining through user fees, carbon credits, and monetization of "ecosystem services." So far, though, it has been almost completely dependent on international funding and dwindling subventions from the five concerned municipalities.

As required by NIPAS, Mantalingahan's management board is composed of some seventy members, including representatives from all levels of government, a host of bureaucratic agencies, two NGOs, and five Indigenous representatives. Although the park's co-management involves many different sectors, Indigenous people are expected to play a uniquely important part. For one thing, they make up an estimate 94 percent of the 12,000 or so people who actually live within its boundaries. Even more important, the existence of ancestral domains and protected landscapes assumes the propensity of Indigenous people to "maintain the ecological balance" of their territory. Including the ancestral domain where Jimi and Bordo live, fourteen different Indigenous tenurial certificates of three different types overlap with Mantalingahan: eleven Certificates of Ancestral Land Claim, two Certificates of Ancestral Domain Claim, and one Certificate of Ancestral Domain Title. These overlapping claims have forced park officials to grapple with the ambivalences lurking beneath the putative "harmony" of ancestral domains and protected areas.

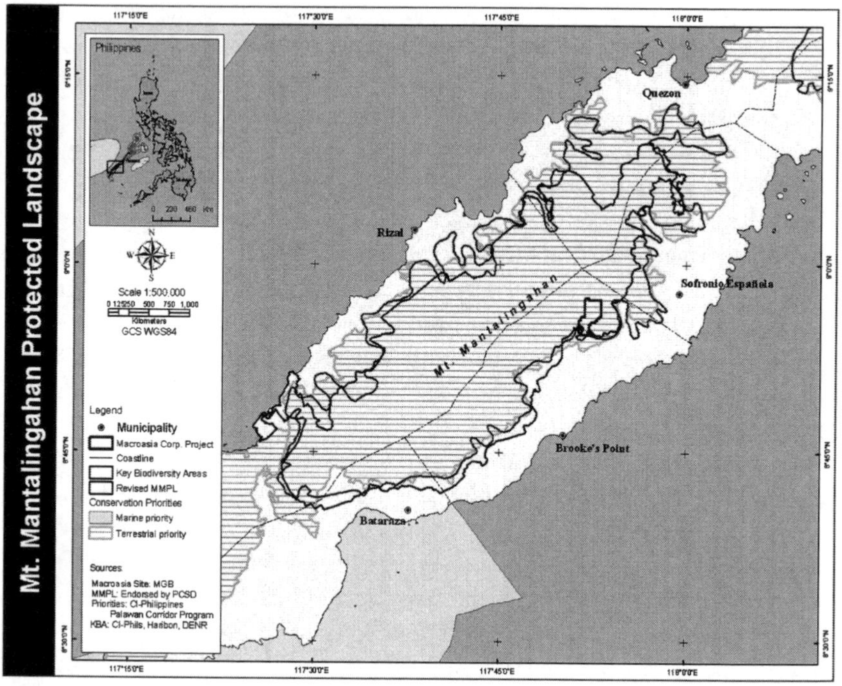

Map 3. Mount Mantalingahan Protected Landscape with overlapping mining interests and additional conservation priority areas. Source: Conservation International—Philippines.

Mantalingahan's management plan adopts the NIPAS zoning scheme, with 76.8 percent classified as "core zone" and another 20.4 percent as various types of "buffer zones." Per the SEP, core zones are off-limits to all "human disruptions" except for traditional Indigenous uses that involve "minimal and soft-impact gathering of forest species for ceremonial and medicinal purposes." The buffer zones offer a bit more leeway, but no one on the ground in villages like Tenga't Gebaq actually knows where one zone ends and the other begins. When I asked officials what Palawan residents were permitted to do within Mantalingahan, most indicated that they were free to engage in "traditional," subsistence-oriented practices. The only exception was clearing swiddens in mature forest, which is strictly prohibited. This policy conflates "traditional" practices with sustainable or "soft-impact" ones and is subject to a great deal of subjective interpretation.[94] Swidden, for example, would definitely qualify as traditional, but most officials see it as anything but soft impact. Some would ban it completely from core zones, but at least one official suggested that this might be a violation of IPRA. Not surprisingly, many Palawan I consulted expressed frustration with this lack of clarity (see chapter 3).

For this reason, Palawan people played a minimal role in Mantalingahan's management during the time of my research. As Tessa Minter found, the legitimacy of Mantalingahan rests on its claims to fully incorporate a population that is, in reality, largely alienated from it.[95] For their part, Mantalingahan's proponents were aware of this alienation. They tried to address it by offering select Palawan communities livelihood assistance and other incentives in exchange for them agreeing to abide by park policies, participate in its activities, and report violators to the authorities. In one case, they helped a Palawan community in southern Rizal successfully apply for an ancestral domain title. Virtually everyone I spoke with, including the Palawan members of the management board, expressed a desire for greater Palawan participation. But the prospects for this seemed rather grim. On the one hand, officials did not have a unified vision of the rights and accountabilities that Palawan have as Indigenous residents of a protected landscape. On the other hand, many Palawan were either unaware of the park's existence or wary of its implications for their livelihood and land tenure. Why, they wondered, should they do the work of conservation when conservation might be but the latest in a long series of efforts to extract value from their lands and livelihoods?

Although ancestral domain recognition and conservation are posited as alternatives to dispossession and degradation, in practice they are deeply entangled with ongoing processes of settlement, land conversion, and market intensification. I noted that migrant settlement proceeded at astonishing rates in the 1980s and 1990s. Although these rates may now be slowing, settlement continues to drive dispossession as established settlers expand their landholdings. One momentous development was the extension, in the early 1990s, of the Palawan circumferential road connecting Rizal to the northern and eastern portions of the island. The "highway" in Rizal was further developed in the late 1990s and 2010s, making it much easier and cheaper to bring consumer commodities in and forest commodities out.

During the time of my research, dramatic processes of land conversion were under way in and around the ancestral domain (see figure 2.3). Investors were purchasing large tracts of land for conversion to rubber, coconut, pineapple, and cassava plantations. Because much of the ancestral domain is enclosed within Mantalingahan, these plantations should theoretically not have extended far into its boundaries. Nevertheless, a significant and growing portion of the domain was already owned by non-Indigenous absentees. Palawan were increasingly converting former swiddens to intensive land uses, such as pineapple farms, as a way to secure their land tenure and provide for their families.

As a result, most Palawan find themselves increasingly relegated to the foothills and mountains. Very much in line with what Karl Marx called "primitive accumulation," Palawan who sell their land to settlers and investors often end up working for them at least part-time as wage laborers. Along the old logging roads downstream of Tenga't Gebaq, tracts of land have been reduced to veritable wastelands to meet the growing demand for charcoal and construction materials in town. The footprint of this demand, which does not always discriminate between mature and immature trees, is gradually working its way into the foothills. Meanwhile, a seemingly insatiable demand for forest products has led to the severe depletion of rattan at lower elevations and overtapped almaciga trees in several areas. Collecting and selling these products has become central to Palawan livelihoods but also a common cause of cyclical debt as collectors accept cash advances from buyers and never manage to fully repay them (see chapter 5).

These transformations are borne on the backs of Palawan laborers whose farm wages, charcoal, house posts, and forest products come at astonishingly low prices given the onerous work involved.[96] By continuing to provide for a significant if declining proportion of their material needs, their subsistence activities subsidize the frontier economy even as government policies and deforestation undermine the viability of these activities.[97]

Figure 2.3. An oil palm plantation in southern Palawan, December 2010. Source: Noah Theriault.

These circumstances are not universal. A small minority of Palawan have successfully established paddy rice fields, coconut farms, and businesses. Those who live close enough to town and can afford supplies send their children to public schools. Even some families in Tenga't Gebaq did so, which meant borrowing money for a motorbike or requiring the students to hike some ninety minutes each way. Palawan from several areas have succeeded in completing secondary and even tertiary education, going on to work for the government or NGOs. Schooling often comes at the cost of having one's Palawan identity denigrated and missing out on the experience of learning from elders. My "nieces" and "nephews" in Tenga't Gebaq told me that their teacher forbade them from speaking Palawan in the classroom and often singled them out for lessons on hygiene and proper appearance. Going to school seemed like a largely negative experience for them. The situation improved somewhat with the opening of the satellite school in the village. Even there, students were not supposed to speak Palawan, focusing instead on the standard elementary curriculum. Even so, many young people considered education crucial to their future. Some of them told me, in between giggles, that they wanted to be teachers or restaurant owners or BMX racers or even police officers, rather than swidden farmers, when they grew up.

Although one would not know from the *New York Times* report, Lindbergh's trip to the Philippines coincided with a period of unprecedented clearing of the archipelago's forests by logging companies, plantations, and small-scale farmers in search of land. Since Lindbergh's visit, policies in the Philippines have shifted from favoring assimilation of minority groups and top-down environmental management to favoring Indigenous rights and cooperative management. This shift has had mixed results, at best, in terms of forest conservation, to say nothing of the ambiguities surrounding Indigenous rights.

In 1969, primary forests covered approximately a third of Philippine territory, down from 70 percent at the turn of the century and 90 percent before Spanish colonization 250 years earlier. In the decades since, clearance of primary forests has continued at an astonishing pace so that as of 2020, they covered less than a quarter of the archipelago.[98] Today, significant tracts of primary forest remain only in eastern Luzon, central Mindanao, and along Palawan's mountainous spine. But Palawan has experienced dramatic losses. By 1992, when the logging moratorium was declared, only some 52 percent of Palawan remained forested; by 2009, that number had fallen to 46 percent.[99] From 2000 to 2020, the island lost another 22,200 hectares of humid primary forest—the most of any province in the archipelago.[100] Since deforestation, dispossession, and impoverishment often go hand in hand, Indigenous people's rights and well-being have not, generally speaking, fared better than the forests.[101]

Whether or not the reforms have been effective, the fact that the Philippines has enacted policies favoring conservation does not mean it has stopped allowing large-scale development. In 1995, the Philippine Congress passed a new Mining Act, which sought to promote large-scale mining by domestic and international companies. As the global demand for rare earths has spiked, mining operations in the Philippines have expanded accordingly. Policies favorable to foreign investment in monocrop plantations, energy development, and dam construction have also remained intact.

At the same time that Palawan was becoming a frontier for conservation, it was also becoming a frontier for eco-tourism, mining, biofuel plantations, and offshore energy production. By 2012, more than 354 mining applications were pending in Palawan, in addition to the four large-scale mining operations already active there. Bolstered by a growing national movement against mining, conservationists and Indigenous rights activists have responded vigorously and with a significant degree of success. Indigenous Palawan and Tagbanua activists have played an important role in this movement, and Indigenous rights laws are an important tool in their repertoire. Unfortunately, the consent process is widely reported to be corrupted by bribes, and Indigenous groups faced with the "choice" of whether to endorse mining have found themselves bitterly divided. The other, demonstrably more effective strategy conservationists have is to promote the expansion of conservation enclosures like Mantalingahan.

Activist accounts of these debates almost invariably invoke the image of Palawan as the last frontier and very often reduce the matter to an existential struggle between conservation enclosures and mining. Even among Indigenous activists, it seems, less polarized visions for the island's future seem to be sidelined. Conserving Palawan's biodiversity is a worthwhile goal, and my point is not to suggest otherwise. Rather, I want to highlight how the last frontier narrative helps underpin an environmental politics in which Indigenous people are symbolically central to the debate but effectively marginal to the decision making. This paradox is a legacy of the colonial era and a reminder that Palawan's colonization remains ongoing.

CHAPTER THREE

Civets, Saplings, and Sweating Rocks

We sat in the shade, wondering how seriously to take the thunder rumbling in the distance. *Barat* (the southwest monsoon) was in full force but also full of empty threats. A breeze carried the comforting scent of toasted new rice along with the rhythmic thud of its threshing. With most of the children in the forest or at school, the village was notably quiet. In the distance, we heard a motorcycle revving its engine as it struggled up the slippery, rocky ascent of an old logging road. It was something of a local pastime to pause and guess who might be arriving. Palaya, in particular, had a keen ear for predicting arrivals by the sound of their motor. "*Duwa*," she muttered, discerning not one but two engines struggling up the hill.

As predicted, two motorcycles soon arrived. Astride them were four government employees—one with the Department of Environment and Natural Resources (DENR) and three with the Southern Palawan Planning Council. All were involved with overseeing the Mount Mantalingahan Protected Landscape, a new national park that surrounded the village on all sides. Visits by park personnel put everyone on edge. Why had they come? Was it to investigate *uma* (swidden farming) or other Palawan uses of the forest? What land would be "protected" now? What did this English word "protected" even mean, beyond a sporadically invoked ban on certain livelihood activities?

Two things made this specific visit particularly nerve-racking. First, one of the motorcycles carried the superintendent of the protected area—a relatively high-ranking DENR official who did not usually accompany her staff in the field. Second, neither of the motorcycles stopped to check in with Jimi, the government-recognized chieftain; instead, they proceeded directly to the trailheads at end of the old logging road.

Word soon came that the bureaucrats had left their vehicles at the end of the road and marched into the forest. Speculation intensified. What were they looking for, and who would wind up in trouble? I had visited an upstream hamlet earlier in the day, so Palaya asked me whether their *uma* clearings were large this year. I nodded that they were. "They're dead," Palaya said hyperbolically, referring to her cousins upstream. "They'd better run and hide."

"They don't know the trails," Jiha offered, referring to the visiting officials. "They won't find anything."

"They've hiked up there before," Palaya retorted. Nervous chatter like this continued as we heard conflicting reports about which trail the officials had taken into the forest.

After about an hour, the bureaucrats emerged from the forest, only to disappear again down a trail leading to the river. That they had yet to explain what they were doing provoked plenty of grumbling but no direct confrontation. Eventually they returned from the river and stopped at Jimi and Palaya's house. Jimi was away at his fields, so they engaged in pleasantries but volunteered nothing about their motives. As the two senior staff waited for their juniors to fetch the motorbikes, they heard a high-pitched cry. It was coming from a wooden cage fastened to the side of Palaya's kitchen. To me the cry sounded like that of a monkey as interpreted by a cat. It was a juvenile civet, a catlike mammal endemic to Palawan's forests (Palawan: *masek;* Tagalog: *musang; Paradoxurus hermaphrodites philippinensis;* see figure 3.1).

"Who delivered that?" asked one of the visitors, assuming that the animal was part of the illegal trade in exotic wildlife. Palaya explained that the children had

Figure 3.1. The juvenile civet whose cries prompted a tense encounter in Tenga't Gebaq. Source: Noah Theriault.

found it in the forest and captured it. It refused to leave and had been allowed to roam free until it started terrorizing her chickens. The civet had eaten at least one chick and caused mayhem when it attacked some roosting hens in the middle of the night. It was agitated by the sound of sweeping and would climb up the legs of anyone wielding a broom. Skeptical of this account, the official suggested that Palaya sell the civet to him so that he could take it to a "reservation" in the provincial capital. Palaya replied that she had no say in the matter: "If it were up to me, I would have killed that thing a long time ago." Her unexpected candor made me snort and laugh, earning me a stern look from the official, who was not amused. We must, he reminded us in Tagalog, protect wild animals, lest we deplete them and thereby destroy nature. His lecture used the inclusive form of the third-person plural pronoun, emphasizing a collective, societal ownership of the animals, of the forest, and of nature (*mga hayop natin, kalikasan natin*).[1]

As he and his companions mounted their motorbikes, Jiha attempted to temper her co-wife's defiant remark. "That *animal*," she said, "was killing off our chickens. We had no choice but to cage it." She later scolded Palaya for her candor, reminding her that the official had really wanted to take the civet and use it as "evidence."

Without ever saying why they had come, the visitors headed back down the mountain. Later that day we learned from Jimi, who passed them on his way back up, what they had come to investigate. They had received reports of swidden fields being cut in old-growth forest. Jimi was agitated by this "investigation," both because he considered *uma* a legally protected Palawan tradition and because he suspected that his rival, Bordo, had a hand in it. He surmised that reporting swiddens in Jimi's area was retribution for his recent successes in an ongoing legal dispute over forest products. In the following days, park personnel returned three times. They gave "tree planting" and "livelihood project monitoring" as their official reasons, but everyone suspected that these activities were cover for further surveillance. Jimi wondered aloud what the National Commission on Indigenous People (NCIP)—an agency often at odds with the DENR—would have to say about this turn of events.

This encounter was fraught with tension: between officials and farmers, between rival Indigenous leaders, between rival bureaucracies, between humans and animals, and between different ways of relating to the environment. Even so, nothing particularly unusual happened that day. Tensions of a more-than-human nature surfaced in many of the daily interactions I witnessed between Palawan people and conservation officials over the course of my research. Pesky wildlife, local disputes, mutual distrust, conflicting legal principles, and thinly veiled surveillance—the actual work of conservation in Palawan comprises all of these factors and more. None of them appear in dominant narratives, such as the park's management plan or the tangle of land use policies that overlap with it. Such accounts instead paint a relatively seamless picture of how the conservation of biodiversity interacts with Indigenous land claims and livelihoods.[2] In the age of co-management, internationally sponsored conservation projects like Mantalingahan must at least claim to operate in a mutually beneficial partnership with Indigenous communities. Jimi was not surprised to learn that surveillance of the community's swidden fields also yielded photos of park personnel planting hardwood saplings alongside their Palawan guides.

Environmental Narratives

Scholars use the term "environmental narrative" to describe a simplistic but authoritative account of environmental change.[3] Environmental narratives matter, in part, because they shape the actions of powerful actors and institution. We most often engage with these simplifications as foils for nuanced scholarly arguments or fine-grained, local knowledge. For example, Fairhead and Leach's classic study of "forest islands" in West Africa challenged the widely accepted narrative that rural Guineans were causing desertification.[4] Savannah farmers, they argued, were actually agents of afforestation. Similarly, Forsyth and Walker have tracked how competing environmental narratives in Thailand portray upland minority groups as either "guardians" or "destroyers" of the forest, misrepresenting complex local realities and fueling misguided policies.[5]

In Palawan, environmental narratives play an important role in legitimating the enclosure of Indigenous people's lands in the name of conservation.[6] As discussed in chapter 2, the portrayal of the island as the last frontier flanks a range of efforts to "save" it by protecting its remaining biological and cultural diversity. What this means in practice is that Palawan's Indigenous people must confront competing efforts to enclose their land for conservation or convert it for other extractive industries. In the words of Clifford Geertz, these narratives offer not just competing models of the world but also competing models *for* it.[7]

But is that all environmental narratives do—oversimplify complex, lived realities in service to misguided, top-down interventions into the lives of marginalized populations? My research suggests that the answer to this question is "no." Environmental narratives also provide people—scholars, bureaucrats, farmers, and so on—with fodder for critical thought and action.[8] We should think of environmental narratives not just as a negativity, as an absence of accurate knowledge that rationalizes dispossession. They are also a generative force in the lives of those whose realities they purport to represent.[9]

In the encounter I described above, we can readily see how the tense micropolitics of conservation diverge from the harmonious relations imagined in policy narratives.[10] We can also see how fragments of those narratives find their way into everyday debates over the role of Indigenous people in environmental management.[11] The official's reprimand, although brief, indexed a familiar narrative about Indigenous people's duty to protect the nation's collective heritage—an example of what I call the nationalist narrative. By contrast, Palaya's defiance and Jimi's indignation drew on a counternarrative that emphasizes Indigenous autonomy and environmental entitlements—part of what I call the rights-based narrative. In Palawan, environmental narratives are debated not just in the legislature, courts, and regulatory agencies but in the everyday lives of those whose lands are at stake. These everyday debates play an important role in shaping larger processes of environmental and social change.

Whether framed as an obligation or as a right, indigeneity carries important symbolic and legal weight in the contemporary Philippines.[12] Palawan and other Indigenous groups find themselves at the center of environmental politics even as their societal position remains marginal.[13] They are constantly asked to consent to and thereby legitimate conservation and development projects that generate value from their land and labor but are offered little in the way of control or compensation. By law, it's their right to withhold consent. But doing so in practice means engaging in direct confrontation with people and organizations that have more power, more money, and more experience with the law. In many cases, overt expressions of consent or refusal mask more subtle negotiations that take place episodically. These negotiations do not happen in a vacuum; they are shaped by profound differences of culture and power. They are also moments in which Indigenous persons creatively and strategically engage with the environmental narratives that place them, however unequally, at the center of struggles over land. Palawan dealings with park personnel are a case in point.

This chapter argues that the microlevel circulation of environmental narratives is an important part of larger societal debates about Indigenous rights and the environment. I begin with a reforestation project convened to mark the anniversary of Mantalingahan's founding as a national park. This vignette will illustrate how public performances of environmental narratives conceal profound differences of culture and power. At the same time, it will reveal how competing ideologies within government complicate efforts to "harmonize" the different interests brought together by the park's co-management. I then turn to the circulation of environmental narratives among Palawan, who have their own knowledge about the causes, effects, and accountabilities of environmental change. Contrary to the notion that environmental narratives are simply the misinformed ideas of elites, Palawan people cite and rework prevailing narratives about themselves to negotiate competing allegiances with external authorities and to build a critical consciousness of power among themselves.[14]

Contrasting Account(abilitie)s

Tenga't Gebaq was a crossroads of sorts for Palawan headed to the coast or back into the mountains. Visitors bearing goods and gossip were never in short supply. It was also remote enough that residents very rarely saw an unfamiliar face. By local standards, June 30, 2011, was an eventful day. It was the second anniversary of Mantalingahan's founding, and to mark the occasion a group of government personnel were touring the protected area and conducting mass tree-planting ceremonies in five "key watersheds." Tenga't Gebaq sat in the middle of one of those watersheds and, being somewhat accessible by road, was selected to host one of the ceremonies. For reasons I will explain, the planting site was just downstream of the village, on a steep mountainside without well-defined trails. Fortunately for the organizers, who were accompanied by the local mayor and dozens of students, it had not rained for a few days, leaving the soil relatively dry. Under muddier conditions, their single-file hike up the mountain, saplings in hand, would likely have become a messy human display of the domino effect.

Residents knew about the tree-planting ceremony in advance because organizers had been there preparing for it. Jimi was the government-recognized chieftain in the area, so he knew he would be expected to participate. He also had errands to run in town that day, so he left early on his motorbike, hoping to make it to the highway before crossing paths with the government caravan. It was too late. By the time he got his things together and left, the horde of clipboard-wielding bureaucrats, photo-snapping students, and M16-toting bodyguards had jammed the old logging road just downstream of the village (see figure 3.2). I arrived on the scene moments after Jimi and could see the surprise in jittery movements as he worked his way through the crowd and greeted the esteemed guests. With no polite way of leaving, he was obliged to stay and participate.

That obligation did not apply to other locals, for whom an unexpected amassing of outsiders was something to be avoided. Before word had spread upstream, a few men and women came walking down the road only to stop, mumble a curse, and turn back away from the crowd. Besides Jimi and me, not a single resident of the village participated in the ceremony. In the days leading up to it, some local men had been paid to clear a trail and prepare the ground for saplings. None of them showed up for the planting activity itself. Even so, the mayor and government officials gave brief speeches in which they mentioned the need to cooperate

Figure 3.2. Students and officials clogging the old logging road just downstream of Tenga't Gebaq during a tree-planting ceremony, June 2011. Source: Noah Theriault.

with Indigenous communities and thanked Jimi for his support. Jimi was called on to give remarks, in which he offered his gratitude for the government's help in protecting the environment.[15] This "public transcript," as James Scott might call it, was a pitch-perfect enactment of Mantalingahan's management plan and of reports made about this and other management activities to international funders.[16]

After the speeches, we picked up a couple of saplings and began a halting march up the small mountain. I positioned myself near a cluster of bureaucrats who were near the mayor. Between their laughing at the mayor's jokes and peppering me with rhetorical questions about how I could possibly suffer life in the village, I struggled to get a word in. When I finally managed to ask a question, it was an impatient, leading one that I regretted before it had even left my mouth: "Isn't it great," I said in Tagalog, "that the Palawan here have donated this land for reforestation?" Sweat stinging my eyes, I prepared myself for a bureaucratically appropriate response—that it was generous of them and very much in keeping with local traditions of stewardship. My question piqued the attention of a man named Arnold, a forester who was among the four officials investigating local swidden a year later. After glancing around to make sure Jimi would not hear him, he corrected my misconception. "No," he said, "this is government land—timberland—and it's inside of a protected area. They didn't donate this [land]." Arnold had complained to me before about the difficulties he faced in getting Palawan communities to cooperate with conservation rules (see chapter 4 for his thoughts on charcoal making). But he had never expressed his views on the legalities of land tenure. Before I could press him on what he meant—"what about the ancestral domain?!"—we were called to pose for photos with the mayor and then led back down the hill in a plodding single file.

Arnold's response surprised me because of how starkly it contrasted with the narrative on display at the ceremony and in Mantalingahan's management plan. It was true that the village and its environs were inside of a protected area. Likewise, most of the municipality was classified as timberland. But the village was also within an ancestral domain that the DENR had established and recognized in the late 1990s. By law, ancestral domains are tantamount to collective land titles and are not abrogated by protected areas. In this part of Rizal, the timberland classification is a legal anachronism that clashes with more recent land classification schemes, including the one according to which Mantalingahan was managed. Where did Arnold's response come from? Why did he ignore the language of Indigenous rights and institutional "harmonization" found in official documents? I believe his response was simply an uneuphemized fragment of the nationalist environmental narrative that I introduced above.

Hearing Arnold say this out loud reminded me of the tensions that often lie beneath the surface when officials seek Indigenous cooperation in conservation activities. These tensions largely owe to the gap between official expectations and local realities. But they also owe to ideological differences among officials. I have suggested that two distinct but sometimes overlapping environmental narratives flanked Mantalingahan's enclosure of Palawan land—one that was nationalist in its orientation and another that was rights-based. Next I examine what these narratives consist of, how they map onto tensions among government agencies, and how residents of Tenga't Gebaq engage with them.

The Nationalist Narrative

Stripped to its essence, the nationalist environmental narrative presents upland-dwelling Indigenous people, including those in Palawan, as occupants of state-owned land and potential threats to forest ecosystems.[17] This narrative rests on a colonial ideology called the regalian doctrine, which was allegedly established by Spain when it claimed the archipelago for the Crown. To this day, the regalian doctrine is cited by jurists in the Philippines and interpreted to mean that all untitled lands are property of the state by default. Legal scholar Owen Lynch describes the regalian doctrine as "mythical" because, he contends, it did not actually become law until 1894, barely four years before Spain lost control of the islands.[18] Mythical or real, this ideology has become the dominant understanding of Spanish colonial policy and has been used to assert public domain for various purposes, from mining to industrial forestry to biodiversity conservation. In short, what legal scholars call "native title" has no standing in the nationalist environmental narrative.

Likewise, this narrative portrays all upland Indigenous people, especially those who practice swidden, as potential antagonists to the goals of environmental regulation, whatever those goals may be. During the Spanish and US colonial periods, the "swidden menace" was primarily seen as a threat to agriculture, logging, and forest products (see chapter 1). These concerns persist in present-day iterations of the nationalist narrative. Nonetheless, since the rise of biodiversity conservation in the 1980s and 1990s, the narrative has also shifted to emphasize biodiversity as part of the nation's "natural heritage." Today, rather than being a threat to logging, Indigenous people are more likely to be a threat to "nature . . . in [its] undisturbed state" (NIPAS Act, Section 4).[19]

The Rights-Based Narrative

The prevailing alternative to this nationalist narrative is what I referred to as the rights-based narrative. This narrative holds, in essence, that Indigenous groups have customary land rights ("native titles") that predate the existence of the colonial state and endure in its wake. Underlying this narrative is the Cariño doctrine, which emerged from a 1909 US Supreme Court ruling. In *Cariño v. Insular Government,* the court found that the regalian doctrine did not apply to all regions of the Philippines, including that of the plaintiff, who belonged to a "savage tribe that never was brought under the civil or military government of the Spanish Crown." Seeking to advance the US mission of benevolent assimilation in the Philippines, *Cariño* instructed the Insular Government to "do justice to the natives" by recognizing native titles in such regions.[20] This decision laid the foundation for later debates about Indigenous rights. It also came seven years after the Insular Government had adopted the Torrens system of land title registration, which makes the state the ultimate arbiter of land ownership through a centralized registry of titles.[21] By instructing the Insular Government to recognize native title under the Torrens system, *Cariño* did more to establish the sovereignty of the colonial state than it did to deliver justice to the natives. As a result, the regalian doctrine prevailed as the state's operating principle in US colonial policy and in subsequent Philippine constitutions.[22]

It wasn't until the post-Marcos reform period that this status quo met a direct challenge. The 1987 constitution maintained the state as the default owner of untitled land, but it obligated the state to respect the rights of Indigenous people to self-govern their ancestral lands. Advocates used this provision to reestablish the principle of native title in the Indigenous Peoples Rights Act of 1997.[23] This important shift in the law has bolstered a rights-based alternative to the nationalist narrative, positioning Indigenous people (rather than the state) as the default owners and managers of their ancestral lands. Ever since, the contradictory implications of these narratives have animated debates among policy makers, Indigenous persons, and those seeking to establish conservation enclosures on their land.[24]

Environmental Narratives in Practice

In the wake of these developments, Indigenous groups in the Philippines find themselves implicated in two competing legal doctrines, each derived from colonial law but favoring a different environmental narrative. On the one hand, their land rights come from the state and depend on their cooperation with conservation and state-sanctioned enclosures. On the other hand, their land rights preexist the state and include a right to environmental self-governance. In theory, these archetypal narratives are mutually exclusive; as Arnold showed us, they sometimes appear so in practice. Generally, however, actual policies and actions are not identical with either but are fraught with the ambivalences and ambiguities that result from their coexistence.[25] These narratives are at distant points on a continuum, not opposite sides of a dichotomy.

Let's consider what this continuum means for major policies pertaining to Tenga't Gebaq, which was within a protected area and a recognized ancestral domain. Arnold's comments notwithstanding, hardcore manifestations of the nationalist narrative are limited largely to anachronistic laws and lawsuits challenging the constitutionality of the Indigenous Peoples Rights Act (IPRA) of 1997. Among the former, the most notable is the Forestry Code of 1975, which places all lands over 18 percent slope in the state's possession as public domain.[26] Among the latter, the most consequential challenge to IPRA came in a 2000 Supreme Court case, on which I comment later. Instead of laws summarily declaring public ownership, laws favoring the nationalist narrative now make subtler appeals to state ownership.

The clearest example of such a law is the National Integrated Protected Areas System (NIPAS) Act, which was passed in 1992. NIPAS established a unified, nationwide system of standards and rules for classifying and managing protected areas. NIPAS falls closer to the nationalist end of the spectrum for several reasons. For one, it invokes the nation's natural heritage, implying public (state) ownership of forests and other "natural" landscapes. This notion of national heritage was, I imagine, the inspiration for the official's lecture about the civet. Some of the protected area categories established by NIPAS (e.g., the Strict Nature Reserve or Natural Park) are supposed to be completely free of human "disturbance," the conceit in such cases being that native title is irrelevant. The authors of NIPAS also had to reconcile the law with concurrent Indigenous rights reforms, including one put into place by the DENR in 1992. Hence the category of a protected landscape. Protected landscapes, including Mantalingahan, "are areas of national significance which are characterized by harmonious interaction of man and land."

In spite of this category, the language in NIPAS presents the state (namely, the DENR) as the primary agent of environmental regulation. Although Indigenous people cannot be involuntarily evicted or relocated by the DENR to make way for a protected area, they appear as nothing more than passive participants in conservation planning. They are part of what needs to be managed, and part of managing them involves giving "notice and hearing" of conservation regulations. NIPAS serves as the legal basis for Mantalingahan. Accordingly, Mantalingahan's management plan and management board reflect the hybrid but mostly regalian composition of the law. The plan presents Indigenous residents as "partners" but adopts a zoning scheme in which large portions of the landscape are assumed to be essentially free of human disturbance.[27] It calls for greater integration with "Indigenous knowledge and practices" and for "cultural preservation" but makes no provision for Indigenous groups who might want to exempt their land from the protected landscape. Meanwhile, the board reserves five seats for Indigenous representatives, but they are outnumbered by non-Indigenous members (even though Indigenous people make up more than 90 percent of those who live within Mantalingahan's boundaries). In my experience and according to what I was told by other board members, their attendance of and participation in meetings has been "weak."

On the rights-based end of the continuum, there are even fewer policies that closely resemble the archetype. The closest is IPRA. Like NIPAS, IPRA is fundamentally hybrid. Although it provides for collective rights to ancestral domain, it also creates a state agency responsible for validating and administering ancestral domain claims. Protections in the law are meant to apply whether or not an Indigenous group has secured a collective land title. But the state ultimately determines who can claim those protections and how. While Indigenous people are meant to formulate a management plan and use customary institutions to regulate their ancestral domains, they are expected to do so in cooperation with the state and to maintain an "ecological balance." This is where IPRA and NIPAS most obviously overlap. As Peter Cuasay has argued, this provision converts native title into a form of eco-governmentality, wherein an

Indigenous group's recognition depends on its ability to self-regulate in line with conservation.[28]

Given the 1987 constitution's tendency toward the nationalist/regalian narrative, it should come as no surprise that IPRA's constitutionality has been challenged. Barely two years after the law was passed, the Supreme Court declared it constitutional by default when the fourteen-member court reached a seven-to-seven tie. Four separate opinions were issued in that case, some invoking the regalian doctrine, others Cariño. Cuasay suggests that the split decision effected an ontological split, wherein minerals and other natural resources were separated from the land rights conferred by native title and revested in the public domain.[29] Clearly, there was and is deep ambivalence about whether and to what extent native title exists. Thus, IPRA—a policy whose gravitation toward the rights-based/Cariño narrative was already ambivalent—remained in force but only after being ambiguously reoriented toward the nationalist/regalian narrative.

As forms of what Cuasay calls "postcolonial legal hybridities," laws like NIPAS and IPRA reflect the dilemmas of Philippine liberalism and of multiculturalism more generally.[30] In Palawan, as I argue throughout this book, these policies have not readily inspired the effective co-management institutions they envision. Instead, they have fostered deeply ambivalent conditions in which asserting Indigenous rights can entail both disempowering obligations and acts of endurance.

If policies like NIPAS and IPRA are fraught with disguised ambivalence, so are the practices of those responsible for implementing them. This is evident in the case of Mantalingahan, which at the time of its founding overlapped with fourteen recognized or pending ancestral domains.[31] According to Mantalingahan's management plan, these overlapping "tenurial instruments" will be "harmonized" by the management board, which includes representatives of all concerned "stakeholder" agencies and constituencies. But the plan does not indicate how harmonization should proceed or what harmony entails. In fact, there are no generally accepted guidelines for reconciling Indigenous land claims with the restrictions of protected areas; it is simply assumed that harmony is immanent. In practice, officials grapple with this question, and how they approach the problem reflects their orientation with respect to the prevailing environmental narratives (nationalist or rights-based). This orientation, in turn, depends on one's understanding of the law, on the agency one represents, and on struggles in the bureaucracy over authority and resources. Protected areas like Mantalingahan are legally derived from the NIPAS Act and overseen by the DENR. As a result, the nationalist environmental narrative is built into the very structure of Mantalingahan and, it seems, is taken for granted by most (but not all) of those involved in its implementation.

I came to this conclusion in part through spontaneous encounters with officials like Arnold and the man who discovered the caged civet. I also interviewed many of the government and nongovernmental organization (NGO) personnel involved with Mantalingahan and asked them directly about the status of Indigenous rights in protected areas. Not surprisingly, in an interview setting, few were as blunt as Arnold. Instead, most appealed to the idea that stewardship is a precondition of Indigenous land rights. The management plan for any Indigenous land claim should already be "harmonized" with that of a protected area,[32] even if the land claim was granted before the protected area's establishment. But what, I asked, would happen if Indigenous people invoked their right to self-determination and simply refused to cooperate with conservation? Most officials dismissed any legal basis for this scenario, suggesting that it might result from Indigenous culture, ignorance, or opportunism. Problems like this, I was told, could be avoided by adjusting uncooperative behavior through education and incentives.

Take the highest-ranking DENR official in Palawan. When I proposed this scenario to him, he laughed knowingly and recounted an experience in another province, where the Indigenous residents—whom he referred with the abbreviation IPs—initially resisted a new protected area. They ultimately changed their mind, he explained, after being taught the value of protecting endangered wildlife. In spite of the "nomad character" that leads "IPs" to search for "greener pastures," Indigenous practices can be "harmonized" with the rules of the protected area through "frequent dialogue." It is important, he added, to make Indigenous people feel that they have priority status in a protected area and make sure they do not go hungry. Otherwise, there will be "rebellion." He acknowledged that Indigenous practices did not result in "significant destruction" in the past but insisted that they should be regulated by government in the present. He gave the examples of hunting and swidden, both of which he said would be forbidden under a strict interpretation of NIPAS. Instead of forbidding them completely, which would run counter to IPRA, he suggested that such traditional practices be allowed in certain zones and regulated. In his account, "harmony" entails a modification of Indigenous practices to fit the rules of conservation, coupled with a prioritization of Indigenous people's subsistence needs.

Similarly, Mantalingahan's superintendent foresaw no such conflicts as long as Palawan residents limited themselves to "traditional" (i.e., subsistence-oriented) practices and avoided cutting large trees for any reason. At the same time, she said it was necessary—and difficult—to "inject" new ideas into Indigenous people's minds. An employee of the Palawan Council for Sustainable

Development, which has a seat on the board, came to the same conclusion from the opposite direction. He argued that Indigenous people have abandoned their traditions of stewardship as a result of being "corrupted" by outside influences. His proposal was to "inculcate" them in the ecologically balanced ways of their own "forefathers."

This view was echoed in part by the project director of the Southern Palawan Planning Council, who described Indigenous residents of Mantalingahan as its "number-one violators." But he did not necessarily see a return to tradition as the answer. Although he agreed that traditional, subsistence-oriented practices were compatible with conservation, he felt that some Palawan abuse the notion of tradition in an effort to have destructive, market-oriented practices exempted from conservation restrictions. Perhaps, he suggested, only Palawan who always wear their traditional loincloth should have any right to invoke tradition. The rest should obey the law.

When I pressed him on how Indigenous rights fit into Mantalingahan, his patience started to wear thin. The matter was simple. Exhuming a scrap of blank paper from his cluttered desk, he drew a large circle and, within it, another, much smaller circle. The former, he said, represented a protected area like Mantalingahan, the latter an ancestral domain. Protected areas are part of a national "system"—NIPAS. Ancestral domains can be integrated into that system but not exempted from it. My thought experiment was irksomely naive. "Who issued their CADT?" he asked, referring to the hypothetical Indigenous group's ancestral domain title. "The government! The land belongs to the state, and it is the state that will prevail." In his account, customary rights are secondary to state ownership of the land.

Though varying in subtle ways, all of these accounts share a set of assumptions derived from the nationalist environmental narrative. They assume that Palawan living in Mantalingahan reside on public land and are therefore legally obliged to cooperate with conservation, even if that means restricting traditional practices like swidden and hunting. Yet it would be unfair to say that park-affiliated personnel disregard Indigenous rights. Most see their work as entirely compatible with IPRA. In these accounts, Indigenous rights do not exist sui generis but as a condition of Palawan cooperation with environmental government. Resistance thus becomes a negation of this social contract, whereas cooperation is thought to flow from a natural inclination toward stewardship, on the one hand, and from the application of regulatory (dis)incentives, on the other hand. Questions of power, sovereignty, coercion, and cosmology are eclipsed by the narrative of harmony.

In the pursuit of harmony, government and NGO personnel have sought to raise public awareness of Mantalingahan's ecosystem services, particularly the role that forests play in protecting watersheds from erosion, among those living in and around the protected area.[33] They have provided livelihood incentives and "cultural preservation" resources to select Palawan communities. Most important, they have followed legal guidelines for protecting Indigenous rights: securing "free and prior informed consent" from Palawan residents, exempting some traditional practices from prohibition, and placing Palawan representatives on Mantalingahan's management board. These practices correspond with an official narrative of cooperation and harmony—one that tempers the politically untenable implications of the nationalist environmental narrative even as it retains nationalist assumptions about difference, rights, and accountability.

We should not confuse dominance with universality. Even in the bureaucracy, there are those who express opposing views. We have already encountered several, like Arnold, who are openly skeptical that cooperation with the Palawan can proceed as imagined in policy. Toward the other end of the continuum are those whose accounts align more closely with the rights-based narrative. In my experience, they are mostly Indigenous rights activists and academics. In fact, among non-Palawan officials involved with Mantalingahan, only one argued that Palawan residents should have greater authority in managing the protected area. Singular though it was, this dissenting voice has important implications for understanding Palawan–government relations.

The voice in question belonged to provincial officer of the NCIP. The officer felt that Mantalingahan put Indigenous people at a "disadvantage" relative to migrants. They were disadvantaged, he said, for two primary reasons. First is that the board was dominated by non-Indigenous people, virtually all of whom live in the lowland towns if not in the provincial capital. Second, and more important, is that NIPAS contained provisions protecting the land tenure of migrants.

Recall how the 1975 Forestry Code often figures prominently in the nationalist environmental narrative because it classified much of the uplands as state-owned timberlands, including virtually all of far southwestern Palawan. In an ironic reworking of such thinking, the NCIP official took this Marcos-era decree to its logical extreme: If all the land in southwestern Palawan is timberland, then everyone there is squatting, including elected officials and municipal government employees. He noted that the Forestry Code contained a provision protecting the land tenure of communities who lived on timberland for the thirty years before 1975—a provision that would, in theory, apply to the Palawan. The fact that NIPAS protects migrant tenure is especially problematic, he argued, because migrants were responsible for destroying the forest. Palawan culture is oriented toward subsistence rather than accumulation and thus leaves the forest intact. In his mind, the best way to protect the forest would be to keep migrants out of it, something for which he saw little political will.

Although he laced his account with sarcasm, the NCIP official made several trenchant points. He highlighted contradictions in how the nationalist narrative invokes the law, found protections for Indigenous land tenure even in the most nationalist legal principles, and shifted blame for forest degradation away from Indigenous people. He did not stop there. His account also invoked IPRA, specifically its requirement of free and prior informed consent. Because Mantalingahan had met only the minimum requirements of consent, it had not yet formally transferred management authority currently vested in Palawan ancestral domains over to the management board. This he described as a "policy clash," in sharp contrast with the language of harmony employed by so many other bureaucrats. Despite his strong interpretation of Indigenous rights, the official hesitated when I asked whether the Palawan had a legal right to refuse to cooperate with conservation. He replied that Indigenous groups could insist on managing a protected area themselves or on imposing protections that exceed those of NIPAS, such as demanding the eviction of migrant settlers. That Palawan rarely assert these rights is not because they are easily harmonized with conservation, but because they are uninformed or intimidated.

If we translate the official's words into those of social theory, he identified what Laura Nader calls "coercive harmony"—a process by which a dominant ideology of "harmony" conceals vast differences of power between conflicting interests, enabling the more powerful interests to dominate others.[34] To me, this is a cogent analysis of what the harmony narrative does for Mantalingahan: It silences the cultural and political tensions that I describe throughout this book. The rights-based narrative, by contrast, foregrounds them. Yet the official's account should not be read uncritically, for it also obscures conflict in its own way.

Two issues in particular—bureaucratic rivalry and mining—lurked between the lines of his account. The rivalry in question mainly concerns the NCIP and the DENR. In 1993, the DENR began recognizing Indigenous ancestral land claims and regulating the use of natural resources in them. Four years later, with the passage of IPRA, the NCIP was created to oversee all aspects of Indigenous rights and land claims. Their ensuing rivalry will unfold in chapter 5. For now, let's just say that questions remained over the role each agency is meant to play in the regulation of Indigenous environmental practices. This becomes an especially problematic issue when DENR-managed protected areas overlap with NCIP-recognized ancestral domains, as we find in Mantalingahan.

NGOs are also implicated in this rivalry. In chapter 2, I described how NGOs have played major roles in establishing Mantalingahan and the ancestral domains in its boundaries.[35] The NCIP official expressed his concern that some of the Palawan representatives on the management board were those recognized by

NGOs rather than by the NCIP. Furthermore, he accused the NGO Conservation International (CI), which has played an instrumental role in Mantalingahan's establishment, of trying to effect "policy change in Third World countries" for its own benefit. He said that CI planned to monetize Mantalingahan through carbon credits, and he doubted this would benefit Indigenous people. For example, CI had declined his request for use of a vehicle, which would have enabled the NCIP to fully support Mantalingahan by conducting community-level consultations.

Entangled with these rivalries, mining is the other important subtext of the official's account.[36] Rising global demand for rare earths has led to a mining rush in Palawan. At the time of my research, mining was among the most politically fraught issues in the province, largely because of the mining claims that overlapped with Mantalingahan and ancestral domains. A coalition of NGOs, including some run by Indigenous people, has mounted a vigorous anti-mining campaign. For its part, the NCIP's Palawan office was widely regarded as supportive of mining. The official I interviewed skirted my question of whether mining would bring greater benefits to Indigenous people than conservation would. He turned the conversation back toward "population pressure" from migrants, which he implied was a much greater threat than mining. He estimated that a majority of the province's Indigenous population supported mining; it was only a few "loud" individuals whose exposure to NGOs led them to oppose it.

When we take stock of these subtexts, we can better appreciate the countervailing political concerns embedded in the NCIP official's account. It was at once a robust critique of the nationalist narrative, a jealous assertion of bureaucratic authority, and a cynical co-optation of Indigenous rights on behalf of mining. We saw how the accounts that favored the nationalist narrative were fraught with veiled ambivalences as to the meaning of Indigenous rights and cooperation. These multiply, at times duplicitously, layered narratives are ciphers for the dilemmas that Palawan communities face as they negotiate with competing government agencies and NGOs. Conservation projects like Mantalingahan—and the narratives that flank them—present Indigenous people with conflicting visions of their rights and responsibilities as well as competing efforts to recruit them into struggles over authority and resources. Indeed, regardless of whether officials favored the nationalist or the rights-based narrative, they all seemed to agree that Indigenous people like the Palawan were in need of benevolent state intervention. Whether this involves (re)orienting them toward environmental stewardship or emboldening them to assert their legal rights, the Palawan face the dilemma of mediating between institutions that claim to represent them but are dominated by external interests.[37]

Even I had to grapple with this dilemma. In August 2012, I gave a periodic presentation of my research findings and recommendations to the research committee of the management board. My main recommendation was that a more diverse set of Palawan people, including *belyan* (healers), have a greater say over how land in the park is zoned for use. I expressed concern about the prohibition of swidden in certain areas and questioned the notion that harmonization would resolve existing problems with compliance. When asked for his response, an NCIP official in attendance emphatically agreed. He and his colleagues, he said, had received many complaints about Mantalingahan from Indigenous communities who found its regulations on swidden and other practices too restrictive. He suggested, in effect, allowing Indigenous groups to opt out of the park. What he did not acknowledge was how such a policy change might serve the interests of mining companies eager to operate in the protected area. Instead, echoing the language of the NCIP official I interviewed, he suggested that the DENR concentrate more on the activities of migrants than on those of Indigenous people. There was an awkward silence. With an incredulous smirk, a DENR representative responded that her agency had utmost respect for Indigenous culture and rights. Nevertheless, the law was the law, and no one was allowed to cut down large trees inside Mantalingahan.

In pushing for greater Indigenous autonomy, I had positioned my research outside the narrative framing of Mantalingahan as an institution and risked aligning it with veiled interests whose motives I did not share. My perspective faced polite dismissal on the one hand and co-optation on the other hand, and thus I got a taste of a dilemma that residents of Tenga't Gebaq must grapple with all the time.

Narrative Alignments

So far we have seen how policy narratives like those in NIPAS, IPRA, and Mantalingahan's management plan, along with public performances like the tree-planting ceremony, mask the tensions of Indigenous–state relations. We have also seen how these tensions reemerge in the practices of individual officials, who are embroiled in the politics of bureaucratic rivalry and resource extraction.[38] This is the complicated political terrain that Indigenous groups like Palawan must negotiate.

With that in mind, let's turn to a brief discussion of how Palawan people engage with competing accounts of their rights and accountabilities. We saw already how spontaneous encounters, such as the civet incident, can reveal underlying tensions between park officials and Palawan people. In my experience, many Palawan had never heard of Mantalingahan, but those who had were generally agnostic (if not suspicious) of its professed aims. It was, some said, just the latest in a series of outside interventions that sought control of their land and resources. Yet, Palawan were neither unanimous in their views of government nor passive in their engagements with it. In what follows, we see how Palawan people approached government with a shared sense of marginality even as they pursued competing agendas.

Let's return briefly to the tree-planting ceremony. Recall the question I posed to conservation officer Arnold about the community having "donated" the mountainside where the saplings were being planted. Although Arnold rebuffed my question, Jimi and Palaya told me that they were "giving" that land to the government (more precisely, that they were doing so on behalf of Palaya's parents). Jimi had even described the mountainside as *lihyen,* a Palawan category for areas that many consider off-limits to swidden. As noted, his selection of this site made for a seamless performance of Indigenous–state cooperation. But Jimi was also making strategic use of the government in ways concealed by the performance of harmony.

Jimi had a number of concerns in mind. Many Palawan I knew were wary of government reforestation. Land planted with government-sponsored trees was, in effect, land that could not be cleared for swidden, collateralized, sold, and so on. To preempt such an outcome, Jimi directed the government toward a mountainside that was, in his view, already off-limits. What's more, this land was at the center of a disagreement between two Palawan couples, who disagreed over whether it was *lihyen.* Jimi's parents-in-law had sold an adjacent plot of land but had thought they had retained the mountainside in question. Meanwhile, the couple who had purchased the land claimed their purchase had included the mountainside. The former saw the land as *lihyen,* the latter as a future swidden. The resulting dispute put Jimi in an awkward position—between his wife's parents and his brother's wife's parents. As the most authoritative dispute mediator in Tenga't Gebaq, he could not simply refer the matter to someone else, nor did he want to show favor to either side. Instead, by guiding the government to plant hardwood saplings there, Jimi deferred the whole affair. As long as the government protects the newly planted saplings, no one would try to clear the land for swidden. The couple who believed they had purchased the land were not especially pleased with this outcome, but there was little they could do.

Performances like the tree-planting ceremony are scripted by policy narratives of harmony, concealing the competing interests and agendas that participants bring to them. We saw, for example, how the ceremony masked tensions among officials and between officials and residents of Tenga't Gebaq. We saw how residents took differing approaches. Jimi was the only Palawan who participated in the ceremony, and even he tried to avoid doing so. Many Palawan I have interacted with distrust conservation, and many officials, like Arnold, see Palawan participation as little more than a formality. Yet Jimi was far from a passive bystander to this event. Working behind the scenes, he guided it in a way that he considered most favorable to local interests, including his own. The event enabled him to defuse a local land dispute while deflecting any related resentment and performing harmonious relations with the state.

In my experience, people in Tenga't Gebaq often responded to unfavorable policies through what James Scott famously called "weapons of the weak"—foot dragging, minor acts of interference, sheer avoidance—which limit the power of state interventions without recourse to outright resistance.[39] To some extent, this is an accurate portrayal of Jimi's behind-the-scenes handling of the tree-planting activity. At the same time, his actions went beyond that. He engaged the state in a proactive and calculated way that is not captured by Scott's notion of resistance. By cooperating publicly while addressing private concerns, Jimi quietly repurposed the authority of the state in a way he deemed most congenial to local interests. In this sense, even as they misrepresent reality and suppress tensions, public performances of environmental narratives may provide a strategic cover for the many competing agendas that Palawan and their government counterparts bring to the table. Harmony, it seems, entails more than a coercive silencing of subordinate interests; it can also provide a convenient subterfuge for their pursuit.[40]

Beyond Concealment

Concealment is not the only role environmental narratives play in Palawan micropolitics. Palawan produce their own environmental narratives that rework and challenge official accounts of their role in environmental change. We can read these narratives as a cipher for how tensions among Palawan people map onto their uneven relations with government. At the same time, Palawan narratives reveal a shared sense of ambivalence and distrust with respect to government in general. In my experience, some of the most interesting and telling narrative work took place when externally recognized Palawan leaders were speaking to fellow Palawan about environmental regulation and its relationship to their *keedatan,* a multifaceted concept that roughly translates as ancestral customs, laws, and practices, as in "the ways of the ancestors" (*keedatan et keguranggurangan*).[41] Environmental narratives in such contexts are, I argue, crucial idioms for mediating relations among Indigenous communities, government agencies, and NGOs. Let's consider this point through a brief anecdote.

On a sweltering July afternoon, I joined a group of Palawan men and women who sought refuge from the sun beneath the thatched roof of a bamboo vending stall. Despite the heat, they had hiked in from their respective villages, some quite far away, to attend the weekly *tabuqan*. The *tabuqan*—an occasion marked as much by socializing and card playing as by commerce—is a Palawan version of the more intensely commercialized "market days" held weekly in lowland towns. *Tabuqan* also provide convenient venues for informal meetings about whatever problems, events, and gossip are on people's minds. Concerns over new environmental regulations were the topic of the conversation when I happened upon it that day.

"In the past," Bordo explained, "there were no laws. Now we have the laws of the DENR, laws of the NCIP, laws of the PCSD, laws of the KSK, even the laws of the PNNI and ELAC."[42] With this flourish of acronyms, Bordo invoked a series of government agencies and two NGOs, whose environmental enforcement activities have implications for Palawan livelihood practices. To denote government-imposed laws, he used the Tagalog word *batas*, emphasizing their foreignness and distinctiveness from Palawan customary law (*adat*). "It's difficult," he continued, "to know which law to follow. One says we have the right to our traditional livelihoods like swidden and hunting of birds and wild pigs. Another says swidden is forbidden, as are birds and pigs. Which are we supposed to follow?"

An elder recognized as a "leader" by the government and NGOs, Bordo was reacting to a poster that had caught his eye during a recent visit to the municipal Environment and Natural Resource Office. The notice, he said, listed the Palawan bearded pig (*Sus ahoenobarbus*) among those species that were legally protected and forbidden to hunt. This classification came as a shock. According to his understanding of the law, Bordo believed that as Indigenous people, Palawan were legally entitled to engage in "traditional" livelihood practices, especially in their ancestral domain. Pig hunting, unlike practices more directly tied to commodity markets, was considered a quintessentially traditional pursuit by many Palawan people, and legally informed elders like Bordo believed that IPRA protects pig hunting as a traditional livelihood. But pig hunting is indeed banned by the Wildlife Act, except when part of Indigenous "religious rituals."

Bordo's speech expressed frustration with the many contradictory signals of environmental policy—an observation I heard frequently not just from Palawan people but also from settler farmers, NGO personnel, and even government officials. I had not yet seen the notice in question, so I asked Bordo whether it had something to do with Mantalingahan. He struggled to remember what the park's abbreviated name referred to (other than the mountain itself) and eventually suggested that Jimi must have given consent for the protected area. He asked me to inquire into the matter of pig hunting during my upcoming visit to the provincial capital, where I would be attending a meeting regarding Mantalingahan.[43]

Municipal environmental officers, he said, had referred his own queries to officials in the capital.

Bordo might have been unfamiliar with Mantalingahan, but he was nonetheless fluent in conservation narratives more generally. His audience that day included a dozen or so Palawan men and women, most of whom were elders. Lest we mistake his opposition to a hunting ban as a condemnation of all environmental regulation, Bordo shifted his tone for the remainder of his impromptu speech. First he publicly scolded his nephew, who had been seen trying to sell myna hatchlings (*Gracula religiosa*). Collecting birds for sale was not part of Palawan customs, he argued. Did they want, he asked rhetorically, to make others rich at their own expense by depleting all the wild birds? His nephew had to promise not to do anything like that again. Bordo offered a cautionary tale of what would happen if his nephew and others did not "follow" their traditions. On his last trip to Manila, he said, what he had encountered was "very bad" (*meyaqat banar*): bald mountains, smoky air, polluted rivers, garbage and sewage in the streets. These conditions explained why typhoons so frequently wreaked havoc in the national capital. By contrast, he continued, Palawan is still "very good" (*menunga banar*), with intact forests, clean water, and no typhoons or floods comparable to those in other parts of the country.[44] His underlying theory—that environmental degradation is a symptom of moral degradation, which invites punishment in the form of adverse events like typhoons—is one I encountered on multiple occasions in my conversations with Palawan elders.

To drive his point home, Bordo invoked a momentous chapter in local history. During the countrywide chaos of the waning Marcos dictatorship, antigovernment rebels were encamped in the foothills and mountains of southern Palawan.[45] The rebels forced the departure of Marcos-affiliated logging companies and thus protected the almaciga trees. The same rebels who demanded food, recruited local youth against the wishes of their parents, and occasionally killed suspected spies turned out to be allies in the defense of resources from predatory elites. Today, Bordo concluded, their ancestral domain claim is what keeps outsiders from taking their land—but even that would not have been possible without the assistance of NGOs and the government.

In Bordo's narrative, Palawan's persistence as a place of goodness has depended not only on Palawan customs but also on alliances, both intentional and involuntary, that have defended the land and resources. Early in his speech, he made a passing reference to mining—an issue that, in other parts of the island, has required communities to engage in difficult and divisive negotiations with government agencies, NGOs, and corporations. Bordo left it up to his audience to decide what to make of this juxtaposition of pig hunting, bird selling, logging, mining, rebels, and government. What he seemed to be saying is that interventions by more powerful others are inevitable but not without their potential advantages.[46] As the rebels did to the loggers of the Marcos era, government conservation may do to the miners of the present. This may seem like a simple truism. For Palawan, the question of how best to navigate the many interventions they face is far from simple. Bordo was grappling with it in his speech, as was Jimi in his participation in the tree-planting ceremony. The paradox of indigeneity requires that Palawan act as arbiters of competing environmental narratives even as they occupy a position of structural and cultural marginality.[47] As Bordo suggests, how Palawan negotiate this paradox will determine their ecological and moral future.

Two different forms of positionality should be addressed here—Bordo's and my own. I suspect, first, that my presence had some influence on what he chose to say that afternoon. By that time we had developed good rapport, but I was nonetheless associated with his rival. Bordo may have wanted to ensure that I would not misconstrue his position as one of total opposition to conservation. In addition, he was obliquely defending his record as a Palawan representative and leader. Bordo promoted the establishment of the ancestral domain in the 1990s and had been in charge of its management since then. During his tenure, the association that oversees the ancestral domain had run up massive debts with financiers of the almaciga resin trade and found itself in a prolonged lawsuit resulting in the suspension of the association's almaciga permits. His allies and opponents alike had complained to me that the boundaries between his business pursuits and those of the association had blurred over the years. In other words, Bordo was an entrepreneur with strong connections to external authorities, including NGOs and government agencies, of which many Palawan are suspicious. It makes sense that he began his speech with a lament about conflicting environmental regulations and ended it with an oblique defense of the ancestral domain and its entanglements.

For my Palawan hosts, environmental narratives were a pliant idiom for negotiating relations with competing government agencies, NGOs, and business interests, and for mediating their internal alliances and enmities. Jimi and Bordo were rivals, enemies even. As I detail in chapter 5, their enmity owed partly to a bitter legal dispute over almaciga trading permits and to their long-standing competition over externally conferred titles and authority. To make a long story short, Jimi was recognized by the NCIP and the municipal government as a "chieftain," while Bordo was recognized by an NGO and the DENR as the "president" of the ancestral domain.[48] Jimi had refused to sign on to on the ancestral domain when it was established due to his distrust of Bordo and the DENR, and he infused his narratives with this distrust while using parental metaphors to characterize the

NCIP's "protection" of Indigenous people. In particular, he contrasted the inherent "rights" (*karapatan*) and "freedoms" (*kalayaan*) of Indigenous people with the DENR's restrictions on swidden and other livelihood practices.

We could read Jimi's and Bordo's narratives as ciphers for conflicting allegiances among Palawan. However, what most interests me are the patterns their accounts share. In particular, I noticed that regardless of their external allegiances, Palawan environmental narratives tended to feature critical commentary on the contradictory environmental narratives of the state.[49] Like many Palawan elders I knew, both Jimi and Bordo pointed to the irony that conservation projects target Palawan lands even though settlers are the ones who have most dramatically transformed the landscape. Likewise, Bordo, Jimi, and many elders narrated the Palawan role in environmental change as one that depended not on benevolent government intervention but on Palawan moral integrity and resourcefulness. In this sense, environmental narratives were also idioms of solidarity within Palawan communities.[50]

Another example of this solidarity came in the form of counternarratives that explicitly challenged the scientific premises of official narratives. I frequently heard Palawan elders discount official claims that swidden, as a cause of deforestation, contributes to floods and landslides. Their counternarratives defended traditional Palawan practices and placed blame on broader changes associated with the mass arrival of Christian migrants, whom Palawan refer to as Kabisayaan.[51] Swidden, they argued, was practiced in Palawan long before the arrival of the Kabisayaan. Thus, they asked: If swidden caused deforestation, flooding, and landslides, why would such phenomena have been so rare in the past? Instead, torrential rain and other adverse events are said to reflect moral lapses in human conduct (i.e., of *adat* or *keedatan*). That is, when people behave immorally (*ba meyaqat it adat diye*), they risk angering deities and powerful beings who can afflict calamities, including typhoons and earthquakes.[52] Unpredictable weather was also said to be a result of this process, since the predictable monsoonal patterns that enable good swidden outcomes were considered a reflection of the overall moral quality of human behavior.[53]

In a variation on this theme, Maman Juhali—a *belyan* who was very critical of government conservation activities—explained to me that the "sweat" of boulders (*linget et kabatuan*) was a source of water that can cause flooding. When bad conduct makes the world "hot," he said, the boulders in the mountains sweat, leading to flooding downstream. (Juhali was drawing on Palawan ancestral knowledge that, for the human body and the land, coolness was associated with health and heat with illness.) In these narratives, immoral behavior included specific actions like excessive drinking, overexploitation of the forest, incest, and interpersonal violence as well as more general attitudinal changes resulting from learning new vices from settlers. Many elders complained that the Palawan were no longer following their own ancestral ways but were practicing those of the Kabisayaan, from whom they are adopting new morals and a radically different lifestyle involving sedentary, intensive agriculture, mass media consumption, and money. Elders surmised that by engaging in these practices by choice or necessity, Palawan were embroiled in a broader process of moral and ecological decline.[54]

Also central to this counternarrative is an irony that Juhali and other elders would highlight with no small measure of resentment. That is, Palawan have never cleared the forest on a scale comparable to what the Kabisayaan have done, and the latter now seek to control swidden and other Palawan uses of the forest. Juhali frequently reminded me and others that Palawan have their own ways of regulating forest use. Contrary to what outsiders believe, Palawan do not clear the forest wherever they please (*misan embe lang*). Instead, he insisted, they practice divination or dream interpretation, which tells them whether it is safe to clear certain areas of forest—that is, whether one has permission from the forest's invisible occupants (*taw't talun*). Kabisayaan, by contrast, clear any expanses of land that suit them. Such actions pay no heed to the claims of invisible beings, who then exact their vengeance in the form of illness, poor harvests, and other hardships (see figure 3.3).

Figure 3.3. Land being cleared and enclosed by settlers, backed by investors from Manila, for coconut and pineapple plantations, a few kilometers downstream of Tenga't Gebaq, April 2011. Source: Noah Theriault.

This ethical critique came as part of a larger narrative in which Juhali interpreted government conservation as a form of negative reciprocity. As Juhali explained it, Palawan were being "squeezed" (*nagipit*) farther into the mountains and then asked to curtail swidden—the basis of their way of life—for the sake of lowland agriculture. Meanwhile, forests in the lowlands were cleared without any regard for the effects on neighboring people, visible or otherwise. The resulting vengeance, Juhali claimed, is borne disproportionately by Palawan, most of whom do not have access to the same protective sorcery (*kependayan*) or medicines (*ubat*) as the Kabisayaan.[55]

An elder woman named Upu Oda agreed with Juhali but had an additional concern. Fewer and fewer Palawan, she explained, took proper "care" (*pang-ipat*) of their swidden rice, which she analogized to the care of children—"if you care badly for your children, your children will be bad; the same for rice" (*ba meyaqat it pang-ipat et meraga, meyaqat it meraga; kwantin gasi it pang-ipat et paray*). Building a "seat" (*pinedungan*) for the rice spirit, ritually washing the rice stalks (*pegtipas*), and avoiding work in the swidden during certain phases of the moon—all such practices were said to be in decline.[56] The same was true for postharvest rituals, including the *basalan* and *panggaw,* at which offerings were made as a form of thanksgiving or recompense to deities, forest beings, and ancestors. By neglecting these rituals in favor of cash-generating activities, church participation, and other "foreign" practices, Oda joined other Palawan elders in locating the decline of the swidden system in broader cultural and environmental changes that have accompanied the arrival of the Kabisayaan.

In short, Palawan counternarratives charged the Kabisayaan with driving the dual degradation of the environment and Palawan society—not simply because ancestral practices were in decline but because newly adopted practices were not seen as morally worthy of favorable environmental conditions. By positing themselves as morally superior but politically subordinate to the Kabisayaan, Palawan assigned themselves a benign role in the drama of environmental and cultural change. By contrast, settlers in the lowlands were cast as the leading culprits of environmental degradation and as the primary beneficiaries of the enclosure of upstream watersheds.[57] This characterization challenged both the efficacy and the justness of conservation-related restrictions on Palawan livelihoods. In this way, elders like Jimi, Bordo, Juhali, and Oda incorporated conservation into an environmental narrative in which it constituted a form of negative reciprocity and moral-*cum*-ecological degradation. As Bordo's narrative suggested, the proliferation of conservation measures was just the latest in a series of efforts to conscript and exploit Palawan. Whether driven by rebels, NGOs, or the state, such interventions may command coercive power but gain legitimacy only when they are seen as providing something in return for what they demand.[58] For instance, the rebels were a threatening presence, but Bordo's memory of them was cut with respect for their resistance against rapacious logging.

We have seen how Palawan people used environmental narratives to navigate the pressures of competing interests, fellow Palawan, and their own ambitions. As a result, their narratives spoke to heterogeneity and even discord among Palawan, particularly when they expressed conflicting allegiances to competing government institutions or business interests. More importantly, Palawan used environmental narratives to make sense of their shared, often difficult experiences of cultural, social, and ecological change. Some, like Bordo, emphasized the importance of balancing skepticism with strategic cooperation. Others, like Juhali, were more cynical and defiant. In my experience, Palawan did not intend their counternarratives as performances for audiences of government officials. (Such performances took place on occasion and were recounted proudly by Juhali and other outspoken elders. But in face-to-face encounters like the tree-planting ceremony, Palawan were far more likely to perform the harmony narrative even if only as a cover for behind-the-scenes maneuvers.) Instead, these counternarratives served primarily as genre for building critical consciousness among Palawan themselves. While specific details of official environmental narratives were sometimes questioned, even more important were matters of accountability, rights, and obligations. By reworking these narratives to tell their own story, Palawan demystified their paradoxical position at the center of environmental politics but the margins of society—a paradox obscured by the harmony narrative and its performances.[59] Particularly when infused with appeals to Indigenous cultural rights, Palawan narratives offered a cogent critique of indigeneity and conservation in the contemporary Philippines.

Prevailing environmental narratives in the Philippines, as elsewhere, are overly simplistic and potentially harmful. In a pattern similar to what Forsyth and Walker have observed in Thailand, Philippine Indigenous groups are often framed—and treated—as the forest's undocumented "destroyers" or as its rights-bearing "guardians."[60] This chapter has tracked how these seemingly opposed accounts find their way into competing policies like NIPAS and IPRA and are reconciled by a third, equally simplistic narrative of "harmony."[61] What results are interventions that claim to serve Palawan interests while extracting value from their land and labor for the benefit of others.[62]

But this chapter has been concerned less with correcting the (in)accuracies of prevailing environmental narratives than with tracing what they do at the level of micropolitics.[63] We have seen how various actors engage with environmental narratives as they navigate, resist, and otherwise seek to influence the larger processes of change in which they are entangled. When we treat environmental narratives solely as macroscale discourses, we disregard their critical role in the material negotiations of everyday life. Likewise, when we see environmental narratives only as a form of (inaccurate) technocratic knowledge, we overlook how actual people—bureaucrats and Indigenous farmers alike—re/produce and rework these narratives to analyze environmental change and the role of various actors therein.[64] The accounts of park officials differed in revealing ways in terms of how they framed Indigenous people's rights and obligations, but they were united in naturalizing the government's regulatory authority. Accounts from Palawan elders living inside Mantalingahan differed from one another in terms of their allegiances but shared a critical analysis of power, moral conduct, and their relationship with environmental change.[65]

Unlike a focus on knowledge, which might posit Indigenous "metis" in radical alterity to bureaucratic technoscience, environmental narratives are a genre in which epistemologically incongruent visions of the world intermingle.[66] This is partly how profound differences of knowledge, culture, and power are masked for the sake of performing cooperation and harmony. But it is also through environmental narratives that particular registers of difference are (re)produced and emphasized. In other words, environmental narratives do more than inspire misguided policies and interventions; they serve as a genre for interpreting those interventions and imagining alternatives to them. Simplified representations of environmental change can convey both universalizing, scientific claims to authority and place-specific, Indigenous counterclaims.

In the Philippines, Palawan and other Indigenous people are socially marginalized yet at the center of contrasting narratives about the past and competing visions for the future.[67] From this paradoxical position, they develop their own critical analyses of indigeneity, conservation, and capitalism, and they use these to pursue their own interests. As will become clear in chapters 4 and 5, the great irony of this situation is that it enables both their empowerment and their dispossession.

CHAPTER FOUR

Forest Dreams, Conservation Fantasies

It was the end of a typical day in the Tenga't Gebaq.[1] As the sun disappeared behind the trees, everyone gathered to watch television in Jimi and Palaya's house. Jimi and Palaya were the only ones in the village with a generator and TV/DVD set. They were also my hosts, so I joined in this nightly routine, no matter how tired I was from a day of research. Except for when I would bring new-to-us episodes of *Planet Earth*—known locally as *bita't ramuramu* (creature TV)—we usually watched either a Korean soap opera or a Filipino action film. Not a big fan of either genre, I often spent this time outside, enjoying the night air and chatting with passers-by. Even then, I tried to keep an ear tuned to the gasps, laughs, and comments of the audience inside the house. Imagine several aunties exclaiming in unison—"But why?!"—as a wealthy character stoically endures her husband's infidelity and abuse. Such moments helped me better understand my hosts' norms around gender, kinship, and moral conduct.

On the night in question, the TV was on for less than an hour before the generator ran dry and sputtered to a stop. Within minutes, everyone had filed out of the house, extricated their cell phones from the tangle of cords around the communal outlet, and walked home in the moonlight. As I settled into my bed, I chatted with Jimi, Palaya, and their kids through the bamboo walls—another part of our routine. We covered some of our usual topics of interest. "Right now it's about six in the morning in America. . . . I don't know if it's sunny there today, but it's usually hot this time of year. . . . Yes, tomorrow I need to do more interviews."

Just as my thoughts were fading to sleep, I heard a rustling somewhere around my bed, then a sinister but indistinct whisper. Before I could react, a bony hand swept across my face and clamped itself over my nose and mouth. Something heavy pressed down on my chest, as if someone were straddling me. Twitching my arms and legs, I found that I was virtually paralyzed. I cried out for help, but my voice was muffled by the powerful hand. What must have been just a few moments seemed to stretch on for hours.

Then I heard a voice. It was Bina, Palaya and Jimi's daughter. "Mom," she cried, "what's going on?!" Her voice quaked with genuine alarm.

As I lay there in a cold sweat, my heart pounding, I realized I had been dreaming. I had no idea how long I had been sleeping or how long my dream had lasted in waking time. Clearly, though, I had been loud enough to frighten Bina.

"He was dreaming," Jimi said, with no small measure of alarm in his own voice. "Noah, are you okay?" he asked. "Yes," I replied, "it was a bad dream." Startled but still exhausted, I soon fell back to sleep, only vaguely aware of an owl hooting somewhere nearby, its call a distinctive cackle unlike any I have heard elsewhere (perhaps *Strix seloputo*).

The next morning, as we sat sipping coffee next to the hearth, I apologized to Palaya and Jimi for disturbing them and the kids. I learned that they had not slept well and that people in nearby households had reported feeling an ominous presence in the air afterward. They smiled humanely at my mortified apologies, saying, "No, we feel sorry for you, that you experienced such a thing here in our place! We thought you were going to die."

"You thought I was going to . . . *die?*" My dream, Jimi explained, was what Palawan call a *deletdet*—a potentially lethal type of nightmare recognized in many East and Southeast Asian societies.[2] Jimi had been rising to intervene when I awoke. If I had not done so on my own, he would have had to fetch a ritual healer (*belyan*) to try and prevent my death.

"It was the owl," Palaya whispered. "The owl?" I asked, confused. Jimi and Palaya elaborated on their theory that the owl had inflicted the nightmare on me. I knew that Palawan considered owls to be bad omens and potentially evil, but this was the first I had heard about an owl attacking a person in a dream. Palaya and Jimi would not venture a guess as to why the owl had attacked me, and their nervous laughs told me not to pursue the matter further until the danger had passed. Sorcery (*kependayan*) was a sensitive matter under normal circumstances, and this moment called for restraint. In due time, I learned that owls were powerful shape-shifters that could smother you in your dream or take the form of traveling kinfolk in need of a place to sleep, only to eat your flesh in the night.

What for me was a fleeting if intense nightmare (and perhaps a side effect of my antimalaria pills) was for my hosts a potentially deadly act of owl sorcery. To them, it was mysterious and difficult to interpret, but it was no less "real" or alarming than if it had happened while I was awake. In this context, my dream was not a figment of a wandering mind whose experiences are materially insulated from waking life. Instead, dreams are what some elements of a person's spirit (*kurudwa*) do and experience while other elements are asleep.[3] Dream experiences can have direct consequences for the dreamer and the community—for example, when one is attacked by an owl or other malevolent being. They can also serve as omens about future events or actions. My nightmare was interpreted not just as an attack but also as a warning that I should limit my travel outside the village. This obliged me to postpone a visit to sites higher up in the mountains, and thus I learned firsthand how, even for a foreign anthropologist, dreams can have very material consequences.

Dreams are a complex matter in any context, and I do not claim to understand the range of how Palawan people and communities experience or interpret them. Even so, dreams permeate this chapter as a source of empirical insight and as a critical metaphor. On the one hand, I look to dream life for insight into how people in Tenga't Gebaq experienced and intervened in processes of social and environmental change. Dreams were one of the primary domains in which my hosts encountered "people of the forest" (*taw't talun*) and other invisible but powerful beings that populated the landscape. These encounters were empirically elusive but, I argue, a crucial factor in how people understood and responded to the changing world.

This chapter also engages with dreams in a metaphorical sense. These are the "dreams" of conservationists, who envision integrating Indigenous people seamlessly into protected areas—in this case, Palawan communities into the Mount Mantalingahan Protected Landscape. Underscoring the colonial in postcolonial, Filipino policy makers have long envisioned "harmonizing" state-mandated conservation zones with their putative "natural partner": Indigenous communities and their "traditions."[4] Under Philippine law, Indigenous people are required to manage their land in cooperation with the state but are also entitled to do so "in accordance with their Indigenous knowledge, beliefs, systems, and practices." This policy assumes that Indigenous practices are compatible (or at least reconcilable) with the laws and logics of bureaucratic regulation.

In practice, efforts to realize this "green development fantasy," as Anna Tsing has called it, have collided with the complex realities and power imbalances that actually exist on the ground.[5] Recall how in chapters 1 and 2, we examined the historical amnesia inherent in this fantasy and contrasted it with how my Palawan hosts theorized their own place in history. We saw in chapter 3 how they engaged creatively with competing and at times contradictory environmental narratives in their pursuit of alternative, even oppositional agendas at the local level.

This chapter adds another dimension to the story. Remaining with my host community in Tenga't Gebaq, we will see how Palawan people grappled with the cosmological and ontological dilemmas that accompanied their entanglements with conservation, capitalism, and Indigenous rights. If the phrase "cosmological and ontological dilemmas" is unclear, bear with me. It will become clear shortly, and I have included an extensive explanation in the notes.[6] For now, think of it this way: My Palawan hosts' interactions with one another, with other communities, and with their surroundings were partly shaped by their relations with invisible beings, including but not limited to the people of the forest and the owl that attacked me in my dream. In this context, these beings are cosmologically and ontologically part of the material world. They are not mere beliefs that exist solely in the human mind. Meanwhile, even as the government demands Palawan cooperation with conservation, it does not recognize their invisible neighbors as part of the landscape that is supposed to be protected. If this statement seems absurd, reconsider it as follows: Most conservation projects, including Mantalingahan, operate according to a scientific cosmology that does not allow for the material existence of forest people and other invisible beings. As a result, these projects ontologically omit a critical part of the ecology that they seek to regulate, creating one of the dilemmas at the center of this chapter.[7]

For people in Tenga't Gebaq, these dilemmas resulted from trying to reconcile the realities of their everyday lives with the demands imposed on them by the government and other well-resourced actors. They did this in part by engaging critically with dominant narratives about Indigenous people, as we saw in chapter 3. These struggles also played out through their dynamic relations with the forest people and other invisible beings. On the surface, these relations sometimes appeared well suited to conservation. My hosts sometimes avoided felling certain large trees for fear of provoking the beings who dwell in them. This was certainly in line with conservation policies and was interpreted by officials as an Indigenous prohibition of felling large trees. But unlike conservation policies, which demand universal compliance with discrete zoning and depersonalized rules, Palawan land use decisions were site-specific, interpersonal, and often discretionary. They were based on constant analysis, not on rote adherence to unchanging rules. Many of the factors involved would be familiar to smallholder farmers everywhere: labor capacity, material needs, future plans, microlevel land use histories, government policies, soil quality, and other landscape characteristics. In Tenga't Gebaq, these factors also included dreams, divination, and other methods to communicate with the invisible realm.

As we will see, my hosts used their own interpersonal, more-than-human analyses in their decisions about how to relate to the land. Yet there was no place for such fine-grained analysis in the rules of conservation, which summarily cordoned off wide swaths of the landscape for protecting everything-but-human biodiversity.[8] Even when Palawan people sought to reconcile their analyses with the government's demands for harmonious cooperation, conservation personnel often interpreted their actions as duplicitous and out of line with Indigenous tradition. As a result, people in Tenga't Gebaq did not find themselves seamlessly integrated into the protected area that surrounded them, nor were their land uses harmonized with its rules. Rather, as we saw in chapter 3 and will further explore here, their interactions with conservation personnel were marked by mutual distrust, doubt, and alienation. This is an important part of how Mantalingahan and similar conservation projects undermine the Indigenous practices that they purport to sustain and uplift.

Palawan World-Making Practices

Despite what Philippine law says about Indigenous people, Palawan communities are not homogenous. In chapters 1 and 2, we learned about how people in Tenga't Gebaq fit into a diverse and historically dynamic social landscape. Most families in the village were among those who had not converted to Islam or Christianity and still practiced swidden in combination with subsistence- and market-oriented collecting of forest products. A few worked for wages, a few set up small dry-goods stores, and a few tried to intensively farm cash crops. Most derived the bulk of their cash income from collecting non-timber forest products like rattan and almaciga. Even so, these people were by no means representatives of "pure" Palawan cultural traditions, whatever those might be. For one thing, even the most distinctive Palawan practices are historically connected to larger regional patterns of material and cultural exchange among cosmologically, linguistically, and ethnically diverse peoples—Hindus, Buddhists, Muslims, Christians, and others from Southeast Asia, China, India, and beyond. This is why we find terms from Sanskrit, Arabic, and English in everyday use among Palawan people, even in the context of self-consciously traditional activities, such as when a respected *ukum* (judge, from Arabic), whom some people address as *tsiptan* (chieftain, from English), settles a dispute through a *bitsara* (a term for customary legal discussions that is derived from Malay and possibly from Sanskrit).[9]

Jimi offers a clear case in point. As someone who played all of these roles, he was vocally critical of organized religion and its proselytizers. This does not mean that he—or other like-minded Palawan—was a hard-line traditionalist who disclaimed all "foreign" influence. For example, Jimi knew that his interpretation of Palawan *keedatan* (customary law) incorporated principles from the *batas* (codified law) of Muslims, Christians, and the nominally secular Philippine state. He tolerated the presence of Christian missionaries and maintained close ties with his kin who joined churches. Meanwhile, Jimi was more heavily engaged with the capitalist economy and government bureaucracy than any Palawan person in the immediate vicinity, as we explore in chapter 5. His seasonal work routine remained organized around the practice of *uma* (swidden farming), but he also experimented with wet-rice farming and planting commodity crops like pineapple. Jimi wanted to secure the future of his family in an increasingly capitalist world, but he also wanted to maintain the rights of his community to their ancestral lands and laws. His outlook was both/and, rather than either/or.

In sum, although Jimi was perhaps more self-conscious in his approach to change than most other Palawan, he was no different from anyone else. Like anyone reading this book, Palawan people think and act in complex, contingent, at times contradictory ways.[10] For this reason, we must remember that the cosmological and ontological theories we encounter here are neither static nor uniform. They change over time and vary not just between Palawan communities but also within them, and this variation is an essential starting point for analyzing contemporary Palawan experiences.

One could attribute this variation to the "disappearance" of Palawan cosmology and related practices. Ethnographic studies by Charles Macdonald and Nicole Revel, who first conducted fieldwork in the 1970s, contain descriptions of an elaborate cosmology, expressed in an extensive tradition of myths (*tuturan et kegurangurangan*), sung epics (*tultul*), and shamanic ritual centered on offerings of rice wine (*tinapey*) or mead (*simbug*). Macdonald concludes that Palawan cosmological knowledge and ritual practices are in a state of decline, as new religious beliefs, medical practices, and livelihoods all marginalize ritual specialists and their knowledge of the cosmos. Many Palawan elders I spoke with drew similar conclusions, arguing that the ways of the ancestors were being replaced by those of Muslim and Christian settlers. As will be discussed, many Palawan also cited the prohibition of swidden farming and the excessive commodification of the landscape as important factors.

Yet my hosts in Tenga't Gebaq were not particularly interested in dwelling on how and why Palawan cosmology might be disappearing. As I shared in the introduction, Jimi admonished me from the start against seeing the dispossession and assimilation of Palawan communities as an inevitability. This is why I do not tell a story of loss or decline but one of change, generativity, and agency amid stark inequalities and real hardships. This chapter focuses on how invisible beings figured into my hosts' everyday, practical relations with their surroundings. These relations remained part of world-making practices in Tenga't Gebaq not despite but because of the profound social and ecological changes people were experiencing.[11] I will further develop this point in a later part of the chapter. First, though, I should explain what I mean by "invisible beings."

The term "invisible beings" is a broad translation of the Palawan term *taw na kaya megkebiri,* which translates more literally to "invisible people." These beings exist in an imprecisely defined invisible realm that overlaps with the visible world and extends into the heavens.[12] As with Palawan cosmology more generally, accounts of these beings vary significantly. In the myths and legends documented by Macdonald and Revel, some beings in the invisible realm go by special names as individuals or groups. In my experience, these specific names are less important than the general categories into which these beings fall. The following discussion emphasizes these general distinctions.

Beyond the earthly realm of invisible people in the strict sense is a set of powerful beings referred to collectively as "masters" or "guardians" (*empuq*)—the Maker (*Empu't Nagbaal*), the Weaver (*Empu't Nagselad*), the Lady of the Monsoon (*Linamin et Barat*), the Guardian of Rice (*Empu't Parey*), and so on. In my experience, these guardians were not referred to as humans (*taw*), and they were generally thought to live in the heavens rather than on earth. Macdonald refers to them as "celestial spirits." I capitalize the names of these beings because despite uncertainties about their ontology, they were generally referred to as specific entities. In some ways, *empuq* remained distant from the day-to-day experience of most Palawan—as referents in myths or legends, thanksgiving rituals, and esoteric shamanic interventions. In other ways, their presence had everyday material consequences. For example, many people said they were supposed to build a small bamboo "seat" (*pinedungan*) for the Rice Guardian in their swiddens and "care" for their rice as they would their children, including ritual bathing and labor restrictions during certain phases of the moon. Ignoring these rules can have short- and long-term consequences for rice harvests. Likewise, Palawan were supposed to make offerings to *empuq* in exchange for healthy and bountiful harvests, and they interpreted scarcity or bad weather as a divine punishment for insufficient offerings and for moral infractions like incest, animal cruelty, child abuse, or neglect of swidden rice. Because of their general remoteness from daily life, *empuq* are of less relevance to this chapter than those classes of invisible beings who inhabit the earth.

Next come the *diwata* (or *taw kewasa*), an ambiguous category of invisible beings who are often said to live at the peaks of mountains. Some accounts placed *diwata* spatially in the heavens and distinguished them from humans in that respect. By all accounts, *diwata* were thought to be essentially good. They were sometimes conflated with the deities of rice, honey, and wild pigs and can be invoked along with *empuq* for help with healing. *Diwata* also served as *gimbaran* or spirit companions for ritual healers. *Diwata* were not cited as givers of illness (or hunters of people). Instead, they were a benevolent if more remote presence with whom good relations depended on making offerings and respecting their spaces in the landscape.

The final class of invisible beings comprises the "people of the forest" or *taw't talun,* who were implicated in my nightmare encounter with the owl sorcerer. In truth, the people of the forest are not exclusively of the forest. They are the occupants of the *talun,* which the English word "forest" only partially captures. The *talun* comprises old-growth forests and other spaces that most Westerners would consider to be wilderness, but this is a misleading translation. Wilderness implies an absence of humans, while the *talun* is occupied (and, by some accounts, cultivated) by invisible persons. *Taw't talun* were generally said to live in old-growth forest, but they could also be along the banks of rivers and streams and in large trees left standing in a clearing. There were different varieties of these beings, such as the generically named *lenggam* and *seytan,* who live in large trees (e.g., *tegas, ginuqu, beringin, rimaraw*), or the Mengeringen, who live along the banks of rivers, where they cultivate seasonal reeds as their "rice" and hunt Palawan people for their meat.[13]

Let's turn to the ontology of forest people in general. Recall the Palawan oral history that I recounted in chapter 1, in which Magellan and Lapu-Lapu discover Palawan Island, fight over its riches, and render it visible to outsiders. According to one elder, a subsequent dispute over sago palm (*betbat*) was what led part of the island's population to revert to invisibility. Whatever their origin, the people of the forest differed from the celestial *empuq* and mighty *diwata* in that they were unambiguously human and inherently dangerous, if not evil. What distinguished them from visible people was their practice of hunting other humans. Being hunted by forest people manifested as illness and death. Furthermore, they were said to use powerful magic to attack people by, for example, possessing them or causing one of their souls (*kurudwa*) to go astray.[14] Although the forest people needed no specific cause for hunting or attacking, they often did so as retribution for a transgression on the part of a person in the visible realm. For example, when a Palawan person overharvested rattan or cleared a forested area without consent, they risked bringing illness and even death upon themselves and their communities. This has important implications for their involvement in markets for forest commodities. Provoking the wrath of the forest people was an especially salient concern for my hosts as they engaged more intensively in marketing forest products like rattan.

In these broad categories of invisible beings, I found that significant ambiguities arose in practice, especially as related to hunting. These ambiguities were most apparent for the guardians of wild pigs, who literally "give" (*begey*) pigs to Palawan hunters and therefore have a more immediate, humanlike presence than other *empuq.* Although the ontology of all invisible beings was shrouded in some mystery, these particular guardians seemed especially varied in their forms. My questions about them yielded conflicting or ambiguous responses as to whether they were more like the Guardian of Rice, the mighty *diwata,* or the menacing forest people. Macdonald suggests that guardians of wild pigs are "forest spirits," which he distinguishes from the "celestial spirits."[15]

This uncertainty has (at least) three sources. The first is that figures bearing names like *Empu't Byek* (Guardian of Wild Pigs) appear as individual characters in ancestral oral histories, whereas colloquial references to the invisible guardian(s) of wild pigs do not necessarily intend to invoke a specific deity. Second, the word *empuq* denotes possession among visible and invisible people. For example, when discussing who owns a machete, a piece of land, or anything else, Palawan referred to its (visible) owner as its *empuq*. They also used *empuq* to refer to the invisible occupants of trees or rattan. Such *empuq* are not necessarily *Empuq* in the sense of the celestial Guardian of Rice but invisible persons who possess the spaces in question.

For the third and final uncertainty: Palawan sometimes conceived of wild pigs as animal doubles for forest spirits (and chickens as animal doubles for visible people). This means that Palawan who hunt wild pigs are hunting (invisible) humans, which complements the notion that Palawan are hunted "like white chickens" by the people of the forest.[16] At the same time, as I will discuss shortly, wild pigs were also said to be "given" to Palawan by the pigs' *empuq*. Among Palawan I knew, this act of giving seemed more salient than the personhood of pigs. For example, the reason for why they should not wantonly kill pigs or sell pig meat was that the *empuq* of pigs would withhold future gifts. I did not hear the personhood of pigs themselves invoked, except for in reference to a form of sorcery whereby a visible person's soul could become trapped in a pig. In any case, the notion of pigs as gifts from invisible beings was not mutually exclusive with the personhood of pigs.[17]

In sum, the landscape around Tenga't Gebaq was inhabited by invisible beings, and their presence was sometimes a significant factor in my hosts' relations with the environment. For example, when deciding where to clear a new swidden field, some Palawan considered not just the soil quality, hydrology, and past land use but the presence of any invisible beings who might be present there. In other words, their relations with the invisible realm had material effects on their lives and environments. Tending to these relations (or failing to do so) can make the difference between health and sickness, bounty and hunger, and even life and death for oneself and one's family. It shapes the landscape itself, as when a large tree is left intact to avoid angering its invisible occupants or an area of older growth is selectively cleared after offerings are made. Accordingly, I have described these relations in terms of onto-cosmological or world-making practices rather than a form of knowledge or ideology. What exactly does that mean?

Revisiting the Concept of Ontology

Let's consider the basic scientific principle that Earth is a planet in our solar system, with all that this implies about our knowledge of outer space. This is not simply a "fact"—it is a cosmological theory deeply embedded in our cultural and political institutions. Nor can it exist independently of those institutions, their technologies of observation, and protocols of interpretation. Ditto for the ontological proposition that the universe is made of particles like protons, electrons, neutrinos, and so on, and for the ontological principle that animals and plants are alive, but rocks and robots are not. These are theories because they provide frameworks for making sense of complex relationships, processes, and phenomena. But they are not just ideas—they are integral to the structure of our society, and in this sense, they are political. This is why encounters between different cosmological and ontological theories—such as those unfolding in places like Palawan—are so politically significant. They aren't simply encounters between different beliefs; they are collisions between different social orders and world-making practices.

Anthropologists have long argued that societies have varying conceptions of reality, and we have defended them as internally coherent, culturally specific forms of "knowledge" and "ideology." But even anthropological approaches have largely treated Indigenous ontological categories as mythological or metaphorical representations. Rappaport's famous formulation distinguished between the "cognized models" developed by local people and the "operational models" developed by scientists—a distinction between how people imagine things to work on the one hand and how things actually work on the other hand.[18] Although Rappaport's brand of functionalism has fallen out of favor, the underlying distinction remains alive and well in environmental anthropology, even as the gaze of critical analysis has increasingly turned back on science. Despite our better intentions, we have often reproduced a hierarchical order in which different "models" of reality can be isolated from one another and, intentionally or otherwise, ranked according to their supposed explanatory power.[19]

To address this problem, recent interventions have urged us to focus on the uncertainty and complexity of everyday material practices rather than on competing sets of narratives or theories.[20] Paul Nadasdy, drawing on an experience he had during fieldwork in the southwestern Yukon, supports the Kluane proposition that animals intentionally "give" themselves to hunters. He urges us to "acknowledge that [Indigenous ontological assumptions] are not just cultural constructions and accept instead the possibility that they may be actually (as well as metaphorically) valid."[21] This argument draws inspiration from Michael Jackson's writing on "radical empiricism," which considers all ontological assumptions as potentially valid. Radical empiricism involves not just participant observation but "radical participation," so that we can "treat [our] own experiences as primary data."[22] In this spirit, I have interpreted my *deletdet* nightmare—and the experiences I describe below—as literal representations of what happened. More generally, I describe Palawan relations with their invisible neighbors not as part of an ideational or "cognized" model of ecology but as a material part of their ecological reality.

Another problem arises here. If we are to treat Indigenous ontological theories as part of material world-making practices and not just metaphorical ideation, what are we to do with accounts of the same event that rest on conflicting ontological assumptions? Latour's solution to this problem is one of the most influential. He proposes that analysts "ontologically flatten" the empirical content of their study.[23] He claims this allows every organism and object to be accounted for as an "actant" without imposing any single set of culturally biased ontological assumptions. I agree that we can and must abandon "nature" as a standard for assessing and intervening in ecological relations. But in my mind, it seems incredibly naive to suggest that we can simply describe "actants" without recourse to our culturally laden ontological assumptions.

This is why, Nadasdy suggests, we ought to deal more directly with ontological "indeterminacy" (or uncertainty).[24] In past work, I have used the concept of ontological multiplicity to describe the interaction of world-making practices in Tenga't Gebaq.[25] In retrospect, indeterminacy would have been a more accurate term and avoids implying that "different peoples inhabit different, incommensurable, and only partially connected realities, or worlds."[26] The conditions in question are, I concur, "far more dynamic, complex, and heterogeneous than can be captured by the multiple-worlds thesis."[27]

Put simply, the world is incredibly complex, and no singular theory of cosmology or ontology can account for all its phenomena. Ontological theories are precisely that—theories. They enable us to conceptualize and interact with profoundly complex, often unstable, even mysterious phenomena. But they do not entail certainty or unanimity, and they do not map neatly onto our day-to-day thoughts and actions. In Tenga't Gebaq, many Palawan considered the invisible realm to be very mysterious, and some claimed to know nothing about it whatsoever. As we saw in chapter 3, it was not unusual for people to integrate "modern" ontological theories—about, say, the role of forests in regional weather patterns—into their accounts of environmental change. Even so, under certain circumstances, these same individuals would attribute an illness to invisible beings or seek a healer's advice about whether to clear a particular area of forest. Relations with the invisible realm were both indeterminate and a material force in everyday life.

Ontological Conflicts

One of the founding myths of the Mount Mantalingahan Protected Landscape, in which an estimated 12,000 Palawan people live, is that the Indigenous people in its boundaries embrace its existence.[28] As required by law, extensive consultations were conducted before Mantalingahan's proclamation as a national park by President Gloria Arroyo in 2009. The nongovernmental organization (NGO) Conservation International (CI) led the consultation process, in which "tribal endorsements" were obtained for the thirty-six affected *barangays* and verified by the National Commission on Indigenous People.[29] In a project report to the Critical Ecosystem Partnership Fund, CI wrote that "the multi-sectoral team made sure that majority of the local communities including the Indigenous peoples in the uplands were properly informed and fully understand the benefits of establishing a protected area." Indigenous people and their rights feature prominently in Mantalingahan's management plan. Five seats on the management board are reserved for Palawan representatives, who are charged with helping ensure that the park's system of land use zoning categories is "harmonized" with Indigenous land claims.[30] The fact that many Palawan live within Mantalingahan's "core zones"—where "human disruption" is strictly prohibited—is not a problem because the law allows "traditional uses of tribal communities for minimal and soft impact gathering of forest species for ceremonial and religious purposes" (PCSD Resolution no. 94-44). Moreover, "refinements [of] zoning [will] take into account Indigenous knowledge systems and practices." On paper, the park is explicitly designated to protect a landscape, and its human residents are supposed to be an integral part of its operation.

In practice, Palawan involvement in Mantalingahan's day-to-day operation remains limited, inconsistent, and fraught with distrust. These challenges came up frequently in my conversations with government and NGO personnel. "It is hard to 'inject' new ideas into the Palawan," said one government official. Another observed that Palawan have been "corrupted" by gambling, drinking, and outside influences, which have led them to clear ever larger areas of the forest without regard for their traditional ethics. Perhaps most common was the notion that Palawan people simply lack the will to make long-term investments or commitments. They lack "discipline," I was told.

Officials had varying views on how faults on the part of Palawan hindered co-management. Perhaps predictably, they were less apt to identify the assumptions of co-management as a problem. For example, consider an NGO employee with whom I interacted regularly (and came to respect deeply). Once, during a frank exchange, I expressed my opinion that conflicting views of swidden were the

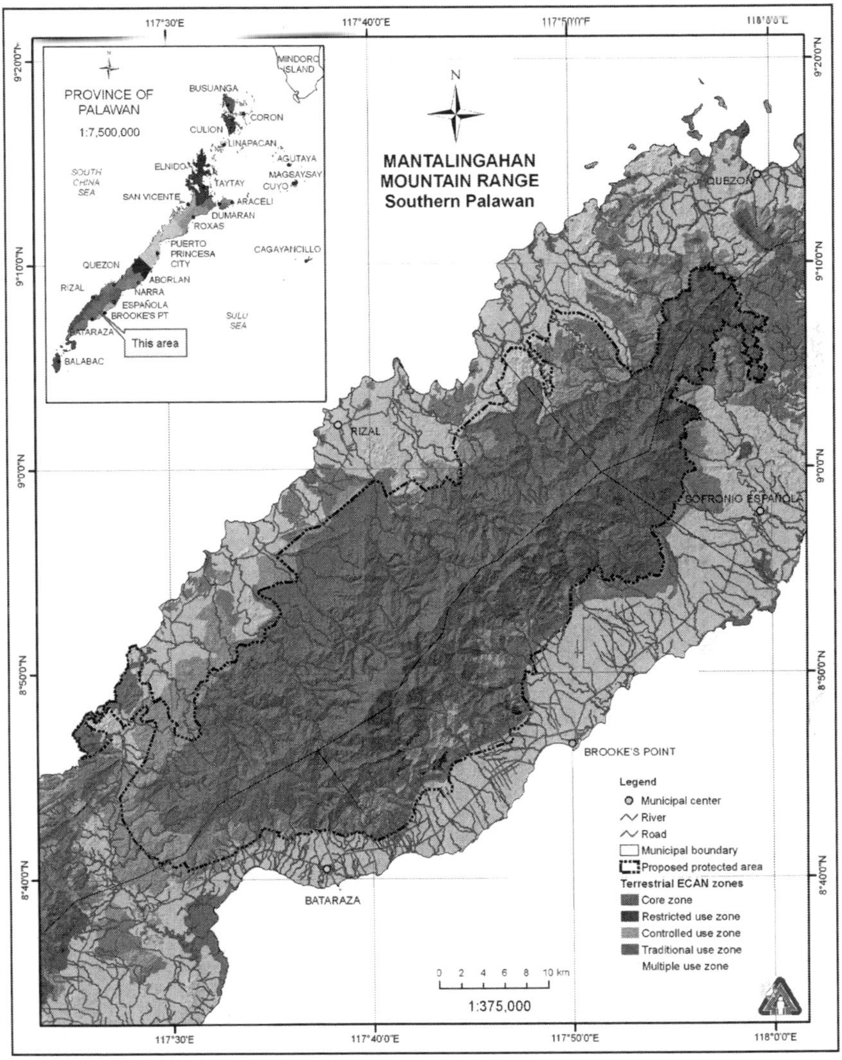

Map 4. Mount Mantalingahan Protected Landscape with land uses zoned under a policy called the Environmentally Critical Areas Network. Source: Palawan Council for Sustainable Development.

greatest barrier to Palawan cooperation with conservation. She countered that Palawan communities had been eager to forge conservation agreements with her organization. She referred me to a letter from a Palawan elder claiming, in effect, that his community only practiced swidden because they were poor. Palawan are "easily brainwashed," she explained, but otherwise they are naturally inclined to protect their ancestral domains. I responded by explaining my understanding of Palawan relations with the people of the forest. Palawan would sometimes seek their permission to clear swiddens in areas that were previously declared taboo. She thought for a moment and then, with an incredulous smile, asked, "But do they *really* believe that?" Her question implied that Palawan might invoke this "belief" as an alibi for disregarding their own tradition of not clearing large trees. She seemed skeptical that invisible beings could actually have an effect on her work.

Dreaming of Angry Giants

Oto was a young bachelor who came and went frequently in Tenga't Gebaq while I lived there. Men of his age, married or unmarried, typically remain attached to the households of their parents or parents-in-law, with whom they build adjacent swiddens and exchange labor to varying degrees. Oto's parents and siblings lived closer to town, in an area that had been hemmed in by migrant plantations and was not suitable for large family swiddens. Instead of trying to attach himself to another household, he floated around as a guest in various homes, earning money for food by collecting almaciga resin and performing wage labor. At one point, he teamed up with another young man in the village to make charcoal to sell in the market.

After sharing a couple of charcoal piles with his friend, Oto began to make his own. The process involves felling small- to medium-sized trees, chopping them into small logs, and arranging them conically around a cavity so that they will burn slowly from the inside out (see figure 4.1). A few days into the process, before he had begun the burn, Oto was confronted in a dream by a pair of giant, angry forest persons. They threatened to kill him if he continued making charcoal, but these beings did not reveal what specifically had offended them—that is, whether the charcoal pile was encroaching on their home or was simply a practice they despised. Either way, Oto said, he would not try to make charcoal again for a long time, if ever. Although he needed money, engaging in this "new" activity was not worth the risk.

Not long before I first arrived there, charcoal making had become a source of income for a significant number of households in and near the village. This laborious practice had gradually spread upstream, following the network of old logging roads, as the town's demand for charcoal grew and more accessible sources of wood were depleted. Just downstream of the village, one cluster of households had become heavily involved in charcoal making. They built their piles in plain sight, seemingly unconcerned that charcoal making was forbidden there. To the field officer who visited regularly, their behavior was anathema. He said he had

Figure 4.1. Logs arranged into a hollow cone, to be burned from the interior cavity to make charcoal, August 2011. Source: Noah Theriault.

considered establishing a biodiversity monitoring project in the village but changed his mind when residents started making charcoal. To him, this development signified a loss of tradition. It also made him wonder how much longer he could go without taking punitive actions.

Given Oto's experience, one might expect to find general agreement between Palawan people and the government on the practice of charcoal making. For Palawan, it can provoke the anger of the forest people and thus transgress the proscription on taking more than one needs. For the government, charcoal making is ecologically destructive and therefore forbidden in a protected area like Mantalingahan. Both see charcoal making as a "nontraditional" or "new" activity. One might note this agreement and conclude, as the field officer did, that charcoal making constitutes an unambiguous violation of both Palawan ethics and government policy. One might draw a similar conclusion about clearing old-growth forest, as was the case with the NGO employee mentioned above. Ultimately, these seemingly harmonious values derive from very different ontological assumptions.

Let's consider more carefully the aversion to "new" or "nontraditional" livelihood activities that Palawan seem to share with government. When Oto told me about his encounter with the angry giants, I asked him if his experience would deter him from other activities that involve cutting trees, namely, swidden. "No," he replied, exaggerating his intonation to highlight the absurdity of my question. The dream, he explained, was not about swidden, nor was swidden a new source of livelihood (*bagung usa*). To the rest of my follow-up questions, Oto would only say "*ista ku kediye*" (I don't know [about] them)—as often happened when I asked young men and women about the people of the forest.[31]

Notwithstanding Oto's reticence, the newness of charcoal seemed to be the problem in his case. Curious how those involved in charcoal making would interpret Oto's dream, I described it to Juhali, the eldest male in the cluster of charcoal-making households, who prided himself on his knowledge of Palawan traditions. Juhali surmised that Oto, by making a charcoal pile near an area of *talun*, had accidentally trespassed on the home of an invisible person. By contrast, Juhali and his neighbors were making charcoal only in *bengley* (relatively immature secondary growth) and thus were not at risk of trespassing. They would take precautions around any large trees in the *bengley* by either leaving them intact or asking their invisible occupants to vacate (more on this practice below).

Was Oto simply more conservative in his ethics than Juhali? Put differently, was the field officer correct to see their contrasting behavior as a matter of differential adherence to "tradition"? One can only answer these questions in the affirmative if one discounts Palawan ontology. Even though Juhali did not see charcoal making as inherently risky, he agreed that it was "new" and thus ethically uncertain. When Palawan describe an activity like charcoal making as "new," they are referring not just to its relatively recent arrival but also to the fact that money is involved. Subsistence activities, particularly swidden, hunting, and gathering wild foods, are considered customary sources of livelihood. Anything that involves selling goods or labor, particularly to outsiders, is considered new. Even an ostensibly ancient activity like rattan gathering is considered new when the rattan is solid at market. Palawan acknowledged that their forebears have been involved in trade since time immemorial, and elders recalled their parents and grandparents trading forest products, particularly almaciga resin, for salt, ceramics, and other luxury items. But the exchange of goods and labor for money is considered a new development (and, for many, a troubling one).

Why should this development be ethically troubling? Their concerns stem from the high value many Palawan place on being *mepekaan*—literally, prone to feeding others. In my experience, many Palawan describe sharing food as the height of moral personhood. Even though Palawan have presumably always varied in enacting this ideal, and even though it seems increasingly out of touch with their lived realities, anything thought to discourage sharing remains subject to ethical stigma. The use of money is of particular concern. Things purchased with money or acquired with the intention of sale often remain outside the gift economy and run counter to the cycle of reciprocal sharing with one's visible kindred and invisible neighbors. For example, Palawan people I knew frequently gave away significant amounts of the rice harvested from their swiddens, but they were much less prone to do so with purchased rice. Palawan elders recounted ruefully how just a generation ago, sharing was done with greater frequency and enthusiasm. Nowadays, they told me, people share begrudgingly or not at all. Instead, they sell forest products and use the money to buy food, which they are loath to share. Similarly, between visible people and their invisible counterparts, monetization leads the former to take in excess of their needs and treat gifts improperly by hoarding and selling them. Just as the gift economy will break down among Palawan if people do not fulfill their obligations to one another, invisible beings will withhold their gifts when they are treated improperly. This was said to be one of the reasons certain wild foods are increasingly scarce. One could certainly translate this ontological proposition into a subsistence ethic or a belief in restraint, but only at the cost of truly understanding the more-than-human social accountabilities that it engenders.

Figure 4.2. Palawan man collecting honey for his family. Source: Noah Theriault.

Before moving on, let's consider how one additional forest product—rattan—fits into Palawan relations with their invisible others. Among visible Palawan, only a few of the many varieties of rattan are considered edible, and even those are used mainly in house construction and to make baskets and a wide variety of other portable objects. When Palawan gather rattan, they do not (in my experience) refer to it as a gift from invisible beings—unlike honey, which was "shown" to them by the *diwata* (see figure 4.2). Instead, rattan is a crop planted by the forest people, who do not give it so much as tolerate it being taken. Thus, if one overharvests rattan in a particular area, the invisible person who planted it is apt to become angry and bring illness on the harvester or their kin. In this respect, most varieties of rattan are different from pig meat or honey; as nonfood items, there is less concern over whether they are shared in the visible community (although this is not to say that rattan harvested for domestic use or food are not frequently shared). Because the people of the forest are angered by excessive taking of their rattan, similar ethical concerns apply to collecting it. Monetized commodification of rattan is, therefore, ethically fraught insofar as it encourages harvesting in excess of need.

For its part, government policy treats these items quite differently. The government has no policy on the sale of swidden rice, provided that old-growth forest is not cleared to grow it. As far as the government is concerned, swidden rice is not a wild organism. However, it is illegal to sell wild pig meat—but not because doing so will offend an invisible being. It is illegal because the Palawan bearded pig, like virtually all wild animals, is a protected species that can only be hunted for traditional subsistence or ritual purposes. Forest honey can be sold with a government permit. In fact, the government and NGOs have long encouraged Indigenous groups to collect and sell honey as a form of sustainable development. The same is true for rattan and almaciga resin, which are among the products for which the government issues permits. Rattan and almaciga have become big business in Palawan, so much so that they have been largely depleted in the northern part of the island. In the southwestern part of the island, the boom did not get under way until the early 2000s. By the time of my research, rattan had been depleted in many areas downstream of Tenga't Gebaq and was being harvested with increasing intensity farther upstream. State agencies mandated to plan, monitor, and enforce the sustainable collection of forest products have devolved many of their responsibilities to NGOs and people's organizations. Their staff and members, meanwhile, are often marginalized and have very limited resources at their disposal.

It is clear that even though they risk illness by participating in it, ready access to an insatiable market for rattan has led many Palawan to risk provoking the rage of their invisible neighbors by taking far in excess of their needs. Some who do so may claim not to believe in such things as invisible people, but during my time in Tenga't Gebaq, I heard regularly of illnesses attributed to overharvesting. Even if one is careful, as most harvesters claimed they were, one does not usually know if one has run afoul of the forest people until after the fact, when a ritual healer determines the cause of an illness. One man I knew had to go through an elaborate seven-week process—including planting bamboo in the forest as compensation and a weekly ritual bathing of himself and a chicken—to rid himself of an illness caused by rattan harvesting. Another man had a tooth removed from his leg by a healer, who determined that an invisible dog of the forest had bitten him while he was collecting its guardian's rattan. The invisible tooth caused a prolonged illness in the man's toddler son. Per the healer's instructions, the man had to make a batch of rice wine, which was offered to the celestial spirits (*empuq*), the angered forest people, and for good measure the ancestors (*keguranggurangan*) (see figures 4.3a and 4.3b).

The varying regulation of forest products by the government seems arbitrary from a Palawan perspective (and vice versa) because the ethical concerns in either case are based on conflicting ontological assumptions. The former revolves around the question of how to protect wild organisms from human exploitation, and the latter revolves around how to coexist with one's visible

Figure 4.3a. A once-invisible dog's tooth, removed by a skilled *belyan* from the leg of a man whose overharvesting of rattan angered the people of the forest, July 2012.

Figure 4.3b. A Palawan elder making an offering of rice wine, June 2011. Source: Noah Theriault.

and invisible fellows. This ambivalence was clear in the differing responses that Oto, Juhali, and the field officer had to charcoal making. If we take Palawan ethical concerns out of their ontological context, we might conclude that Palawan ethics mirror government policy and that Oto's response marks him as more "traditional" or "authentic" than Juhali. But when we take ontological indeterminacy into account, we find that such variation depends partly on how people navigate the more-than-human social relations in which they are embedded. These relations unfold through a pragmatic process of negotiation and appeasement, not an impersonalized list of rules. Such situational contingency is also important in the context of swidden.

Contingency and Forest Clearance

As forms of territorialization, conservation projects like Mantalingahan involve imposing abstract spatial categories, such as land, natural resources, and property, onto place-based world-making practices, such as those in Tenga't Gebaq.[32] This involves not just surveying the land or registering property but materially producing the conditions for their existence as fungible spatial categories.[33] As with the regulation of forest products, complications arise when official categories miss the array of concerns informing Palawan decisions about where to cut their swidden fields. For example, consider the land that Palawan consider *lihyen* or forbidden—parts of the forest that are off-limits to swidden and potentially other activities. *Lihyen* most often comprise specific parts of the landscape, such as where certain types of trees grow (e.g., ficus or *nunuk*), along the banks of rivers and streams, in places associated with particular stories, or in places where invisible people have refused requests to vacate.[34] In government and NGO documents, *lihyen* is usually translated as "sacred places." They are thought to be ideally suited for conservation and are often invoked by Palawan and non-Indigenous activists in efforts to counter outside interests like mining companies. In practice, the notion of sacredness provides a potentially misleading translation of *lihyen* because it implies a degree of fixity and consensus not necessarily present among Palawan persons and their invisible neighbors.[35] As I will show, places acquire meaning through relations that are ontologically incompatible with the spatial practices of the state.

Just upstream of Tenga't Gebaq was an area that virtually everyone agreed was *lihyen*. Upu Isu, the most influential healer in the area considered it *lihyen*, and he said it had been so since his parents' time at least. The distinguishing characteristic of this particular area, which was on a small mountain at least seven kilometers inland, was that it contained a grove of a tree species (*buneg* [*Garcinia* sp.]) that Palawan associate with lower elevations. Forest people must have cultivated these fruit-bearing trees on the mountain and thus would be angered if the trees were cut down. Over the years, Upu Isu said, the *lihyen* nature of this area was confirmed by dreams and divination. This area had wider recognition as *lihyen* than any other I heard mentioned. Even so, its boundaries reflected an analysis of interpersonal, place-based contingencies, not some kind of dogma, doctrine, or standardized code.

Jimi had experienced these contingencies for himself. Once, about ten years before I came to live with him, he had wanted to cut a swidden near the *lihyen* in question. He went to the spots that would have marked the boundaries of the swidden and called on (*tinkeg*) the invisible occupants of the place to make their will known either in his dream (*peteginep*) or by upsetting a tripod of small branches he built on the ground (*petendaq*, see figure 4.4). A few nights later, he had a mysterious but frightening dream in which his toddler son went missing. He searched desperately in the forest, only to find the boy sitting alone on the opposite side of a rushing river. Jimi reported this dream to Upu Isu, his wife's uncle, who advised him not to clear the area in question because its occupants had threatened to take his son. The area was evidently also *lihyen*.

Figure 4.4. A divination tool (*petendaq*) used to request permission from people of the forest before felling a specific tree or clearing an area.

Jimi could have asked a ritual healer to attempt an offering to the invisible occupants, or he could have tried to do so himself.[36] For example, he could have made the request again, accompanied by a promise of, say, seven offerings of rice wine. In such a case, Jimi said, one should try to make at least one of the offerings up front—what he analogized to a down payment on a motorbike—and then make the rest of the offerings after the harvest. Such negotiations are not especially common because the people of the forest may not accept the offer, and most people hesitate to make such promises without knowing what the harvest will be like. Jimi was wary of endangering his son, so he decided not to pursue the matter further.

In this case, translating *lihyen* as a "sacred place" would partially encapsulate its significance, but it would also be misleading. By the time of my fieldwork, part of the area in question had been cleared by a related kin group, who had built half a dozen swiddens and houses there. The eldest couple in that group told me that they had called on the invisible occupants before clearing the land and had not cleared anything that was *lihyen*. For that matter, they did not consider what they cleared to be old growth (*gebaq*) but immature secondary growth (*bengley*), which does not typically contain trees large enough to be of interest to forest people.

Contrary to the fixity implied by "sacred" places, the boundaries of *lihyen* may be subject to contingencies at the microlevel. Healers have an important role in determining which areas are *lihyen*, but their classifications are not always universally recognized, and it is not really their role to compel people's cooperation. Invisible beings are the ones who actually punish Palawan for their trespasses, but whether they will do so in a particular case is difficult to predict. For this reason, Palawan practices around *lihyen* are much less standardized than what the government's land use zones would indicate. Those zones are based on discrete, territorial categories of land use that do not consider more-than-human social accountabilities or the high degree of personal discretion that Palawan exercise in negotiation of those accountabilities.

As first mentioned in chapter 3, I encountered another interesting example of this ontological friction just downstream of the village. A couple had purchased land from another Palawan family and started clearing it for swidden. A disagreement emerged between the families about the precise boundaries of the purchased land. The original family claimed they had retained a forested part of the land. When the dispute emerged, the purchasers had not yet cleared the whole lot, but they had started to fell some of the more mature trees. (Prior to this clearing activity, the area was a mix of *bengley* and *tering gebaqan* [moderately mature secondary growth].) When one of the purchasers became seriously ill, her husband blamed it on the sellers for having promised not to clear the land. Claiming the insight of a ritual healer, he learned in a dream that the sellers had promised only to clear the land up to a certain point, a practice known as *peseked*. He made an offering of rice wine in an attempt to undo the *peseked* and make up for the "debt" (*utang*) owed by the sellers to the area's invisible occupants. The sellers denied that they owed any such debt.

This area was not *lihyen* in the sense that its invisible occupants had made their will known through a Palawan healer. Nevertheless, according to at least one family, it was claimed by angry people of the forest. In the end, the disagreement was not resolved, nor was the land cleared. Instead, Jimi donated the area to the government for an *ipil* (*tegas; Intsia bijuga*) reforestation project. It became off-limits to all and was suitable for inclusion in government and NGO reports as a "sacred place."

As such outcomes suggest, the people of the forest had material consequences in the lives of Palawan people in Tenga't Gebaq and in those of bureaucrats in the capital and their agents in the field. Like many postcolonial states, the Philippine government envisions a world where Indigenous ancestral domains can readily double as conservation enclosures because of their residents' adherence to a subsistence ethic. To the extent that Palawan practice a subsistence ethic, it coincides only superficially with the logic of bureaucratic conservation. Instead, their interactions with the landscape reflect a host of factors, not the least of which are their relations with the invisible beings with whom they share it. The importance of dreams, divination, and propitiation in these more-than-human social relations contrasts starkly with the state's bureaucratic approach to delineating discrete land use zones and regulating human actions therein. Such high levels of interpersonal, spatial, and temporal variability run headlong into official expectations of uniformity.

Dario Novellino has made a similar argument about relations between conservation officials and Indigenous Batak people in central Palawan.[37] Unlike Novellino's analysis, mine has not emphasized the breakdown of Indigenous ontological practices in the face of social and ecological upheaval. Rather, I aimed to show their continued relevance in shaping both Palawan engagements with change and their relations with government institutions seeking their cooperation. Crucially, Palawan are not simply abandoning their world-making practices as they engage with those of settlers and the state. Instead, for many Palawan men and women, rapid social and ecological change intensifies their interactions with the invisible people who live in and around the forest. The more Palawan people are embroiled in the commodification of land and forest products—and the more they deviate from the ethics and laws of the ancestors (*keedatan et kegurangurangan*)—the more they have to worry about provoking the wrath of their invisible counterparts.

In July 2015, I met with my friend Bon, a Palawan man who served in the legislative assembly of a southern municipality. We discussed his ongoing effort to formulate a new municipal ordinance that recognizes Indigenous practices regarding the placement of swidden fields. A major challenge in this is deciding how best to codify the sorts of practices I have described here, including those determining which parts of the landscape are *lihyen*. Because such determinations often emerge through relations with the people of the forest, I asked Bon whether the ordinance would include provisions recognizing their presence. He had considered this, of course, but he chuckled wearily at the prospect of translating the complexity of those relations into the language of law. After all, what would such a translation entail? Would it force him to reduce the lived reality of his fellow Palawan into the terms of a system that does not recognize that reality as such?

Probably so. This is among the dilemmas that Palawan and other Indigenous groups face in their dealings with the state. These dealings, even when framed by laws protecting Indigenous rights, are "always already conditioned by unequal relations of social power."[38] The spatial manifestations of this paradox are relatively well documented. Wainwright and Bryan have argued that "cartographic-legal strategies" for asserting Indigenous rights in Central America end up "literally helping the [state] to *see* indigenous people and places [and thereby] align [them] with the expectations of state institutions."[39] In Southeast Asia, where policies of Indigenous recognition are comparatively rare, scholars have focused primarily on how state regulation of minoritized populations and their environments reinforces broader processes of internal colonization and capitalist expansion. The Philippines is no exception, even though it was the first country in the region to afford special rights on the basis of indigeneity. But this is not the whole story. As Wainwright and Bryan suggest, collisions between different world-making practices remain common in our neocolonial times, and they do not have definite analytical, ontological, or political endpoints. They call for "radical questioning" with an eye to "new possibilities for political struggle and more radical forms of geographical justice."[40]

We have seen here why it is risky to relegate certain ontological propositions to the realm of the "supernatural" or merely "symbolic." This boundary impoverishes our empirical understanding of more-than-human assemblages, and it naturalizes ontological propositions that in turn favor the expansion of (neo)colonial institutions and capitalism. It is equally risky to imply that different "ontologies" are homogeneous unto themselves and only practiced in isolation. Much to the contrary, we can (and must) avoid treating the world-making practices of state interventions as separate from or impervious to those of Indigenous peoples. I agree with E. Richard Atleo that both are part of a "unified but polarized reality" in which varying ontological propositions meet one another in unequal but mutually transformative encounters.[41] These are not "cultural conflicts" but what Marisol de la Cadena calls "pluriversal politics"—spaces in which Indigenous world-making practices interact with, complicate, and potentially subvert those of (neo)colonial states and extractive industries.[42]

In her work on efforts to control a fungal "bananapocalypse" afflicting the plantation lands of Mindanao, Alyssa Paredes traces how a "backyard scientist" of humble origins combined biological materials from the forest and divine inspiration from his dreams to develop a crop vaccine against the fungus. Where well-funded corporate teams and government scientists have utterly failed, this vaccine has had miraculous success. This is significant, Paredes concludes, because of the challenge to corporate plantation power that it capacitates. "As industrial agricultural regimes reach toward moments of apocalypse in the twenty-first century," she writes, "unprecedented methodologies reaching for scientific, divine, microbial, and political collaboration may continue to burst open entrenched paradigms."[43]

Not unlike the crop vaccine, my hosts' relations with the forest reflect an embodied, place-based analysis that draws on putatively "supernatural" sources of information. In either case, insisting on conventional ontological theories about what is real and what is supernatural may inhibit our understanding of what is happening on the ground. This is not a naive suggestion that we simply cast aside our ontological propositions and adopt new world-making practices. Instead, it reminds us that, whether or not we "believe" in invisible beings, they are having a material effect on the world. This matters not just to people in Tenga't Gebaq, who must contend with these beings as they contend with conservationists, capitalists, and other actors vying for their land. It also matters to those conservationists, capitalists, and other actors whose fantasies of a universal ontology collide with the demands of invisible beings who inhabit the forest and appear in dreams. It matters to anyone reading this book as we all face global-scale ecological crises rooted in ontological theories that we would do well to reconsider.

An elder named Lido loved to tell me about the time a non-Palawan farmer learned not to ignore the people of the forest. Before selling his land and moving farther into the mountains, Lido used to live on flatter land near the municipal road. Over the years, the land around his house was bought up by migrant settlers, and eventually he was living side by side with a fairly well-off settler who hired him periodically to help clear and plant the land. One night Lido had a dream that prompted him to advise his neighbor against felling a large ficus tree (*beringin*) standing in the middle of what would become a rice paddy. Lido and other Palawan workers refused to clear the tree, but his neighbor dismissed them and said he would do it himself. That night, the man saw a blinding white light appear above the tree and got a call on his cellphone from a "crazy" (*gila*) woman speaking English. Thoroughly disturbed, the man told Lido what he had experienced and that he had changed his mind about the tree.

Lido laughed every time he told this tale, recalling proudly how he had pointed at the tree and reminded his neighbor that "we have a neighbor here . . . even if you can't see them."[44] When I first heard this story, I asked Lido whether his neighbor had dreamed this experience or whether it had happened while he was awake. He hesitated before replying that the man had dreamed it, dismissed the dream, and then had the experience again while awake. His hesitation reminded me that from a Palawan perspective, this question was entirely beside the point. The tree lived on, and the man had learned to take his invisible neighbors seriously.

CHAPTER FIVE

Indigenous Rights in the Orbit of Capital

Early one morning in August 2008, Jimi and I set out on a brisk hike through the forest, hoping to visit his relatives at the base of the mountain and return by the afternoon. Along the way, he patiently indulged my interest in learning local names for wildlife. He smiled warmly, with just a hint of incredulity in his furrowed brow, when I struggled to distinguish the calls of insects from those of birds. As he helped me navigate the slick, coppery clay of the footpath, I had a chance to ask him some of the interview questions I had prepared for the day. Armed with a wry, cynical sense of humor, Jimi spoke frankly about his experiences dealing with nongovernmental organizations (NGOs) and government agencies. He recalled meetings, workshops, and photo shoots at which he and fellow Palawan had been instructed to don the traditional *baqag* (loincloth) rather than the shorts and T-shirts they usually wear. These encounters, he complained, had resulted in a multitude of promises but little else.

After spending a few hours with Jimi's relatives, we headed back toward his house, this time taking a long-abandoned, muddy logging road instead of the slippery forest path. Despite being a good foot shorter than I am, Jimi moved much more quickly in this terrain, and I struggled to keep up. To my relief, we eventually came across a settlement clustered around a large, ramada-like structure built from wood, bamboo, and nipa palm thatch—a perfect excuse for me to stop, rest, and take some photographs. Nailed to the rafters on one side of the structure was a hand-painted placard bearing the following message in Tagalog (see figure 5.1):

> NOTICE
>
> - This is the ancestral domain of the Indigenous Palawan of *barangay* Punta Baja in Rizal, Palawan.[1]
> - Anyone entering this area without the permission of the recognized leader of the community will be penalized according to our Indigenous laws.
> - The purchase of land within our ancestral domain is strictly forbidden.
> - Any agreement made without community consultation is invalid.[2]

Figure 5.1. Placard at the boundary of the ancestral domain, July 2012. Source: Noah Theriault.

As an artifact of Indigenous rights laws in the contemporary Philippines, this placard spoke directly to the issues I was there to research. It claimed the local Palawan "ancestral domain" using the language of government policy, it referred to a "recognized leader" in the singular, and it used the exclusive first-person plural pronoun.[3] This was an explicit message to non-Palawan people that the land belonged to "us [not you]" and that anyone entering it would be accountable to "our [not your]" laws. I planned to ask Jimi about the placard—about whether anyone was ever punished "according to Indigenous law," about the recognition of leaders, and so on—but before I had a chance to do so, these matters came up on their own.

Later that day, as Jimi and I sipped syrupy-sweet instant coffee in front of his house, a man came walking down the dirt road and stopped abruptly when he saw me. Unlike Jimi, who wore old basketball shorts, rubber sandals, and a faded T-shirt, the passerby wore a collared shirt, slacks, and had spectacles hanging from a lanyard around his neck. "Who's that?" the man asked. Jimi explained who I was and what we had done that day, to which the man responded that I should have gotten his permission. After a brief discussion, the man shot me a final dubious glance and continued on his way. As soon as he was out of earshot, Jimi explained that I did not, in fact, need that man's permission because he was merely the "president" of an NGO-affiliated group and, unlike Jimi, was not recognized as a "chieftain" by the National Commission on Indigenous People. When I asked Jimi to elaborate, he shrugged and said, "In the past, the Muslims organized us. Now it's the NCIP and NGOs."[4] He went on to elaborate, but his laconic, matter-of-fact statement stuck with me because it actually said a great deal about local history.

This encounter took place the day after I met Jimi for the first time. I had traveled to Rizal—the municipality in which Jimi lived—as part of preliminary research into prospective research sites. Three years later, when I returned for my long-term fieldwork, I found that tensions had escalated between Jimi and the other man, Bordo, whom we first met in chapter 3. They were involved in a prolonged legal dispute over permits to market almaciga (a valuable tree resin; Palawan: *begtik*) extracted in the ancestral domain. Their dispute was a central concern in Jimi's life during my stay, and it came to figure even more centrally in my research than I anticipated.

During my many visits to Palawan between 2010 and 2018, I learned of disputes over almaciga permits up and down the island. But the feud between Jimi and Bordo was remarkable for its protracted nature and the legal questions it raised. Their court case dragged on for years without a clear resolution, leading to an informal settlement in 2017. Meanwhile, on the other side of the mountains, something no less remarkable was happening: Members of a Palawan community managed to settle their almaciga-related disputes and gain an advantageous position in the almaciga trade. As recounted to me by Palawan elder and community organizer Norlita Colili, Palawan residents in the municipality of Amas established a direct relationship with a factory that processes almaciga, thereby bypassing the middle merchants to whom Jimi, Bordo, and other Palawan traders were beholden.

These contrasting examples suggest some of the different strategies that Palawan people have used as participants in the trade of almaciga and other "minor" or "non-timber" forest products (sometimes abbreviated as NTFPs). Philippine policy makers have given Indigenous people priority access to permits for the trade in these commodities. This policy is meant to help incentivize and sustain Indigenous resource management practices and thereby realize the dual dream of Indigenous rights and biodiversity conservation. In practice, forests have been depleted in many parts of island, and the competition for what remains only magnifies the dispossessory pressures that Indigenous communities face.[5]

In this chapter, we learn how the intensifying commodification of forest products has unfolded in two different locales: Jimi and Bordo's hometown in the Malambunga watershed and Norli's hometown in Amas. How have Palawan people crafted entrepreneurial strategies in each case? How do their strategies compare with the designs that conservationists, capitalists, and bureaucrats have for Indigenous peoples' participation in the forest product trade? As we will see, Jimi's use of the court system in his dispute with Bordo offers a compelling example of how the state's imposition of collective Indigenous rights can be strategically engaged to assert an individual right to participate in commerce. For Jimi, Indigenous rights are a tool for navigating intense competition among powerful government agencies, wealthy merchants, and their Indigenous agents. His approach has challenged dominant assumptions about how "homogeneous" Indigenous communities develop consensus and speak with one representative voice. It has also invited close scrutiny from lawyers and officials, who brought their own agendas to the case.

Meanwhile, in Amas, Norli and her collaborators have drawn on their connections to NGOs to circumvent the debt trap through which merchants control the trade in forest products. Their approach more closely resembles the sort of collective enterprise envisioned in the dominant framework of Indigenous rights.

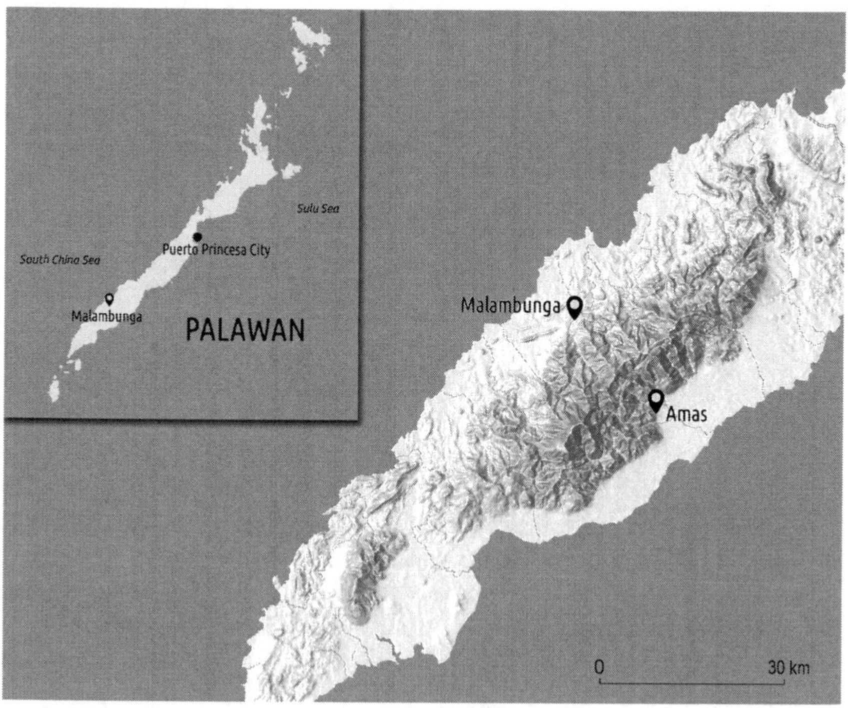

Map 5. Relief map of southern Palawan Island showing the location of Malambunga and Amas.

But they, too, are thinking and acting critically as they pursue resources that can help them resist rather than simply manage their dispossession.

Neither of these experiences can be reduced to a simple story of Indigenous subjection or resistance. Instead, these are two approaches that Palawan people have taken to assert their interests and defend their land rights, even as they are inevitably drawn into the resource frenzy that surrounds them. The results are transformative, but not necessarily in the way that proponents and critics of the trade in forest commodities might expect.

Commodifying the Forest

Imagine hiking up a densely forested mountain in a tropical climate, sleeping two nights in an improvised shelter, and then hiking back down with fifty kilograms of crystallized tree sap, worth approximately US$30, strapped to your back.[6] This is what it takes to harvest almaciga, a hard, flammable resin exuded by towering agathis trees (*Agathis philippinensis*) in the highland forests of the Philippine archipelago. In addition to its artisanal uses as an incense, fire accelerant, and sealant, almaciga has long been used in the industrial production of a variety of paints and adhesives. Today, as a result of deforestation and overexploitation, almaciga gathering is only possible in a few remote parts of the archipelago. The mountains of southern Palawan are one such place. There, many Palawan families rely on almaciga harvesting as their main source of cash income.[7] Those who cannot harvest almaciga or need additional income may, depending on local conditions, have recourse to a variety of other forest products, such as wild honey, rattan, bamboo, and tiger grass. By bringing these materials to market, Palawan families are important actors in the global trade of forest products.[8]

In Palawan today, forest commodities are big business, but the trade itself is nothing new. Almaciga, rattan, camphor, and other Southeast Asian forest products have a long history as commodities in long-distance trade. For centuries, upland Indigenous communities like those in Palawan have fostered, harvested, and traded forest products as a way to supplement their farming, hunting, gathering, and artisanal craft production. Over the past century, rapid deforestation and surging commodity markets have led to a vicious boom-and-bust cycle of unsustainable extraction in the region's remaining forests.[9] Ironically, this has only escalated since a moratorium was placed on commercial logging in 1992. With large-scale timber concessions no longer an option, efforts to extract value from Palawan's forests has become increasingly focused on "minor" commodities, including regulated ones like honey, rattan, and almaciga and banned ones like exotic animals. As in other parts of the world, this shift has driven a scramble to extract, cultivate, and regulate these resources. Palawan's forests are an important interface where the interests of states, NGOs, capitalists, and rural communities variously coalesce and collide. The United Nations, conservationists, and Indigenous rights advocates have all promoted the sustainable extraction of forest commodities as a "low volume, high value" approach to improving upland livelihoods, incentivizing forest protection, and buttressing ancestral land claims. The results of their efforts have been mixed, at best.

Almaciga as a "Leading Edge" Commodity

Derived from the Nahuatl word for incense, *copal* is a generic term referring to aromatic exudates that are produced by a range of tree species around the world.[10] Numerous varieties of copal have a long history of circulation in regional and global trade. Only the variety exported from insular Southeast Asia is known in the industry as almaciga (or Manila copal).[11] Because almaciga is often exported as a raw material, its economic importance is said to be small compared with that of rattan furniture (e.g., US$222,000 for almaciga versus US$98.2 million for rattan furniture in 2004, although a more meaningful comparison would factor in the export value of goods manufactured from almaciga).[12] Recently, anti-mining activists, carbon-credit programmers, and development NGOs have shown growing interest in Palawan's almaciga. They hope almaciga will offer a better source of sustainable upland livelihood than rattan, which has been depleted in many parts of the island and cannot provide a long-term incentive for the protection of old-growth forest in the same way as almaciga. Almaciga can, however, be overtapped. Overtapping can and does result in the death of the overexploited tree. Scientists have documented significant rates of agathis tree mortality in central and northern Palawan, and similar trends have been anecdotally reported in the south.[13]

In the old-growth forests along Palawan's spine, most of the towering, resin-producing agathis trees grow at elevations above 750 meters.[14] Official records indicate that 9,321 metric tons of almaciga were collected in the Philippines between 2001 and 2021.[15] In recent years, Palawan has been the sole source of this resin, most of it collected by Palawan people from their ancestral lands in the southern part of the island (see figure 5.2).[16] Most government permits for almaciga collection are issued to Palawan tribal councils, which oversee recognized ancestral domains and have priority access to permits. Yet during my research, Palawan men and women worked in the almaciga trade almost exclusively as collectors, rather than merchants. A few, like Jimi and Bordo, acted as local middlemen, but only the cooperative in Amas had a direct link to a processing facility, and that relationship did not take shape until 2018. Instead, most

Figure 5.2. Palawan man climbing an almaciga-producing agathis tree, August 2011. Source: Noah Theriault.

tribal councils sold their almaciga to regional traders, who trucked it to the provincial capital for transport by ship to Manila and beyond. For their part, regional traders lived in the provincial capital or Manila and used debt to control a patronage network of local middlemen at the collection sites. Some traders were said to conduct their business illegally by smuggling resin to Malaysia or through a combination of legal and illegal means involving the fraudulent use of legitimate permits.

As with other forest commodities, the extraction and sale of almaciga is subject to different environmental regulations depending on where the extraction takes place and who carries it out. What sets almaciga apart is that its commodity chain has consisted primarily of a single strand leading out of Palawan, making it especially prone to monopolization. An Indigenous council or association can hold permits to collect and sell forest commodities, but only if it represents a recognized ancestral domain claim or title, as was the case in Malambunga and Amas. Permits issued to Indigenous associations, unlike those issued to individuals, come with the condition that the pertinent resources and any revenues arising from them are managed cooperatively. This approach is supposed to make the trade in forest commodities more beneficial and equitable for Indigenous people. In my experience, however, almaciga's journey as a commodity was largely the same whether it originated from a permit held by an individual merchant or one held by an Indigenous group. In most cases, including in Malambunga, permit holders sold only to one trader and did not transact directly with the facilities in other provinces where almaciga is processed for commercial use and export. This meant that even when a tribal council officially held the permit to trade in almaciga, their ancestral domain became a de facto concession of a wealthy trader.

The commercial value of Palawan's forest commodities pales in comparison to that of the minerals extracted on the island. Nevertheless, in places like Malambunga and Amas, the intensified extraction of these commodities has been part of what Anna Tsing calls the "leading edges" of capitalism's expansion.[17] Leading-edge commodities are typically those that can be monopolized by a small set of capitalists and yield high profit margins with minimal investment.[18] Which commodities play this role varies across space and time. At one point in Palawan, timber led the way, serving to attract capitalists and create the conditions for capitalist relations of production going forward. "Minor" forest products, such as almaciga and rattan, were extracted along with timber, but their significance was smaller by comparison. In the latter twentieth century, with hardwoods increasingly depleted or protected, the focus of extraction shifted to minor products and to the labor of those who collect it.

By and large, the trade in Palawan's forest commodities was (and is) controlled by a small number of capitalists who extract value from the land, labor, and knowledge of Indigenous communities far in excess of what is returned in compensation. This fact is well known among Palawan almaciga collectors in Malambunga and, according to Norli, it is well known in Amas. When it comes to almaciga, however, it would be a mistake to conclude that collectors see themselves as victims. To be sure, collectors return haggard from their overnight trips into the mountains—their necks stiff from having supported a *kiba* (rattan backpack) strap across their forehead, their backsides caked in mud from losing their footing on slick trails, and their hair glistening with tiny, sticky flakes of resin sent flying as larger clots are hacked off the side of the tree. For this they are paid 25 pesos per kilo if it is high-quality almaciga (i.e., ~US$0.50 per kilo as of March 2023).

Nevertheless, most of the Palawan people I consulted preferred almaciga collection to virtually all other possible ways of generating cash income. As an elderly couple explained,

> Almaciga is good. Selling it is not forbidden, unlike honey or wild pigs [whose invisible owners are angered by commodification]. It doesn't rot or run out, unlike rattan. As long as you take care of the trees, you won't become ill [i.e., be made ill by their invisible owners, as is the case with overextraction of rattan]. Our ancestors collected almaciga, and we sell it today to buy rice, salt, clothing, everything. We are grateful to the rebels who drove away the logging companies [in the early 1980s]. Things were better in the past, when people were generous and shared food with each other. If it weren't for almaciga, we Palawan would probably die of hunger.[19]

A simple (and simplistic) way of interpreting such statements is that almaciga is worth more to people when it is sold than when it is used or that collecting it yields higher returns than other income-generating activities. There is some truth to such statements. Almaciga is inedible, making it more attractive for sale than cassava and other cultigens grown in the swidden. Unlike rattan and food crops, almaciga cannot be attacked by mold. Although a trader told me that she will not pay as much for almaciga that has been sitting in storage for a long time, no one else saw almaciga as having a "shelf life" as long as it was stored properly. This durability enables strategic timing of sales and reduces risks. Compared with casual wage labor, moreover, my observations suggest that almaciga offers, on average, a higher daily return.[20]

Even so, economistic explanations are insufficient on their own. Beyond exchange value and opportunity calculation, I found that Palawan favored almaciga because of the autonomy they had to decide where, when, and how much to gather. As Charles Macdonald has observed, Palawan people tend to treat personal autonomy as an essential ethical principle in everything from child-rearing and gender norms to residential mobility and customary law.[21] For this reason, performing wage labor for the Kabisayaan or other migrants was something many Palawan disdained, even as their growing dependence on money made it difficult to turn down any opportunity to make cash.

Such autonomy would arguably apply to collecting any forest product, but from a Palawan perspective, not all forest products are created equal. In contrast to the stories I heard about rattan, honey, bushmeat, and charcoal making, I never heard anyone mention a fear of negative consequences from overtapping almaciga. Three characteristics of almaciga help account for this perception. First, because almaciga can be tapped without causing serious harm to the tree, Palawan tended not to see its collection as requiring the consent of the tree's invisible occupants (*taw't talun*). Second, because agathis trees only thrive at high elevations, most of them are located far enough away from human settlements to discourage overtapping by nonlocals with less of an interest in taking proper care of the trees.[22] Third, the resin's heft makes it difficult to carry down steep, often slippery mountain trails. This factor largely rules out daily collection trips of the sort one might make to collect rattan. Fourth and finally, like other forest commodities, opportunities to collect almaciga vary in relation to the weather and competing labor commitments. However, unlike honey or wild fruit, its availability does not fluctuate seasonally or annually, making it less likely to be exhausted in a frenzy of collection. Nor is it perishable, reducing the risk that it will rot on the way to market.

Almaciga productivity is high in Palawan because of the relatively dry climate.[23] Both the agathis tree and its resin are called *begtik* in Palawan. Most Palawan I consulted reported that a large, healthy *begtik* tree can be gainfully tapped monthly or even biweekly. As long as they practice appropriate "care" (*pang-ipat*) for the tree, they need not worry about attracting the enmity of the people of the forest. Most kin networks claimed exclusive rights to significant stands of *begitk* trees through their caretaking activities. At least in the area where I lived, the yields from such stands seemed abundant enough to keep them occupied, though never flush with cash. My interlocutors acknowledged that killing a tree by overtapping it would constitute a potentially dangerous transgression. Such danger was usually associated with ethically reckless others who would steal from other people's trees or overtap trees in areas where claims had become unclear. For all of these reasons, Palawan described *begtik* as less likely than, say, rattan to be extracted in excess.

In sum, more so than with other forest commodities, the proper care for *begtik* trees can mean stable access to cash that neither undermines personal autonomy nor pushes the boundaries of socioecological ethics. *Begtik*'s transformation into almaciga, a "leading edge" commodity, is not propelled solely by the external force of global markets. Rather, its materiality operates within an "assemblage" that comes together through the ecological and cultural processes of its production.[24] Difficulty of access, durability, inedibility, and sustainability through care—these and other features assembled almaciga as a commodity and make it possible for us to trace its trajectory in a broader field of transformations (see figure 5.3).

Seeking the "Freedom" to Do Business

"But do people own money or does money own people? In the past, it seemed like people owned money, but today it seems like money owns people." Aban offered this observation to his brother Jimi as they squatted in the shade of a mango tree. They were discussing the lawsuit Jimi had filed against Bordo, the tribal council of the ancestral domain, and the Department of Environment and Natural Resources

Figure 5.3. A view toward forests with almaciga-producing agathis trees (*kebegtikan*) from a hill near the Malambunga River, April 2011. Source: Noah Theriault.

for denying him access to almaciga permits. In this and other conversations, Jimi framed his legal struggle as one for the economic freedom to which he was legally entitled as an Indigenous person—in his words, "the freedom to do business." But Aban was skeptical. Even with legal protections for Indigenous people, whom (or what) did "business" really empower? His doubts echoed those of many others I met during my research. If Indigenous rights have come in tandem with intensified commodification, monetization, and regulation, what does all of this mean for Palawan "freedom"? Local history offers one way of answering this question.

Government Chiefdoms

Accounts vary as to when the title of "chieftain" first entered into the Palawan repertoire in southwestern Palawan. Some accounts attributed the first appointment of chieftains to an NGO, the Office of the Presidential Assistant on National Minorities (PANAMIN), which was active during the Marcos years, while others cited the Office of Southern Cultural Communities under the Aquino administration. A former PANAMIN worker I interviewed denied that his employer had appointed chieftains, but a former official from the Office of Southern Cultural Communities said that the agency had simply carried on a practice begun by PANAMIN. The only documentary evidence I found was in one of the office's annual reports, which dated the establishment of a tribal council in Punta Baja to 1990. Whatever the precise sequence of events, the first chieftain in the Malambunga area was Bordo.[25] At that point, chieftains and other tribal council members were appointed through government-supervised elections, though that practice was later abandoned when it was deemed incompatible with local customs.

A few years after being elected chieftain, Bordo resigned when it became clear to him that the government was not responsive to Palawan needs. Instead, he aligned himself with an NGO, NATRIPAL (United Tribes of Palawan), which at that time was working on securing ancestral domains for Indigenous groups throughout Palawan. As noted in chapter 2, Palawan was arguably the epicenter of efforts to secure ancestral domains in the wake of the national government's issuance of Department Administrative Order 2 in 1992.

Dozens of ancestral domain applications were initiated in the province, with those covering the municipality of Rizal being the most ambitious. Backed with funding from a variety of international funders, NATRIPAL worked with several other NGOs to secure a contiguous string of ancestral domains that would include Palawan residents living in all eleven *barangay* in Rizal. Why Rizal was chosen for this ambitious plan is a question to which I have never found a complete answer. Clearly, it was then (and remains) an area with a relatively large Palawan minority and some of the island's most extensive forests. Rizal was (and remains) a "critical area" for Indigenous rights. In 1991, the Philippine marines allegedly intimated and assaulted members of a Palawan community who had reported illegal logging and timber smuggling to an NGO (Human Rights Watch).[26] Finally, there was a factor that cannot possibly be a coincidence: Rizal still had vast "inventories" of forest commodities.

Throughout Palawan, a key goal of establishing ancestral domains was to gain more control of markets that had long been dominated by non-Indigenous, often absentee concessionaires. Because forest commodity permits are issued on a territorial basis, Indigenous groups with recognized ancestral domains would, in effect, take over existing concessions. Not surprisingly, this was not welcome news to concessionaires or traders, particularly those in the almaciga business, who sought to block the recognition of ancestral domains.[27] As McDermott has chronicled, the almaciga traders were politically well connected.[28] In one case, a almaciga trade association (the Palawan Bagtik Association) petitioned the Palawan Council for Sustainable Development, arguing that their families had been involved in the trade for generations.[29]

Ultimately, only one Certificate of Ancestral Domain Claim was awarded in Rizal, covering some 15,092.88 hectares in *barangay* Campung Ulay and *barangay* Punta Baja. Because this area was so large and spanned two *barangays,* two separate tribal councils were organized to oversee it, with their respective jurisdiction corresponding to *barangay* boundaries. Following an approach favored by its international funders, NATRIPAL established a Community-Based Conservation and Enterprise Program for each of the ancestral domains, including the one in Rizal.[30] According to Pinto's detailed study, this approach were intended to test "the hypothesis that if local communities receive sufficient benefits from a biodiversity-linked enterprise, then they will act to conserve the resources it depends on."[31] In other words, it was an experiment in eco-governmentality.[32]

Each ancestral domain's enterprise program, including the one in Rizal, involved establishing a tribal council, creating an "area servicing unit" to serve as its headquarters, and preparing a resource management plan based on the sustainable harvesting of resources like rattan, honey, almaciga, and palm leaves used for thatch (see also chapter 2). These councils were treated by the Department of Environment and Natural Resources (DENR) as legal permit holders and were supposed to ensure that the management plan was followed. Pinto's study makes clear that this process was fraught with complications from the beginning, including resistance from concessionaires and traders, tensions among the various NGOs and government agencies involved, and competing factions in Indigenous communities.[33] The dispute between Jimi and Bordo was a direct legacy of these complications.

To make a long story short, Bordo became the first president or *satya* of the tribal council for the Punta Baja portion of the ancestral domain in Rizal. At the time the ancestral domain was proposed, Jimi's father held the title of chieftain, which he received from the Office for Southern Cultural Communities. These chieftains and the tribal councils they led were generally not chosen to represent the new ancestral domain, leading to competition between parallel councils and rivalry among their members. Jimi and others reported that his father had, in fact, chosen not to endorse the ancestral domain shortly before his death in 1996. The reasons for his refusal remained unclear to me no matter how many people I asked. What was clear was that Jimi sustained his father's suspicion of the ancestral domain and did not participate in its management.[34]

After 1997, the Office of Southern Cultural Communities was shuttered, and the administration of Indigenous people and ancestral domains was transferred to the National Commission on Indigenous People (NCIP). In 2002, reportedly in response to a petition of the municipal government, the NCIP appointed Jimi as chieftain. The NCIP had adopted a policy favoring Indigenous leaders who could claim inheritance, and Jimi had a claim based on his father having held the position.[35]

Bordo remained the president of the tribal council from its founding in 1997 until his death in 2017. The council staked its legitimacy on its relationship with NATRIPAL and with the national government agency that was responsible for recognizing ancestral domains until 1997 (DENR). When the ancestral domain was founded, the tribal council came into possession of the DENR-issued permits for trade in almaciga, rattan, and other forest commodities. Financing for the council's almaciga-buying business was advanced by the regional merchant concessionaire who had already previously controlled the permits for this area. In exchange for those loans, Bordo signed a contract granting the merchant exclusive rights to almaciga collected in the ancestral domain. As of 2019, the initial advance was never fully repaid, growing in principal and interest over the years and creating a local monopoly. Bordo and his followers, despite nominally controlling the permits, found themselves beholden to one merchant and could not transact with any others.

Jimi was recognized as a chieftain by the NCIP and was Bordo's only real rival when it came to external recognition. The ancestral domain was established before the existence of the NCIP, and over the years it remained associated with DENR and NATRIPAL even as the NCIP took over responsibility for Indigenous rights. When the ancestral domain was established, most of Jimi's lineage declined to endorse it or participate in its activities. They were suspicious, they now say, of Bordo's motives since he was neither born in Malambunga nor a blood member of the lineages he was claiming to represent. I also believe they did not want to go through Bordo's association to access regional markets for forest products.

Over the years, tensions simmered, but outright conflict was held at bay by begrudging cooperation with the tribal council and occasional smuggling of products. This détente eventually ran its course. In 2009, one of the merchant's employees broke away and started her own enterprise. She approached Jimi and invited him to be her agent in the area. Jimi, a determined and ambitious man, could not let go of the opportunity and convinced Bordo to give him access to the ancestral domain's almaciga-trading permits on a trial basis.

Because Jimi was already part of the network of agents for the tribal council, he could expand his operation without attracting too much attention. But his efforts were thwarted when the first merchant found out and ordered the council to deny Jimi further access to permits. By then, Jimi was in deep with the renegade merchant, and she urged him to take the matter to court. He first sought redress through the NCIP, which has quasi-judicial authority to intervene in disputes among Indigenous people. After a series of failed mediations, the NCIP advised both sides to stop selling almaciga pending resolution of the dispute. When Bordo's organization failed to comply, the NCIP ceased playing the role of a neutral mediator. It confiscated a large shipment and issued a memo that questioned the legality of Bordo's council and the DENR's basis for issuing permits to it. Such decisive action escalated the dispute to the national level. At stake now was the long-vexing question of which agency—the DENR or the NCIP—has ultimate authority to regulate Indigenous people's environmental activities.

Also at issue are legal ambiguities surrounding the resolution of disputes among Indigenous people. The law favors "customary" dispute resolution through Indigenous institutions but only gives vague guidelines for the NCIP's intervention in cases where this fails. If Indigenous groups are recognized as a homogeneous, self-regulating collectivity, what is the state to do when a member of that collectivity presents himself as an individual and seeks legal adjudication of his rights? As their case dragged on, Jimi and Bordo watched their stocks of almaciga pile up, leaving them to ponder the uncertain boundary between special cultural rights for minority groups and the sort of institutional exclusion one might find in a bifurcated colonial state.

"Wala na tayong pag-asa. Mali ang witnis ko." We have no hope. My witness was wrong. Jimi dictated this text message, in Tagalog rather than Palawan, to a companion during a hearing of his case in the provincial capital. It was then sent to his family in the village, where it caused much speculation and alarm. Jimi was two days away from coming home, and between his resistance to sending text messages and the village's weak cell-phone signal, we had no way to find out what exactly this message meant. At the hearing in question, we later learned, one of Jimi's cousins humiliated him by botching his testimony. His cousin did not understand that to testify successfully as an Indigenous person before the NCIP, one must vastly oversimplify one's life so that it meets official criteria for authentic indigeneity. "What is your main source of income?" the attorney asked. "Well," he said, "I often perform wage labor, I sometimes make charcoal, I sometimes collect rattan or almaciga." That was the wrong answer. Indigenous people worthy of holding permits should not rely on wage labor or charcoal making. Jimi's text message was melodramatic for good reason: If he and his witnesses were less adept than their opponents at performing their indigeneity, they could lose their case. Such an outcome would leave Jimi buried in debts he could never repay.

At one point, it looked as if Jimi's suit might reach the Supreme Court, which could have set a precedent for future decisions regarding Indigenous rights. Even though the case was not picked up by the court, Jimi was quite bemused that it has grown to such proportions. He was, he insisted, just defending his legally guaranteed "freedom" (*kalayaan*). That the "freedom" he seeks will likely involve an inescapable cycle of debt, accompanied by more intensive contact with government regulation, represents another example of the paradox of Indigenous rights, which I explore throughout this book. When Indigenous rights come linked to greater dependence on commodities, asserting those rights pushes people like Jimi further into the orbit of capital. Yet we can also see how Indigenous rights offered him an idiom for contesting capitalist control of Indigenous people's land and labor.

When Jimi articulated his position as a matter of "freedom," he invoked a classic argument in debates over the role of the state in economic affairs. Readers will likely find the equation of liberty with free markets a familiar ideological proposition. When I first heard this rhetoric, I wondered whether Jimi was drawing on language used by his NCIP-assigned attorney. From the NCIP's standpoint, Jimi was standing up for the collective right of his community to make decisions about development under conditions of "free and prior informed consent," as dictated by law. And there was Jimi, using a Tagalog word that I never otherwise heard in colloquial Palawan speech.[36]

Later, though, I was surprised when I heard Jimi correct a settler who praised him for standing up for Indigenous rights. Even as he warranted his position by citing the Indigenous Peoples Rights Act (IPRA), Jimi made it clear that he did not file his suit for the sake of collective Indigenous rights but for his personal freedom to conduct business as an Indigenous person. I eventually realized that for Jimi and many of his fellow Palawan, expressions of bureaucratic power, including permits and NGO projects, did not constitute what one might call the rule of law. They were, instead, the arbitrary acts of an external state that exercises its coercive power according to the needs of those who control it.[37] This did not prevent Jimi from maintaining allies connected to the state. Nor did it mean that he perceived no potential benefits in the state's regulatory power. It meant that he acted cautiously, knowing that the *gubyerno* as a whole served the interests of the Kabisayaan, not those of Indigenous people.[38] From Jimi's perspective, he was using an alliance with one part of the state to limit intervention by another.

Coupled with his cousin's testimony, Jimi's self-fashioning as an individual entrepreneur would seem to disappoint bureaucratic expectations for homogeneous Indigenous collectivities. Yet Jimi ultimately prevailed when Bordo's side gave in and agreed to grant access to the permits. An NCIP attorney explained to me that the judge was prepared to side with Jimi because, he reasoned, an ancestral domain is meant to benefit the entire Indigenous group living in it, not a single individual or subgroup. Somehow, Jimi deployed the apparatus of indigeneity in his favor even as he rejected (or simply failed to conform to) the practices and categories that apparatus calls into being.

Does Jimi's lawsuit constitute a challenge to the "bureaucratic Orientalism" of recognition? Has he manipulated the state into undermining the categories on which its authority depends? My answer to these questions remains deeply ambivalent. Answering them in the affirmative would, I think, vastly oversimplify things. On the one hand, the freedom Jimi seeks is achieved through the marketing of a particular commodity and the regulatory apparatus that sharpens its leading edge. For Foucault, such a notion of freedom "no longer [calls forth] the exemptions and privileges attached to a person, but the possibility of movement, change of place, and processes of circulation of both people and things. It is in terms of this option of circulation, that we should understand the word freedom, and understand it as one of the facets, aspects, or dimensions of the deployment of apparatuses of [government]."[39]

Indeed, the power of Indigenous rights is not necessarily that it produces uniform subjectivities. Its power inheres in the way it draws forth desires—desires that, whether in keeping with the law or not, reproduce the logic of commodity capitalism through their expression.[40] That these desires often contradict the expectations of Indigenous recognition does not subvert the overarching regulatory system of which recognition is a part. But it does open up space for people like Jimi to assert a claim to personal autonomy that answers to their moral vision and to the demands of making a living in a changing world. It is an act of endurance, even if it also redounds to the power of capitalism and the state.

Cutting Out the Middleman

Norlita Colili is a Palawan elder and community organizer from Amas, a municipality on the eastern side of the Mantalingahan range, opposite Malambunga. As a child, Norli learned from her elders how to farm and harvest forest products, but she also had the opportunity to attend school, where she learned skills very different from those of her elders. For twenty-five years, she has worked in the NGO sector, first as a project facilitator and agriculturalist for the Palawan Tropical Forest Protection Program and later as an area coordinator for the Non-Timber Forest Product Exchange Program (hereafter Exchange Program). She was drawn to advocacy by a desire to help Indigenous communities, including her own, defend themselves from a range of forces seeking to control their land and transform their way of life (e.g., migrant settlers, extractive industries, and government agencies). Her work has long focused on promoting traditional handicrafts as a way to maintain Indigenous knowledge, support sustainable land uses, and generate cash income. Over the years, she has worked with practitioners, scholars, and activists from across the Philippines and around the world to raise awareness of how Palawan weaving is connected to their cosmology, land care practices, and social relations.

Norli's career in advocacy began just as the Philippines became the first country in Asia to recognize and legally codify Indigenous rights, first in the 1987 constitution and later in IPRA. She has seen firsthand what has—and has not—changed as a result of the law. As seen throughout this book, IPRA has created new legal mechanisms for asserting Indigenous land claims, and at the same time it has further entangled Indigenous communities in capitalist resource politics and elite-dominated bureaucratic processes. When the first round of ancestral domains was delineated in the mid-1990s, advocates saw control of forest commodities as crucial to empowering Indigenous communities and enabling sustainable development. For each ancestral domain, they created extensive documentation of forest resources, produced a detailed management plan, and secured trading permits for the tribal council. Remember that both Amas and Malambunga were in one of these original ancestral domains. In neither case, however, did Indigenous residents secure control of forest commodities. Only after several years of constant advocacy by NATRIPAL and other NGOs did provincial policy makers agree to prioritize Indigenous applicants over prior concessionaires when issuing permits.[41] As we learned already, concessionaires vigorously resisted this policy and have found ways to subvert it.

We already know what happened in Malambunga as a result of these struggles. The story of Amas is similar until around 2014, when NATRIPAL helped

Norli and other residents revive the Samahan ng mga Palawano sa Amas Brooke's Point (Association of Palawan in Amas, Brooke's Point), a "multipurpose cooperative" designed to process almaciga and other commodities harvested in the ancestral domain. NATRIPAL also tried to establish its own Indigenous-led almaciga-buying business to bolster the income of harvesters and bypass the non-Indigenous merchants. When this strategy failed, cooperative members in Amas turned to the Exchange Program, with whom they had an existing partnership. With funding from the World Conservation Congress and other sources, the Exchange Program helped the cooperative strengthen its business capacity, secure its own permits, and establish a direct relationship with a varnish-making factory in Cebu. The cooperative has been selling directly to the factory since 2018. This has increased the price paid to harvesters and provided wage-earning opportunities for Palawan who cannot physically harvest almaciga or who have no ancestral claims to almaciga-producing trees.[42] The wages paid for weighing, sorting, and packing almaciga have been especially important for women, elders, and families who have lost their ancestral lands and trees (see figure 5.4).[43]

Almaciga remains a key source of cash income for many Palawan families in both Malambunga and Amas. The difference is that in Amas, the community

Figure 5.4. A handmade backpack (*kiba*) filled with high-quality almaciga (*tipak*), April 2011. Source: Noah Theriault.

formed a consensus around the cooperative and successfully leveraged the support of the Exchange Program in establishing a direct link to the varnish factory. Why don't Malambunga and other Palawan communities simply follow the Amas model? The answer is simple: Some have tried, but well-financed merchants continue to sponsor middlepersons who oppose the cooperative model. When the Exchange Program tried to help a community just north of Malambunga, it encountered divisions in the Palawan community as to the desirability of a cooperative model. This in itself would not rule out establishing a cooperative, particularly if the different camps could agree to share use of almaciga shipping permits. However, when the merchants have allies in local government, they can block some of the clearances the cooperative needs to operate. In avoiding such a situation, Amas is the exception, not the rule.[44]

Clearly, it matters who controls the infrastructure through which forest commodities are traded. But this is not the only thing that matters. Equally important are the overall livelihood conditions of families, especially their level of food security and their access to land. Norli has observed—and I concur—that Palawan families who live higher in the mountains seem to benefit more from almaciga than those who live in the foothills or lowlands. This is not just because they live closer to the trees and can therefore more easily care for and tap them. It is also because they tend to have more land at their disposal for hunting, gathering, and the ancestral practice of *uma* or swidden farming. In addition to its cosmological and ecological significance, *uma* is a vital source of food. Except for those who have settled in towns or transitioned to sedentary farms, such as rice paddies, most Palawan families still practice *uma*. Nowadays, Palawan who live in the lowlands and foothills tend to have less land at their disposal than those living higher in the mountains (and certainly less land than their ancestors did). This loss of land means that these families can only fallow their *uma* fields for a few years in between each cycle of clearing, burning, and planting. Over time, this reduces soil fertility and encourages the growth of invasive grasses, which hinder forest regrowth and choke out cultigens. Declining *uma* productivity weakens these families' food security. Meanwhile, they live in closer proximity to settler-owned farms and businesses, where they can perform low-wage labor and purchase food. This increasing dependence on waged work and purchased food becomes a vicious circle because it reduces the time/energy available for *uma*-related work and creates new desires that require money to satisfy.

Generally speaking, Palawan families who live higher in the mountains are able to satisfy most of their food needs without money, whereas those who live at lower elevations depend more on money earned by working for settlers. The former sell almaciga and other forest commodities as a supplement to their independent, *uma*-based food security—a way to access goods like cell phones, clothing, medicine, tools, and special foods but not their primary way to meet basic needs. Although their lives are by no means free of hardship and toil, they ultimately decide how they use their time, and they have a choice about how and when to earn money by harvesting almaciga, making crafts, and otherwise producing commodities. The latter, because they have lost some or all of their land, must constantly "chase" money. Producing forest commodities may afford these families some independence from exploitative wage labor, but it is unlikely to be enough to sustain them, especially if they are harvesting sustainably. Without measures in place to protect Palawan land claims and ensure their food security, forest products alone cannot stave off dispossession and proletarianization, even if the marketing infrastructure is locally controlled.

Forest commodities have long been integral to the globalization of capitalism. They are leading-edge commodities that help drive the expansion of capitalism into new regions by laying the groundwork for dispossession. For Palawan communities facing the rapid loss of ancestral land, producing forest commodities for merchant concessionaires serves as a transitional occupation in a larger process that leaves them dispossessed and dependent on exploitative wage labor. But forest commodities are also part of an effort to promote inclusive, sustainable development. If effectively regulated, they could support rural livelihoods while incentivizing sound forest management. If people received a fair price for the forest commodities they produce, they could pursue a better future for their families without selling their land or labor to extractive industries.

I believe, along with Norli, that both perspectives are valid. In Palawan, forest commodities have yielded fortunes for non-Indigenous capitalists while Indigenous communities have lost their land and become increasingly dependent on wage labor. Even after the legal recognition of Indigenous rights, Palawan communities have continued to face entrapment in debt and exploitative pricing at the hands of merchants. But Palawan communities—along with their Tagbanua and Batak brethren in central and northern Palawan—have managed to wrest back some control of the market. With support from organizations like NATRIPAL and the Exchange Program, Palawan have adopted and adapted new economic practices, including the cooperative model at Amas; they have stood up for their constitutional rights; and they have advocated for themselves at all levels of government.

A "low volume, high value" approach to forest commodities cannot in itself counteract the forces that push Indigenous communities into dependency on the exploitation of their labor. As the differences between Amas and Malambunga make clear, Indigenous control of marketing infrastructure is crucial. These cases also underscore the broader importance of land, labor, and food security. Even if Indigenous communities control their marketing infrastructure and have direct links to wholesale buyers, families who have already lost control of their land face exploitation in their efforts to shelter, feed, clothe, heal, and advance themselves.

These findings are similar to those of Michael Dove, who has examined the long history of upland commodity production and trade in Southeast Asia.[45] His research has shown that highland peoples, such as those in Palawan, have long been crucial participants in this trade, because it is their labor and knowledge that bring the products to market. This has strengthened these communities' independent livelihoods, but only when it is part of a "dual economy." In a dual economy, Indigenous families harvest forest products and grow select commodity crops like rubber or bamboo, but they also maintain robust subsistence-oriented practices of farming and foraging. This strategy affords access to the market economy without making them dependent on it for their survival. As Dove writes, "the degree of worker autonomy made possible by the presence of other resources is anathema to the state-supported plantation sector because it affects a basic dimension of power—who controls the mobilization of labor."[46]

As developments in Malambunga and Amas make clear, Palawan elders like Jimi and Norli are keenly aware of how forest commodities connect their communities to larger political and economic systems (including but not limited to the Philippine state and global capitalism). They know that their legal recognition as Indigenous people does not insulate them from these systems but deepens their entanglements. This is the paradox of Indigenous rights in the contemporary Philippines—and a dilemma faced by Indigenous people around the world.[47] Elizabeth Povinelli has invoked "the cunning of recognition" to explain how states use the bestowal of Indigenous rights to strengthen colonial institutions.[48] Paul Nadasdy has argued that when "empowerment" forces "disempowered peoples to alter their personhood and society as a prerequisite for the exercise of that power, [it] must also be viewed as a form of subjection."[49] These authors were referring to conditions in Canada and Australia, respectively, but they could just as well have been writing about the Philippines.

Focusing only on these subjugating effects can reinforce the idea that Indigenous assimilation and dispossession are inevitable. In this chapter, we have seen how Palawan people themselves interpret and navigate the dilemmas of recognition, with varying strategies and outcomes. These pragmatic maneuvers may not look like heroic acts of resistance, but they are nonetheless forms of endurance. In her work on Mohawk history, Audra Simpson reminds us not to reduce Indigenous people's political agency to the all-or-nothing pursuit or refusal of state recognition. This framing, she argues, presumes that colonization is already complete and obscures the complex conditions, strategies, and negotiations unfolding in practice.[50]

Simpson focuses on the overt and subtle ways in which Mohawk people have refused the terms of recognition imposed on them by Canada and the United States. Her argument holds even in a place like Palawan, where outright refusal is a less common strategy. As our encounters with Boro, Jimi, and Norli suggest, engaging selectively with the obligations and ambiguities of recognition can open up space for contesting the demands of extractive industry, the state, and conservation. These engagements are transformative, but why assume that they are transformative only for Bordo, Jimi, Norli, and other Palawan? It is true that the "juridification of indigenous politics" extends the reach of capitalist-state power as much if not more than to defend Indigenous self-determination.[51] But acts of Indigenous endurance can and do exceed the terms imposed on them. Even when they act within those bounds, people like Jimi and Norli continue to enact and defend social formations very different from the ones that colonial institutions expect. Wherever indigeneity has been codified to serve the interests of (post)colonial governments and capitalists, the cunning of recognition is absolutely at work. But we should not let it overwhelm our sensitivity to the microlevel practices that contest and perhaps even subvert it.

Conclusion

One day, not long after I first arrived in Tenga't Gebaq, a meeting was called during the weekly *tabuqan*.[1] Heading up the meeting was Carlos, a Visayan man who had migrated to southern Palawan in the 1990s, married a Palawan woman, and now lived about a half hour's walk downstream of the village. He had recently become the Purok president after petitioning the local government to reinstate Tenga't Gebaq as a *purok*.[2] Carlos called this meeting because the annual town fiesta was coming up, and he was hoping to organize a group to participate in the parade. There would be a prize for the best Palawan group, and to win it they would need not just a strong turnout but a strong display of *tradisyon* (tradition). Men would need to wear the *baqag* (loincloth), women the *tapis* (sarong skirt), and some would need to dance, play gongs, or sing.

Carlos's appeal prompted much laughter and chatter among the two dozen or so Palawan people gathered around him. The prospect of parading through town was mortifying by itself, let alone while wearing garments they knew to be objects of fascination and ridicule among Kabisayaan.[3] Undeterred, Carlos reminded everyone that he could appeal to the local government for assistance with, say, fueling a generator at the *tabuqan* or improving the road to the village. For such requests to be effective, "we must show that we are united as a *purok*." The parade presented an opportunity to do just that.

Carlos gave his speech in Tagalog, but his audience responded in Palawan. At the time I did not speak Palawan well enough to follow all the commentary, but I got the gist of one young man's response. Before Carlos finished, the young man stood, hiked up his basketball shorts to simulate a loincloth, and then gyrated his pelvis in a suggestive manner. His wife sighed, as if she had seen this gag one too many times, but most of the group was in stitches. Carlos was starting to look a bit exasperated. He appealed individually to men and women, asking them to promise that they would accompany him to town for the parade. After the meeting, I asked several people whether they planned to participate. Some said they would, but no one seemed especially enthusiastic. "They'll probably just laugh at us," one man said, voicing a concern that many seemed to have. "*He* should wear a *baqag!*" a young woman joked, referring to Carlos.

I ultimately missed the parade because of a meeting in the provincial capital. When I returned to Tenga't Gebaq a few days later, I learned that a dozen or so men and boys had accompanied Carlos, and a few had even worn the *baqag*. Had their experience been as humiliating as some had feared? It turned out that no one had much to say about it. It had been a bit embarrassing, but mostly it was disappointing because they had not won the prize. Their group had been overshadowed by a much larger one organized by a neighboring *purok*.

A few weeks later, I went to visit the group that had won the prize and spent the day at their *tabuqan*. When I returned to Tenga't Gebaq late in the afternoon, Jimi asked me what I had done and seen there. In the course of recounting the day, I mentioned that a trio of men had played gongs for me when I first arrived. "Ah, so they performed again?" Jimi asked with a smile, referring to their award-winning show in the town parade. Then, without explanation, he started preparing a performance of his own. With the help of his wife, sister, and brother-in-law, Jimi had his son, daughter, niece, and nephew dressed in traditional attire. The boys wore loincloths and headbands, the girls tied sarongs around their waste, and each child was adorned with a traditional item: woven *tabig* baskets for the girls, a *kiba* rattan backpack for the older boy, and a sprig of a medicinal herb called *ruku-ruku* in the headband of his younger cousin. The "show," which I was encouraged to photograph, consisted mostly of the four kids parading around the yard while everyone, including the four performers, laughed riotously. I joined in the laughter, but I was also puzzled. I knew that Jimi had little patience for events like the town parade, so I wondered why he had reenacted it in miniature with the children.

As the setting sun bathed the giggling children in golden light and stretched their shadows farther and farther across the garden, I asked Jimi what had prompted him to stage this show. "Nothing," he said, "it's just for fun." Eventually, our conversation turned to more serious matters, particularly Jimi's wariness of government officials, nongovernmental organizations, and other outsiders who ask Palawan to don traditional garb and perform for public events. Jimi believed that outsiders "used" these performances for purposes that rarely benefited Palawan people. Why else would they want Palawan to dress in a manner that his parents' generation had been pressured to abandon and that continued to be an object of derision in certain contexts?

This performance was neither a simple joke nor a crude act of self-ridicule. It was a comic satire of how outsiders exoticize Palawan people and of the practical dilemmas that this creates for Palawan. It was also a cue for me to reflect on my role as an outsider who authors and circulates representations of Palawan. When I first met Jimi and he suggested that I become *sibilais,* he meant civilized not in the colonial sense but in the sense of learning to communicate and collaborate across linguistic, cosmological, and social differences (see introduction). This was how, he said, I would learn to tell the "truth" about what I experienced during my research, instead of just using Palawan people for personal gain. That "truth," however partial and positioned, is what I have tried to convey in this book. Like Jimi, I believe that the story of his community matters. It matters not just for the inherent significance of their lives or that of their biodiverse lands but also for the critical insight that he and other residents have to offer about Indigenous rights, capitalism, and conservation. Jimi and his neighbors are not just experiencing these forces—they are critical thinkers and actors who have their own analyses and debates about their place in world history. Together we generated knowledge that, I hope, will help inform larger debates.

Palawan in the "Transit" of Empire

On February 20, 2023, the *New Yorker* ran an essay by evolutionary biologist Manvir Singh, who argues that indigeneity is a primitivist, colonial concept that perpetuates "discredited stereotypes" about marginalized populations. Over the past fifty years, according to Singh, "the indigenous identity" was taken up by and imposed on marginalized rural populations throughout the Global South.[4] "Indigeneity is a project of hope," he writes, "a politics of the oppressed, aiming to protect land and sovereignty, to turn 'backward' natives into respected stewards."[5] Proponents of the concept, including many Indigenous persons, succumbed to "the natural temptation . . . to stretch the concept until it covered as many disempowered peoples as possible, even at the cost of coherence."[6] Amid this incoherence, Singh concludes, the only common denominator is the trope of primitiveness: "Even if you are not aboriginal, you can count as Indigenous if you come across as simple, egalitarian, culturally encapsulated, spiritually attuned to nature, and somehow isolated from history and civilization."[7]

It's not every day that a prestigious magazine like the *New Yorker* features critical reflections on indigeneity. In this case, the article does a disservice to this complex matter and the realities of the peoples it implicates. The author makes one important point: Indigeneity is a concept onto which powerful people and institutions project their biases and desires. It is often defined and institutionalized in ways that perpetuate colonial political structures and further subjugate Indigenous peoples. And it is, indeed, often associated with primitivism and the commodification of difference.

All of this is true. But it's no revelation, and it represents only a small fraction of what indigeneity means and does in the world. Consider the moments I described above, when residents of Tenga't Gebaq responded critically and creatively to demands that they perform a specific kind of Indigenous difference. Their responses were much more incisive and nuanced than Singh's take. As we have seen throughout this book, Jimi and many people in Tenga't Gebaq had a critical, sometimes even cynical, view of government-defined Indigenous rights. Some did not even know what the English word "Indigenous" really meant. Yet these same people had critical questions and insights about how their experiences were connected with those of similarly positioned people around the world. Recall Palaya's question from the introduction: "Are there Palawan in America?" That exchange was part of a larger conversation in the community about how societal structures and historical processes affected their lives. The same was true for the satirical play that Jimi staged and for other moments recounted in these pages. These moments have revealed critical perspectives on what it means to be marked as *netibo, katutubo,* tribal, and Indigenous amid an ongoing frenzy for the region's resources. They have also revealed a Palawan analysis of how this frenzy fits into a longer history of successive, interrelated imperial projects. This analysis, I have argued, understands the paradoxical nature of indigeneity in Palawan and elsewhere. It shows how the codification and manipulation of indigeneity by governing elites reinscribes transimperial structures of rule in the postcolonial language of Indigenous rights. It also generates insights into those structures and enables critical engagement with them.

With due respect to Singh, there is no such thing as "the indigenous identity." As a range of scholars have argued, indigeneity is an analytic, not an identity.[8] Jodi Byrd, for example, has described indigeneity as a "transit of empire," through which the subjugation of Native peoples has been legitimated but also resisted and at times disrupted.[9] Although referring specifically to the US empire, this theory of transit aptly describes how discourses and policies of indigeneity operate more broadly in the contemporary world, including postcolonial contexts like the Philippines. On the one hand, the transit of indigeneity enables transnational capitalist interests to extend their power across disparate people and geographies. Indigeneity is one way different people's specific histories are selectively recognized, instrumentalized, exploited, and ruled. (Recall from the introduction Mark Goodale's concept of "dark matter."[10]) On the other hand, these disparate peoples also engage with the transit of indigeneity to develop critical theories, analyses, solidarities, and transits. Their transits, in turn, are "attuned to the local conditions of colonialism that might speak across geopolitical boundaries [and] provide a diagnostic way of reading and interpreting the colonial logics that underpin cultural, intellectual, and political discourses."[11] My argument in this book is that this critical work takes place not only among Indigenous scholars and their interlocutors but also among Palawan people and theirs.

As one of their interlocutors, I have sought to listen to their analyses, share my own, and pursue the questions, conundrums, and theories that result. This book is one such result. Residents of Tenga't Gebaq do not have special wisdom that can save us from capitalism or the climate crisis. Nor do they have definite solutions to the dilemmas they face. But they do have generative responses to those dilemmas, and their responses are part of the "transit" of indigeneity across peoples, places, and political boundaries. Much recent scholarship on indigeneity in Southeast Asia dwells on the limits of the concept as an identity, as an analytic, or as both. My aim here has been to show that this is not just an academic debate.

Professional scholars are not the only ones aware of the transimperial forces that yoke the recognition of Indigenous rights in the twenty-first-century Philippines to hundreds of years of colonial history. Nor are we the only ones capable of developing critical theories and actions based on that knowledge. In their oral histories of colonialism (chapter 1), differing responses to conservation (chapter 2), production of environmental narratives (chapter 3), relations with forest beings (chapter 4), and uses of the court system (chapter 5), we have seen how Palawan people in and around Tenga't Gebaq think and act critically in their efforts to survive and thrive in a rapidly changing world. Their story is, I believe, as relevant to Southeast Asian studies as it is to Indigenous studies.

Research as Interpersonal Responsibility

Isu and Neli were an elder couple whose main residence was about a half-hour hike upstream from Tenga't Gebaq. I loved visiting them. It was just close enough for me to go it alone, but far enough that I could cool my heels in a spring and let my senses wander into the sights, sounds, and smells of the forest. Mostly I loved visiting them because they were so kind to me. Their kindness wasn't performative, nor did it manifest in a material form. Neli rarely spoke directly to me, and I usually brought the provisions for our shared meals. Theirs was a kindness made of patience and curiosity. They humored me through many hours of conversations about local history, ancestral knowledge, and their lives. This often meant helping me figure out how to express myself comprehensibly in Palawan and repeatedly explaining certain things so I could understand them. They took me to see their fields, let me help with the harvest, introduced me to their visiting kin, and designated me as a sort of stenographer in ceremonies, disputes, and nuptials that Isu oversaw in his capacity as a *belyan* and *pegibutan* (ritual healer and respected elder). I responded as best I could to their questions about America, Manila, World War II, the meaning of various terms like "protected area," and so on. When I didn't know the answer to a question—for example, how much profit do wealthy almaciga traders make by underpaying Palawan collectors?—I would try to find out before my next visit.

I harbor no illusions about the broader context of our exchanges. I had access to more wealth and power than they did, and the knowledge we exchanged has almost certainly done more to advance my livelihood than it has to advance theirs. We did not somehow transcend the historical forces that brought us together. Instead, we engaged as intellectual equals with a mutual interest in what each other knew about the world. This is what Jimi meant when he invited me to become *sibilais*—to think beyond one-sided research methods like interviews, focus groups, surveys, and even participant observation. It was an invitation to make my time in Tenga't Gebaq an end in itself, rather than a means of generating academic knowledge artifacts. This wasn't easy for me. I had a book to write and plans for an expansive project covering multiple areas. Instead, I stayed in Tenga't Gebaq and had the privilege of becoming *sibilais* with Isu, Neli, and many others whose presence is felt in these pages.

There's no single correct way to do research in Palawan or anywhere else. The approach I took, thanks to Jimi, prioritized developing interpersonal relationships and finding shared matters of concern. This is a "more than research" approach in that the research is predicated on relationships rather than the other way around.[12] These relationships take a lot of effort to form and sustain, yet they are often devalued in favor of methods that yield larger, more systematic datasets. This bias, I believe, says more about the productivity demands of the academy than about the intellectual value of the research itself. We cannot ignore the academy's demands, but we can resist them by changing how we approach and value our work. I invite readers to consider how a more-than-research approach might inform your work as students, educators, activists, and scholars.[13]

Isu died from pneumonia in 2018. No one knew exactly how old he was in calendar years, but he had been born before the Japanese occupation of Palawan during World War II. With him went a tremendous amount of knowledge, skill, and history. When I visited Tenga't Gebaq some months after his death, I spent a day with Neli and their eldest son, Iteng. We played video and audio recordings I had made with Isu and reminisced over old photos. Four generations of Isu's kin chatted, worked, cooked, dozed, and played around us. At some point, I asked what would happen to the *rurungan* without him as a *pegibuten*.[14] Iteng paused and looked around. "Father died," he said, "but he's still here—in my body, in theirs, in his uma fields, even in your recordings. It's up to us."

Notes

Introduction

1. Except for public figures, all personal names used in this book are pseudonyms.

2. He asked, in Palawan, "Embe't kantu't America?"

3. For my benefit, Palaya spoke in a mix of Tagalog and Palawan. At this relatively early point in my research, though I was starting to understand basic Palawan, I was still mostly conversing with people in Tagalog. For "Indigenous," she used the Tagalog word *katutubo*.

4. I capitalize the term "Indigenous" when it refers to peoples, such as my Palawan hosts, who can claim indigeneity under national and international law. This helps avoid conflation with lower-case "indigenous," which is often used colloquially to describe humans, animals, plants, and products that originate in a particular place. See Paredes, "More Indigenous than Others."

5. As explained later in the introduction, my Palawan hosts redefined *sibilais* to describe any act of gaining fluency in the language and customs of others. In this way, they subtly reject civilizational narratives that cast them as primitive. In their usage, becoming *sibilais* is not an assimilative process whereby "uncivilized" peoples adopt the "civilized" ways of others. Rather, it's a potentially mutual process of observing, learning, and adapting that occurs across linguistic and cultural differences. Becoming *sibilais* was often described as a one-sided process, where Palawan had to learn the ways of others and not vice versa. This was seen as a concession to unequal power rather than a result of their own inferiority.

6. In particular, I was reminded of Tania Li's observation that our ideas about who we are emerge recursively—that is, through dialogue with others—in this case through two-way interviews with an anthropologist. See Li, "Ethnic Cleansing, Recursive Knowledge."

7. Kumar, "Nation-States as Empires, Empires as Nation-States."

8. A variety of specific events are seen as leading to the internationalization of indigeneity, such as actions of the International Labour Organization in the 1950s, early alliances between the Inuit and the Sierra Club in the late 1960s, the founding of the first international Indigenous organizations in the 1970s, or the World Bank's embrace of Indigenous knowledge in the 1990s. This history has been addressed by other scholars, whose choices of emphasis inevitably reflect their broader theoretical interests. See Dove, "Indigenous People and Environmental Politics"; Igoe, "Global Indigenism and Spaceship Earth"; Kirsch, "Juridification of Indigenous Politics"; Lightfoot, *Global Indigenous Politics;* Merlan, "Indigeneity"; Morgan, *Transforming Law and Institution;* Niezen, *The Origins of Indigenism*; and Stewart-Harawira, *The New Imperial Order.*

9. See Baviskar, "Indian Indigeneities"; Casumbal-Salazar, "The Indeterminacy of the Philippine Indigenous Subject"; Hodgson, *Being Maasai, Becoming Indigenous;* Igoe,

"Becoming Indigenous Peoples"; Maruyama, "From 'Displaced Peoples' to 'Indigenous Peoples'"; Morton and Baird, "From Hill Tribes to Indigenous Peoples"; Paredes, "Between Rights Protection and Development Aggression"; Uddin, "In Search of Self."

10. See Dressler and Guieb, "Violent Enclosures, Violated Livelihoods"; Hagen and Minter, "Displacement in the Name of Development"; Hirtz, "It Takes Modern Means to Be Traditional"; Holden, Nadeau, and Jacobson, "Exemplifying Accumulation by Dispossession"; Montefrio, "Land Control Dynamics and Social-Ecological Transformations"; Paredes, "Preserving 'Tradition'"; Peñalba, "Indigenous Peoples versus the State"; Smith and Dressler, "Forged in Flames."

11. Dressler and Smith, "Blood, Timber and Plantations"; Eder, *On the Road to Tribal Extinction*; Eder and Evangelista, *Palawan and Its Global Connections;* Montefrio, "Cooperation and Resistance"; Novellino, "From Local Struggles to Global Advocacy"; Smith, *Mountains of Blame.*

12. Macdonald, *Uncultural Behavior.*

13. See Cattelino, "The Double Bind of American Indian Need-Based Sovereignty"; Ludlow et al., "The Double Binds of Indigeneity and Indigenous Resistance." The concept of a double bind is useful for understanding contemporary Indigenous experiences in many contexts. When it comes to dealing with colonial states, Indigenous peoples are too often "damned if they do, and damned if they don't." What I hope to do is explore the moments in which such dilemmas come to the surface and provoke critical engagement.

14. Brewer, "Microhistory and the Histories of Everyday Life"; Putnam, "To Study the Fragments/Whole."

15. Paredes, "More Indigenous than Others."

16. Tsing, "Natural Resources and Capitalist Frontiers," 5102; see also Tsing, "How to Make Resources in Order to Destroy Them."

17. See Baviskar, *In the Belly of the River;* Blaser, Feit, and McRae, *In the Way of Development;* Cadena, "Indigenous Cosmopolitics in the Andes"; Cepek, *A Future for Amazonia;* Deloria, *Indians in Unexpected Places;* Dizon, *Reciprocal Mobilities;* Estes, *Our History Is the Future;* Montefrio, "Cooperation and Resistance"; Paredes, *A Mountain of Difference*; Rubis and Theriault, "Concealing Protocols"; Sawyer, *Crude Chronicles;* Simpson, *Mohawk Interruptus;* White, *The Middle Ground.*

18. Dressler, *For the Sake of Forests and Gods;* Parreñas, "From Decolonial Indigenous Knowledges to Vernacular Ideas"; Simon, *Truly Human;* Smith, *Mountains of Blame.*

19. Berlant, *Cruel Optimism.*

20. Casumbal-Salazar, "The Indeterminacy of the Philippine Indigenous Subject"; Theriault, "Unravelling the Strings Attached." As Li has written, "In parts of Asia where colonial authorities had created a distinct legal category 'tribe,' as they did in India and the Philippines, the colonial category transmuted relatively easily into the transnational category 'Indigenous,' at least from the perspective of the Indigenous peoples' movement." Li, "Indigeneity, Capitalism," 395.

21. Hoganson and Sexton, "Introduction."

22. Escobar, *Territories of Difference;* Hall, "The Meaning of New Times 1989"; Kirsch, *Mining Capitalism;* Melucci, "The New Social Movements."

23. Niezen, *The Origins of Indigenism.*

24. Povinelli, *The Cunning of Recognition.*

25. Daytec-Yangot, "Transcending Aboriginality and Minority"; Gatmaytan, "Indigenous Autonomy amid Counter-Insurgency"; Li, "Indigeneity, Capitalism."

26. Gatmaytan, "Living with the Promise of Violence."

27. Foster, "The Financialization of Capitalism."

28. Foster, "The Financialization of Capitalism."

29. Camba, "From Colonialism to Neoliberalism"; Edelman, Oya, and Borras, "Global Land Grabs"; Franco and Borras, "The Global Climate of Land Politics"; Li, "What Is Land?"; McMichael, "The Land Grab and Corporate Food Regime Restructuring"; Montefrio, "Land Control Dynamics and Social-Ecological Transformations"; Rosales, "Radical Rentierism."

30. Bracking, "Financialization and the Environmental Frontier"; Büscher, "Derivative Nature"; Dressler et al., "Land Sharing Not Sparing in the 'Green Economy'"; Kelly, "Conservation Practice as Primitive Accumulation"; Lunstrum, "Capitalism, Wealth, and Conservation in the Age of Security"; Massé and Lunstrum, "Accumulation by Securitization"; Mitchell, *Revenant Ecologies.*

31. Anthias, "Indigenous Peoples and the New Extraction"; Beban, So, and Un, "From Force to Legitimation"; Goodale, "Dark Matter."

32. Gatmaytan, "Advocacy as Translation"; Hagen and Minter, "Displacement in the Name of Development"; Novellino, "'Talking about Kultura and Signing Contracts'"; Rubis, "The Orang Utan Is Not an Indigenous Name"; Rubis and Theriault, "Concealing Protocols."

33. Bello, "How Neoliberalism Killed the Philippines' EDSA Republic"; Harvey, *A Short History of Neoliberalism;* Larner, "Neoliberalism"; Peck and Tickell, "Neoliberalizing Space."

34. Cooke and Kothari, *Participation;* Goldman, *Imperial Nature;* Junge, "NGOs as Shadow Pseudopublics"; Alejandro Leal, "Participation."

35. Büscher, Dressler, and Fletcher, *Nature Inc.*

36. Reid, "Poverty Alleviation and Participatory Development"; Resurreccion, "Gender, Identity and Agency"; Seki, "Green Neoliberalism, Ecogovernmentality, and Emergent Community"; Seki, *Ethnographies of Development and Globalization in the Philippines.*

37. Theriault, "Environmental Politics and the Burden of Authenticity."

38. Cramb et al., "Swidden Transformations and Rural Livelihoods"; McDermott, "Boundaries and Pathways."

39. Brown, "Defending Society."

40. Goodale, "Dark Matter," 441.

41. Republic of the Philippines, Republic Act 8371.

42. Theriault, "Environmental Politics and the Burden of Authenticity."

43. Hirtz, "It Takes Modern Means to Be Traditional"; McDermott, "Invoking Community"; Minter, "The Agta of the Northern Sierra Madre"; Paredes, "Preserving 'Tradition.'"

44. Arquiza et al., "From Barter Trade to Brad Pitt's Bed"; Eder, "Zoning Resources, Zoning People."

45. McDermott, "Boundaries and Pathways."

46. Tebtebba, "Indigenous Peoples and the Sustainable Development Goals."

47. Bello, "The Subversion of the Philippines' Indigenous People's Rights Act"; Gozum, "Dumagat-Remontados Begin 9-Day March"; Ilagan, "Palawan IPs Seek to Stop Consent Process"; Lapniten, "Collusion, Corruption Allegations Hound Dam Projects."

48. Survival International, "Philippine Mining Plans Blocked."

49. See Simon, *Truly Human.*

50. Warren, *The Sulu Zone, 1768–1898;* Warren, *Iranun and Balangingi.*

51. Macdonald, *Uncultural Behavior.*

52. Li, "Ethnic Cleansing, Recursive Knowledge."

53. Dove, *The Banana Tree at the Gate;* Padwe, *Disturbed Forests, Fragmented Memories;* Tsing, *In the Realm of the Diamond Queen;* Tsing, *Friction.*

54. Dove, *The Banana Tree at the Gate;* Zakaria, *The Camphor Tree and the Elephant.*

55. Aguilar, "The Triumph of Instrumental Citizenship?"; Duncan, *Civilizing the Margins;* Thongchai, *Siam Mapped.*

56. Scott, *The Art of Not Being Governed,* 20.

57. Scott, *The Art of Not Being Governed.*

58. Jonsson, "Paths to Freedom," 167.

59. Jonsson, "Paths to Freedom," 167.

60. Zakaria, *The Camphor Tree and the Elephant.*

61. Dove, "Hybrid Histories and Indigenous Knowledge"; Dove, *The Banana Tree at the Gate.*

62. Dressler, Smith, and Montefrio, "Ungovernable?"; Paredes, *A Mountain of Difference;* Rigg, Salamanca, and Thompson, "The Puzzle of East and Southeast Asia's Persistent Smallholder."

63. Li, *Land's End,* 15.

64. Li, *Land's End,* 179.

65. The term "salvage frontier" comes from Tsing, "Natural Resources and Capitalist Frontiers," 5102. See also Chao, *In the Shadow of the Palms;* Holden, Nadeau, and Jacobson, "Exemplifying Accumulation by Dispossession"; Jacka, *Alchemy in the Rain Forest;* Kirsch, "Indigenous Movements and the Risks of Counterglobalization"; Prasse-Freeman, "Necroeconomics"; Tsing, "Natural Resources and Capitalist Frontiers."

66. See also Kirsch, *Reverse Anthropology.*

67. Aguilar, *Clash of Spirits.*

68. West, *Kupilikula.*

69. Beban and Work, "The Spirits Are Crying"; Chao, *In the Shadow of the Palms;* Paredes, "Experimental Science for the 'Bananapocalypse'"; Rubis and Theriault, "Concealing Protocols."

70. Blaser, "Ontological Conflicts and the Stories of Peoples in Spite of Europe"; Cadena, "Indigenous Cosmopolitics in the Andes"; Cadena, *Earth Beings;* Escobar, *Designs for the Pluriverse;* Nadasdy, "The Gift in the Animal"; Nadasdy, "How Many Worlds Are There?"; Povinelli, *Geontologies.*

71. Jackson, *Paths toward a Clearing;* Latour, "Whose Cosmos, Which Cosmopolitics?"; Stengers, "The Cosmopolitical Proposal"; Viveiros de Castro, "Perspectival Anthropology and the Method of Controlled Equivocation."

72. Nadasdy, "How Many Worlds Are There?," 358. See also Bessire and Bond, "Ontological Anthropology and the Deferral of Critique"; Ramos, "The Politics of Perspectivism"; Todd, "An Indigenous Feminist's Take on the Ontological Turn."

73. Nadasdy, "How Many Worlds Are There?," 363; Cepek, "There Might Be Blood."

74. Atleo, *Principles of Tsawalk.*

75. Paredes, "More Indigenous than Others."

76. Simon, *Truly Human;* Watson, *Japan's Ainu Minority in Tokyo.*

77. Chua and Idrus, "Introduction"; Cooke and Johari, "Positioning of Murut and Bajau Identities"; Keating, "Kuy Alterities"; Shah, *In the Shadows of the State;* Uddin, "In Search of Self."

78. Parreñas, "From Decolonial Indigenous Knowledges to Vernacular Ideas in Southeast Asia."

79. Smith, *Mountains of Blame*. Hannah Bulloch, *In Pursuit of Progress*, makes a similar argument about how Christian communities in Siquijor understand uneven development.

80. Schreer, "The Absent Agent."

81. Smith, *Mountains of Blame*, 5.

82. Coulthard, *Red Skin, White Masks;* Simpson, *Mohawk Interruptus;* Vizenor, *Native Liberty*.

83. Whitman, "Lindbergh Traveling Widely as Conservationist."

Chapter 1. Colonial Sorcery

1. Pigafetta, *The First Voyage around the World, 1519–1522*, 57–58.

2. Mojares, "Lapulapu in Folk Tradition," 61.

3. The Battle of Mactan, as this encounter is known in Philippine historiography, has inspired a number of thoughtful essays over the years. In 2021, for the 500th anniversary of the battle, President Rodrigo Duterte organized a national celebration, in which he insinuated he was an heir to Lapu-Lapu's nationalist legacy. See Aquino, "Rethinking Magellan and Rediscovering the Philippines"; Candelaria, "1521, Duterte, and the Politics of Commemoration in the Philippines"; Joaquin, "Lapu-Lapu and Humabon"; Mojares, "Lapulapu in Folk Tradition."

4. Anthropologists Charles Macdonald and Nicole Revel, who have been doing ethnographic research with Palawan communities since the 1970s, have written extensively in French and English on the dynamism of Palawan oral traditions. They have analyzed Palawan accounts of the creation of the seven-tiered cosmos by a deity called the Weaver. For an English translation of this account, see Revel, "The 'Gifts of the Weaver' and Their Becoming." While some Palawan elders were familiar with this story, it was not the one they first thought of when I asked about how the world came to be. Among other topics, Macdonald's and Revel's works also address Palawan oral epic traditions, ritual practices, natural history, kinship, and social organization. See Macdonald, "Mythe de création Palawan"; Macdonald, *Une société simple;* Macdonald, "Bons et mauvais coups de tonnerre"; Macdonald, "Kinship and Fellowship among the Palawan"; Revel, *Fleurs de paroles;* Revel, "Kudaman"; Revel, "Corps en jeu (je) ou la chasse généralisée."

5. Michael Cullinane pointed out that this story reflects Palawan exposure to the postcolonial Philippine education system (because the Magellan/Lapu-Lapu episode was not widely known in the Philippines until nationalists reformed public school curriculum after independence). Palawan oral histories also contain accounts of their ancestors' battles against Muslim traders and raiders, identified by various names. When I asked how those accounts fit into the story about Lapu-Lapu and Magellan, I was told that the Muslims were able to find Palawan thanks to its earlier discovery by the Visayan-Spanish duo.

6. Broad and Cavanagh, *Plundering Paradise*, 39.

7. Municipality of Rizal, "Greetings from the Mayor!" A slightly different version of this passage is also cited by Fabinyi in his discussion of last frontier rhetoric. Fabinyi, *Fishing for Fairness*.

8. This passage comes from a caption associated with a video documentary posted to YouTube by Ancestral Land/Domain Watch (ALDAW), a Palawan-based Indigenous rights

organization founded in 2009. ALDAW's main activities include opposition to mining and large plantation development on Palawan lands. ALDAW, "Palawan: Our Struggle for Nature and Culture."

9. World Wildlife Fund, "A Biodiversity Hotspot in the Philippines"; World Wildlife Fund, "Palawan Moist Forests."

10. Oona Paredes makes a similar argument about representations of Indigenous Lumad peoples in Mindanao. Paredes, *A Mountain of Difference.*

11. I have borrowed the term "liberal exceptionalism" from Julian Go, for whom it signifies an American ideology that "admits that the United States has been an empire, but insists that the empire has been unique." Go, "The Provinciality of American Empire," 75.

12. Forsyth and Walker, *Forest Guardians, Forest Destroyers,* 17. Nora Haenn offers a similar concept with "regime of nature," which, following Escobar, she defines as "a story that condenses and attempts to direct the intersection of history, cultural mediation, and ecology." Haenn, "Nature Regimes in Southern Mexico," 2; Escobar, "After Nature."

13. Foucault, "Of Other Spaces"; Kavanagh, "Haunting Remains."

14. Smith, *The New Urban Frontier,* xvi.

15. The most in-depth study, published in Tagalog in 1985, is Nilo Ocampo's *Katutubo, Muslim, Kristyano.* Some other recent works include a chapter on the Culion leper colony in Anderson, *Colonial Pathologies;* Salman, "'The Prison that Makes Men Free'"; and Romanillos, "Augustinian Recollect Contributions."

16. See Dressler, *Old Thoughts in New Ideas;* Eder, *On the Road to Tribal Extinction;* Eder, *A Generation Later;* McDermott, "Boundaries and Pathways"; Montefrio, "Cooperation and Resistance"; Smith, *Mountains of Blame;* Webb, "Domestic 'Eco' Tourism and the Production of a Wondrous Nature in the Philippines."

17. Fabinyi, *Fishing for Fairness,* 23.

18. Ocampo, *Katutubo, Muslim, Kristyano;* Ocampo, "A History of Palawan."

19. Ocampo, "A History of Palawan," 24.

20. The province of Palawan encompasses some 1,800 smaller islands, such as the Calamianes group, Busuanga, Cuyo, Dumaran, Cagayancillo, and Balabac.

21. Concepcion, "General History of the Discalced Augustinian Fathers," 310.

22. Bellwood, "Southeast Asia before History."

23. Eder and Fernandez, "Introduction," 2.

24. Eder, *On the Road to Tribal Extinction,* 24.

25. Bellwood, "Southeast Asia before History," 6.

26. Eder, *On the Road to Tribal Extinction,* 25.

27. Southern Palawan is the only place in the Philippines where manggis trees (*Koompassia excelsa*)—the tallest trees in Southeast Asia—grow wild. It is also home to one of the Philippines' only remaining lowland forests that runs contiguously from the mangroves to the mountains.

28. Barrera, *Soil Survey of Palawan Province.*

29. Eder, "Coastal Resource Management and Social Differences in Philippine Fishing Communities"; Kummer, "Measuring Forest Decline in the Philippines."

30. Hutterer, "Prehistoric Trade and the Evolution of Philippine Societies."

31. Scott, *Prehispanic Source Materials for the Study of Philippine History.*

32. Kress, "Contemporary and Prehistoric Subsistence Patterns on Palawan." See also Eder, *On the Road to Tribal Extinction,* 48–51, for a summary.

33. Concepcion, "General History of the Discalced Augustinian Fathers," 309–310.

34. In the Sulu Zone, these products mainly included things like beeswax, trepang, gutta-percha, camphor, rattan, various resins, tortoiseshell, pearls, mother of pearl, and edible birds nests. See Warren, *The Sulu Zone, 1768–1898.*

35. Warren, *The Sulu Zone, 1768–1898.*

36. Warren, *The Sulu Zone, 1768–1898.*

37. Warren, *The Sulu Zone, 1768–1898;* Warren, *Iranun and Balangingi.*

38. Of these, perhaps the most widely known is Dean Worcester, who visited Palawan in 1887 and 1892, was appointed by President McKinley to both Philippine commissions, and served as secretary of the interior for the Insular Government from 1901 to 1913. Except for a short stopover in Balabac, Worcester stayed in the vicinity of Puerto Princesa during his initial expeditions.

39. Whitehead, "Notes on the Birds of Palawan," 38.

40. Whitehead, *Exploration of Mount Kinabalu, North Borneo.*

41. Whitehead (*Exploration of Mount Kinabalu, North Borneo,* 180–181) describes the Orang Sungei thus: "[They] are settled on the various rivers, and are, like the Sulus, Mohammedans. They work harder than the Sulus, not having the trade monopoly, are dark-skinned, usually ugly, and badly dressed in Sulu fashion, being poor."

42. Macdonald, *Uncultural Behavior,* 13–14.

43. Magellan had been commissioned by King Charles V of Spain to find a western route to the Spice Islands.

44. Toponyms reflect modern usage. With reference to Palawan, Spanish documents alternate between Paragua, which was its official Spanish colonial name, and various iterations of Palawan.

45. Pigafetta, *The First Voyage around the World, 1519–1522,* 66.

46. Andaya and Ishii, "Religious Developments in Southeast Asia, c. 1500–1800," 13.

47. Schurz, *The Manila Galleon,* 43–44.

48. In a 1569 *relación* addressed to King Philip II, Legazpi wrote, "I believe that if the land is settled and peopled by Spaniards, we shall be able to get plenty of gold, pearls, and other valuable articles." Legazpi, "Letter to Felipe II."

49. Bankoff, "One Island Too Many."

50. Andaya and Ishii, "Religious Developments in Southeast Asia, c. 1500–1800"; Paredes, *A Mountain of Difference.*

51. Concepcion, "General History of the Discalced Augustinian Fathers," 315–316. The term "Moro" refers to a collection of Muslim ethnic groups indigenous to Mindanao and Sulu. Although the term is of Spanish origin and was imported from Spain to legitimate imperial conquest, it is self-ascribed today. In the case of seventeenth-, eighteenth-, and nineteenth-century Palawan, the Moros and Sulus in question were most likely of Malay, Tausug, or Samal ethnicity.

52. Concepcion, "General History of the Discalced Augustinian Fathers," 319.

53. In 1752, Spain sent a military contingent to secure the island, but it eventually had to turn back due to illness. This expedition is mentioned in the Philippine Commission Report for 1900 as part of a chronological summary of the Spanish period.

54. Legazpi, "Letter to Felipe II," 242.

55. Bankoff, "One Island Too Many."

56. Quirante, "Expedition to the Mines of the Igorotes, Alingayen, 5 June 1624," 267–268.

57. Bankoff, "One Island Too Many," 317.

58. Jordana y Morera, *Estudio forestal acerca de la India inglesa, Java y Filipinas;* Vidal y Soler, *Memoria sobre el ramo de montes en las islas Filipinas,* 67–68; cited in Bankoff, "One Island Too Many," 319.

59. Quoted in Bankoff, "One Island Too Many," 320.

60. Ocampo, "A History of Palawan."

61. Fox, *Religion and Society among the Tagbanuwa,* 2.

62. Worcester, *The Philippine Islands and Their People,* 82.

63. Scott, *Slavery in the Spanish Philippines,* 39.

64. Amoroso and Abinales, *State and Society in the Philippines;* Phelan, *The Hispanization of the Philippines;* Scott, *Slavery in the Spanish Philippines.*

65. Abinales, *Making Mindanao;* Amoroso and Abinales, *State and Society in the Philippines;* Anderson, "Cacique Democracy in the Philippines"; McCoy, *An Anarchy of Families;* Sidel, *Capital, Coercion, and Crime.*

66. Salman, *The Embarrassment of Slavery;* Scott, *Slavery in the Spanish Philippines.*

67. Lynch, "Concepts and Strategies for Promoting Legal Recognition," 397.

68. In chapter 3, I address how the legacy of these and other policies live on in contemporary environmental narratives concerning the rights and obligations of Indigenous people vis-à-vis the state.

69. Agoncillo, *The Revolt of the Masses;* Aguilar, "What Made the Masses Revolutionary?"

70. Immerwahr, *How to Hide an Empire.*

71. Philippine Commission, *Report to the President, Volume 3,* 288.

72. At the time, Bankoff writes, "the nascent U.S. conservation movement was split between preservationists and the so-called utilitarian conservationists." The leading exponent of the latter school of thought was Gifford Pinchot. Prior to serving as the first chief of the US Forest Service from 1905 to 1910, he traveled to his government's new colony in 1902 to inspect its forests. In addition to vast amounts of commercially valuable timber, Pinchot saw an opportunity to realize his vision of scientific, utilitarian forestry. Under the leadership of George Ahearn, a close Pinchot associate, the Insular Bureau of Forestry became an experiment in undiluted utilitarian conservation—something that was impossible in the United States because of political pressure from preservationists. Bankoff, "Conservation and Colonialism."

73. Potter, "Forests versus Agriculture"; Tucker, *Insatiable Appetite.*

74. In 1914, Worcester wrote that "Philippine forests should be like money in the bank for the inhabitants of the islands" (*The Philippines Past and Present, vol. 2,* 847). See also Worcester, "Philippine Forest Wealth."

75. Philippine Commission, *Report to the President, Volume 1,* 159.

76. Philippine Commission, *Report to the President, Volume 3,* 124.

77. Rice, *Dean Worcester's Fantasy Islands.*

78. Worcester, *The Philippine Islands and Their People,* 120, emphasis added.

79. Bureau of Forestry, *Annual Reports* (1924).

80. According to the Director's Annual Report, 28,642 cubic meters of lumber were "utilized" from Palawan in 1921, accounting for approximately 4.4 percent of the total utilization that year, 653,944 cubic feet. Numbers for other years suggest that this share remained steady over time—4.7 percent in 1907 and 4.3 percent in 1923—even as Palawan's logging operations grew, confirming that logging in the colony as a whole was growing during this period. Bureau of Forestry, *Annual Reports* (1921, 1924).

81. Philippine Commission, *Report to the President, Volume 3*, 288.

82. Bureau of Forestry, *Annual Reports* (1921).

83. Bureau of Forestry, *Annual Reports* (1916), 17.

84. The Bureau of Non-Christian Tribes was replaced with the Ethnological Survey of the Philippines, only to be reinstated again in 1917. Throughout this period, "non-Christian provinces" were governed under the supervision of the Department of the Interior (Griffin, "National Policy on Minority Cultural Communities").

85. Barrows, *The Bureau of Non-Christian Tribes for the Philippine Islands*, 3.

86. Charbonneau, *Civilizational Imperatives;* Finin, *The Making of the Igorot;* Hawkins, *Making Moros.*

87. McCoy, *Policing America's Empire.* See also Abinales, "The U.S. Army as Occupying Force in Muslim Mindanao, 1899–1913"; Lynch, "Disenfranchisement qua Paternalism."

88. This was not the only such experiment in social engineering undertaken on Palawan. The Iwahig Penal Colony, established near Puerta Princesa in 1904, was an experiment in reformatory penology that predated and helped inform important penal reforms in the United States. Salman, "'The Prison that Makes Men Free.'"

89. Bureau of Forestry, *Annual Reports* (1914).

90. Philippine Commission, *Report of the Philippine Commission to the Secretary of War* (1912), 81.

91. Philippine Commission, *Report of the Philippine Commission to the Secretary of War* (1910), 65.

92. Bankoff, "Conservation and Colonialism."

93. Dressler, *Old Thoughts in New Ideas*, 42–46; Lynch, "Native Title, Private Right and Tribal Land Law."

94. See Philippine Commission, *Report of the Philippine Commission to the Secretary of War* (1912), 75, 80–82.

95. Eder, *A Generation Later*, 23.

96. Eder, "Converts to Islam and the Muslim Community in the Christian Philippines."

97. Eder, *A Generation Later*, 27.

98. Li, *The Will to Improve;* Scott, *Seeing like a State.*

99. Bender, "The Father, the Son, and the Aswang"; Burow, Brock, and Dove, "Unsettling the Land"; Coulthard, *Red Skin, White Masks;* King, "New World Grammars"; Kirsch, "Insular Territories"; Povinelli, *Geontologies;* Rafael, *Contracting Colonialism;* Rubis and Theriault, "Concealing Protocols"; Todd, "An Indigenous Feminist's Take on the Ontological Turn."

100. In this respect, my findings differ significantly from those of Smith, *Mountains of Blame*, who finds that Palawan blame and, in a sense, punish themselves for the social, ecological, and climatic dislocations they are experiencing. It also dovetails with the Palawan moral condemnation of greed. In a different myth, greed among Palawan—specifically a dispute over sago palm—is said to be what led half the population to become visible, while the other half remained invisible and became the *taw't talun* (people of the forest, see chapter 4).

101. No one could say how many generations it had been since Palawan was rendered visible.

Chapter 2. Producing and Consuming the "Last Frontier"

1. Whitman, "Lindbergh Traveling Widely as Conservationist."
2. Whitman, "Lindbergh Traveling Widely as Conservationist."

3. Macdonald, *Uncultural Behavior.*

4. Alternative spellings reflect local variations in pronunciation, which correspond with dialectical varieties of spoken Palawan (Macdonald, *Uncultural Behavior,* 12). I follow Macdonald's spelling because it seems the most inclusive.

5. Some of these crops originate in the New World, but that does not make them nontraditional. I resist coming up with a technical definition for the word "tradition" because I am hoping not to define an "essential" set of Palawan characteristics but to identify some of those that have existed since time immemorial from their perspective.

6. Macdonald, *Uncultural Behavior;* see also Dove, *The Banana Tree at the Gate;* Ocampo, *Katutubo, Muslim, Kristyano;* Warren, *The Sulu Zone.*

7. Macdonald, "Indigenous Peoples as Agents of Change."

8. Macdonald, "Kinship and Fellowship among the Palawan."

9. Palawan share this fear with other "nonviolent" peoples of Southeast Asia, including the Buid of Mindoro, the Semai and Temiar of the Malay Peninsula, and the Punan of Sarawak. Benjamin, "Process and Structure in Temiar Social Organization"; Dentan, *Overwhelming Terror;* Gibson, *Sacrifice and Sharing;* Sellato, *Nomads of the Borneo Rainforest.*

10. Macdonald, *Uncultural Behavior,* 12.

11. Palawan do not have an elaborated system of clans, lineages, or ranks. Like much of Southeast Asia, individuals reckon genealogy bilaterally and with few exceptions have a shallow historical memory of specific ancestors.

12. Different Palawan people have told me different things about the history of polygamy in their communities. Some say it has always been an acceptable if relatively rare practice, others that it has been more common recently. What's certain is that it is stigmatized among Christian lowlanders and increasingly among Palawan men and women who convert to Christianity or live alongside Christians.

13. It seems that the ethnogenesis of the Penimusan is following a similar pattern to that of the Molbog people of Balabac Island, who were once a Palawan subgroup but became increasingly distinct through intensive contacts with Muslim traders and settlers beginning in the eighteenth century. See Blanchetti-Revelli, "Sea Harvesters, Traders, and Corporations."

14. Macdonald, *Uncultural Behavior.*

15. Customary law experts are referred to variously as *memimitsara, panglima,* and *menunukum. Panglima* is clearly derived from the Sulu sultanate—a trace of that state's influence on Palawan social organization.

16. Macdonald, *Uncultural Behavior.*

17. Macdonald, "Kinship and Fellowship among the Palawan."

18. This is a pseudonym. My residence in the village was punctuated by trips to the provincial capital and, on occasion, other regions. I typically spent two to five weeks in the village at a time.

19. *Barangay* are the smallest administrative units in the Philippines. In rural areas, villages and hamlets within *barangay* are referred to as *sitio.* In urban areas, *barangay* are subdivided into *purok.* Some rural *sitios* are organized as *purok*, which can elect a representative to liaise with the *barangay* council but do not have formal political authority.

20. Such distinctions were generally of minor significance in daily life. When they did become significant, it was usually as an exonym. For example, one Palawan might refer to another (most likely not to the person's face) as a "downstream person" (*taw't napan*) to emphasize how the person had strayed from Palawan traditions. Someone might be referred

to as "really an upstream person" (*taw't daya banar*) to emphasize their avoidance of outsiders. I also found that Palawan in one area often expressed varying sentiments of trust and fellowship with Palawan in other areas. Many people in the Malambunga area said that Palawan in Iraan and Ilog-Ilog were trustworthy and "just like us," whereas those in Ransang and on the eastern side of the mountains were prone to sorcery and violence. Such stereotyping, I believe, is mostly an index of familiarity, with the nearer Palawan subgroups more likely to be trusted than those farther away. In some cases, these views had interpersonal origins. One woman told me that she would never travel to the eastern side of the mountains because her father had died after being poisoned during a visit there (presumably through sorcery).

21. When I first arrived in the village, they had separate stores that competed. This soon proved financially unviable, so they combined them. Although they helped each other out here and there with everyday chores, like tending the swidden and fishing, they lived separately in many ways. They frequently shared food but rarely ate together. They maintained separate swiddens and separate finances.

22. Many people in rural Palawan believe that the Japanese hid gold in the mountains during World War II, and apparently some foreigners believe this as well. I met a German man who said he had brought a metal detector with him when he first came to the area in hopes of finding buried treasure.

23. For the record, Isu claimed that he would not want the title since it meant having to deal with outsiders all the time.

24. Republic of the Philippines, *Republic Act 1888*.

25. Eder, *On the Road to Tribal Extinction,* 170.

26. At this point, the regulation of non-Christian minorities was bifurcated so that Muslim minority groups were dealt with by one agency (Southern Philippine Development Authority, which later became the Ministry of Muslim Affairs) and tribal minorities (i.e., those once known as pagans by the Spanish and Americans) by another (PANAMIN).

27. Eder and McKenna, "Minorities in the Philippines," 61.

28. Presidential Decree 1414, 1978.

29. In 1974–1975, for example, PANAMIN was dispatched to Mountain Province to try and convince the Kalinga and other Indigenous groups to cease their tireless opposition to the Chico Dam. Ironically, the movement against the Chico Dam was pivotal for galvanizing support for the legal recognition of Indigenous rights in the postauthoritarian period, as I discuss later. Griffin, "National Policy on Minority Cultural Communities"; Rocamora, "The Political Uses of PANAMIN."

30. Headland, *The Tasaday Controversy*.

31. Fay, *Counter-Insurgency and Tribal Peoples in the Philippines;* Griffin, "National Policy on Minority Cultural Communities"; Rocamora, "The Political Uses of PANAMIN."

32. Presidential Proclamation 219, 1967.

33. Presidential Decree 705, 1975.

34. McDermott, "Invoking Community," 101.

35. Gatmaytan, "A Critical Appraisal of the Social Forestry Program," 10.

36. As discussed elsewhere, my Palawan hosts did not use this term to signify the superiority of the Americans or any other groups to whom they have become *sibilais*. Rather, they used it to mean "accustomed to" or "fluent in the ways of."

37. Eder, *A Generation Later,* 31.

38. Chapter 3 offers an analysis of how this episode has become part of Palawan narratives about the accountabilities of environmental change.

39. Covering 125,647 hectares, the new municipality was first named for Marcos but was renamed Rizal in 1988.

40. Dressler, *Old Thoughts in New Ideas;* Fox et al., "Policies, Political-Economy, and Swidden in Southeast Asia."

41. Montefrio, "Land Control Dynamics and Social-Ecological Transformations"; Smith, *Mountains of Blame.*

42. Eder provides a contrasting example from more heavily logged parts of northern Palawan. Eder, *Migrants to the Coasts.*

43. Arquiza et al., "From Barter Trade to Brad Pitt's Bed"; Lacuna-Richman, "Subsistence Strategies of an Indigenous Minority"; McDermott, "Boundaries and Pathways."

44. Fox, *Religion and Society among the Tagbanuwa.*

45. Charbonneau, *Civilizational Imperatives;* Eder, "Muslim Palawan Diversity and Difference."

46. Macdonald, *Uncultural Behavior,* 15; Whitehead, *Exploration of Mount Kinabalu.*

47. Palawan refer to all Christian settlers with the collective demonym for people from the Visayas.

48. Rico, "Civil Society Groups and the Legislative Process."

49. "Cultural community" and "tribe" remain in wide usage, but they are usually modified by "Indigenous." The Tagalog word *katutubo* is considered to be synonymous with Indigenous. Gatmaytan, "Advocacy as Translation"; Rico, "Civil Society Groups and the Legislative Process."

50. Erni, *The Concept of Indigenous Peoples in Asia.*

51. Hilhorst, *The Real World of NGOs.*

52. Article XII, Section 2.

53. Eder and McKenna, "Minorities in the Philippines," 62.

54. McDermott, "Boundaries and Pathways," 110.

55. McDermott identifies these groups as the Cordilleran People's Alliance and the Indigenous People's Federation of the Philippines. McDermott, "Boundaries and Pathways," 110.

56. McDermott, "Boundaries and Pathways," 113.

57. See McDermott for a detailed account of how Certificates of Ancestral Domain Claim were implemented in Palawan. McDermott, "Boundaries and Pathways," 109–114.

58. Eder and McKenna, "Minorities in the Philippines," 66.

59. Philippine law distinguishes between ancestral *land* and ancestral *domain,* resulting in Certification of Ancestral Land Claims and Titles in addition to ancestral domain counterparts. The difference is that land claims/titles can be awarded to "individuals, families or class," while the domains can only be awarded to "Indigenous cultural communities." Land claims and land titles, moreover, only cover the land itself, not the resources contained there.

60. This personal communication was relayed to me by Maria Paz Luna.

61. Gatmaytan, "Advocacy as Translation."

62. Republic of the Philippines, *Republic Act 8371,* chapter 2, section 3, emphasis added.

63. These classes of rights are elaborated as follows. (1) Rights to "ancestral domains," including attendant rights to ownership of land and resources, to self-determination in the development and management of the same, to regulate the entry of outsiders, to refuse

displacement, and to have certain individually owned agricultural lands classified as alienable and disposable. (2) Rights to "self-governance and empowerment," including attendant rights to maintain customary juridical institutions (within the bounds of national laws and human rights), to form their own local governments in areas where they are the minority, and to participate in political decision making at all levels (including mandatory Indigenous representation in all legislative and policy-making bodies). (3) Rights to "social justice and human rights," including attendant rights to basic services, to culturally appropriate education, to equal opportunity in employment, and to equal opportunity for women and youth. (4) Rights to "cultural integrity," including attendant rights to legal protection of distinctive cultural traditions, knowledge systems, ceremonial practices, and biological and genetic resources.

64. Free and prior informed consent is defined as "consensus of all members of the ICCs/IPs to be determined in accordance with their respective customary laws and practices, free from any external manipulation, interference and coercion, and obtained after fully disclosing the intent and scope of the activity, in a language and process understandable to the community."

65. Theriault, "The Micropolitics of Indigenous Environmental Movements."

66. Theriault, "Environmental Politics."

67. Hirtz, "It Takes Modern Means to Be Traditional."

68. McDermott, "Boundaries and Pathways"; Pinto, "Contesting Frontier Lands in Palawan, Philippines."

69. Bello, "The Subversion of the Philippines' Indigenous People's Rights Act"; Ilagan, "Palawan IPs Seek to Stop Consent Process"; Lapniten, "Collusion, Corruption Allegations Hound Dam Projects."

70. Casumbal-Salazar, "The Indeterminacy of the Philippine Indigenous Subject."

71. Eder, *Migrants to the Coasts;* Kummer, "Deforestation in the Philippines, 1950–2000."

72. Hammond, "Asia-Pacific Forestry Sector Outlook Study."

73. For example, a REDD+ carbon offset program was implemented in central Palawan. Dressler et al., "REDD Policy Impacts on Indigenous Property Rights Regimes on Palawan Island."

74. Ilagan, "7M Hectares of Philippine Land Are Forested."

75. This program sought to consolidate and expand several DENR initiatives, including its supervision of ancestral domain claims and the Integrated Social Forestry Program it inherited from the Marcos administration. Through community-based forest management agreements, rural communities can obtain twenty-five-year leases to public forest land in exchange for serving as stewards. These agreements rarely allow logging, but they do facilitate access to permits for selling forest products.

76. The DENR also reported for 2022 that it recognized forty-eight integrated forestry management agreements, covering some 470,023 hectares.

77. Cagalanan, "Governance Challenges in Community-Based Forest Management in the Philippines"; Pulhin and Tapia, "Devolving Bundles of Rights or Bundles of Responsibilities?"

78. It is important not to oversimplify the thrust of reforms after 1986. Though some have favored progressive agendas, such as recognizing Indigenous rights and conserving biodiversity, others have continued to favor extractive industries and the powerful vested interests that promote them. In 1995, environmentalists, along with economic nationalists, were outraged when the government passed a mining act that encourages large-scale, privately owned

mining operations on public land, including by foreign-owned corporations, and imposes relatively low taxes on mining revenue.

79. Republic of the Philippines, *Republic Act 7586.*

80. Igoe, Neves, and Brockington, "A Spectacular Eco-Tour around the Historic Bloc."

81. Though I did not mention it, foreign and domestic NGOs, often supported by international funding, played a pivotal role in lobbying for ancestral domain policy and carrying out its implemented.

82. Bryant, "Non-Governmental Organizations and Governmentality," 274.

83. Dressler, *Old Thoughts in New Ideas;* Minter, "The Agta of the Northern Sierra Madre."

84. Republic of the Philippines, *Republic Act 7586.*

85. In 2018, the Duterte administration signed into law an expanded version of the NIPAS Act, adding ninety-four new protected areas to those specifically listed under NIPAS (see Republic of the Philippines, *Republic Act 11038*). It also delisted or excluded some, including five in Palawan, thereby eliminating the island from the act entirely. The Mount Mantalingahan Protected Landscape was among those excluded. This was widely seen as a concession to mining companies and other powerful interests looking to remove barriers to extractive development. Nevertheless, the presidential proclamations that created Mantalingahan and other protected areas in Palawan remain in place. For this reason, their status has not effectively changed even as it remains somewhat ambiguous.

86. Austin and Eder, "Environmentalism, Development, and Participation."

87. Funding for a second phase of this project (1990–1999) came from the Asian Development Bank.

88. The SEP defines sustainable development as improvement in the quality of life of the present and future generations through the complementation of development and environmental protection activities.

89. Several other NGOs, including Legal Assistance for Indigenous Filipinos, the Indigenous People's Apostolate, and Haribon-Palawan were also involved in ancestral domain delineation. Funding sources for these activities came from an array of international funders, including USAID (Biodiversity Conservation Network), the Vienna Institute for Development and Cooperation, the International Union for the Conservation of Nature, and the European Union (Philippine Tropical Forest Protection Program).

90. Pinto, "Contesting Frontier Lands in Palawan."

91. The combined ancestral domain includes some 15,092.88 hectares. See Pinto, "Contesting Frontier Lands in Palawan."

92. Although the DENR is officially responsible for Mantalingahan, the park's establishment and management have depended heavily on the work and funding of Conservation International.

93. The title of the grant was "Building the Governance Structure and Strengthening Inter-LGU Collaborative Conservation and Resource Management Initiatives in Mt. Mantalingahan Protected Landscape," and it amounted to US$498,799.

94. See Minter, "The Agta of the Northern Sierra Madre."

95. Minter, "The Agta of the Northern Sierra Madre"; Hagen and Minter, "Displacement in the Name of Development."

96. In 2012, house posts could be sold for PHP3.00–20.00 (US$0.07–0.47) depending on their girth. Charcoal could be sold in town for PHP45.00–50.00 (US$1.05–1.16) per sack. A full day's labor earned PHP100.00–200.00 (US$2.32–4.65). A kilogram of almaciga (of which

a single collection trip could yield fifteen to fifty kilograms) could be sold for PHP10.00–14.00 (US$0.23–0.33) depending on the quality and point of sale. Rare finds of "class A" or "export-quality" almaciga could bring up to PHP20.00 (US$0.54) per kilogram. Dollar equivalents were approximated based on the prevailing exchange rate at the time: 43.00 PHP = US$1.00.

97. Li, *Land's End;* Tsing, "Natural Resources and Capitalist Frontiers"; Tsing, "Contingent Commodities."

98. Kummer stresses that estimates of forest cover, particularly for the past twenty years, are very rough estimates. He writes, "As of 2003, the situation for national forest cover in the Philippines is as follows: 1. it would appear that no one in the world knows how much forest cover there is and whether it is increasing or decreasing; [and] 2. regardless of the first point, everyone involved with environmental issues in the Philippines is convinced that forests are continuing to decrease." Kummer, "Deforestation in the Philippines, 1950–2000," 313; Ilagan, "7M Hectares of Philippine Land Are Forested."

99. Palawan Council for Sustainable Development, *State the Environment.*

100. Esquire Philippines, "Palawan Leads Deforestation in the Philippines."

101. Eder, "Deforestation and Detribalization in the Philippines."

Chapter 3. Civets, Saplings, and Sweating Rocks

1. He spoke Tagalog to Palaya. Her responses combined Tagalog and Palawan in a manner she knew he would comprehend because he visited the village regularly.

2. Minter, "The Agta of the Northern Sierra Madre"; Novellino, "'Talking about Kultura and Signing Contracts.'"

3. Forsyth and Walker define environmental narratives as "simplified explanations of environmental cause and effect that emerge in contexts where environmental knowledge and social order are mutually dependent." Forsyth and Walker, *Forest Guardians, Forest Destroyers.*

4. Fairhead and Leach, *Misreading the African Landscape.*

5. Forsyth and Walker, *Forest Guardians, Forest Destroyers.*

6. Perez, "Living with the Problem of National Parks"; Perez, *Green Entanglements.*

7. Geertz, *The Interpretation of Cultures;* see Carrier and Miller, *Virtualism.*

8. Alatout, "Towards a Bio-Territorial Conception of Power."

9. Perez, "Living with the Problem of National Parks."

10. See Milne, *Corporate Nature.*

11. Montefrio, "State versus Indigenous Peoples' Rights."

12. Paredes, "Preserving 'Tradition'"; Theriault, "Unravelling the Strings Attached."

13. Tsing, *In the Realm of the Diamond Queen.*

14. See Cepek, "Foucault in the Forest."

15. During the speeches, I was being questioned by the local police, so unfortunately I was not able to document in detail what was said. The police had heard that a foreigner was living in the village and were taking the opportunity to find out why. I made many courtesy calls at the beginning of my research, but I had not visited the police station. Lesson learned.

16. Scott, *Domination and the Arts of Resistance.*

17. Dressler, *Old Thoughts in New Ideas.*

18. Lynch, "Native Title, Private Right and Tribal Land Law"; Lynch, "Concepts and Strategies for Promoting Legal Recognition."

19. In chapter 2, I touched on the global political-economic context of this shift.

20. Cuasay, "Indigenizing Law or Legalizing Governmentality?"

21. Dressler, *Old Thoughts in New Ideas.*

22. Cuasay, "Indigenizing Law or Legalizing Governmentality?"; Dressler, *Old Thoughts in New Ideas.*

23. Gatmaytan, "Advocacy as Translation."

24. Bryant, *Nongovernmental Organizations in Environmental Struggles;* Cuasay, "Indigenizing Law or Legalizing Governmentality?"

25. Montefrio, "State versus Indigenous Peoples' Rights"; Tsing, "Agrarian Allegory and Global Futures."

26. Lands that have occupied for more than thirty years before the decree's issuance were exempt from the 18 percent rule; however, the occupant had to be eligible for a free patent under the Public Land Act. Indigenous rights were not a consideration.

27. The zoning scheme, known as the Environmentally Critical Areas Network, was established by the Palawan Council for Sustainable Development. This special regulatory body was founded in 1992 with assistance from the European Union. It exists only in Palawan and duplicates many of the functions of the DENR. I delve deeper into this matter in chapter 4.

28. Cuasay, "Indigenizing Law or Legalizing Governmentality?"

29. Cuasay, "Indigenizing Law or Legalizing Governmentality?"

30. Cuasay, "Indigenizing Law or Legalizing Governmentality?," 72.

31. In the 2010 management plan for Mantalingahan, these recognized ancestral domains included seven Certificates of Ancestral Land Claim and two Certificates of Ancestral Domain Claim. An additional four ancestral land claims were listed as "pending" in the Mantalingahan management plan. The plan omits one ancestral domain title, which was pending at the time. Legally speaking, ancestral claims are different from ancestral titles insofar as the former were awarded before the passage of IPRA under a 1993 DENR administrative order (DENR DAO 02 1993).

32. Each officially recognized Certificate of Ancestral Domain Claim or Certificate of Ancestral Domain Title has a corresponding management plan or sustainable development and protection plan, which codifies customary law and sets out regulations for land tenure and use of natural resources.

33. See also Büscher, Dressler, and Fletcher, *Nature Inc.;* Fletcher, *Failing Forward;* Milne, *Corporate Nature.*

34. Nader, "Controlling Process"; see also Dietrich, "Coercive Harmony, Deep Capture and Environmental Justice."

35. See also Austin and Eder, "Environmentalism, Development, and Participation"; Novellino and Dressler, "The Role of 'Hybrid' NGOs."

36. For insightful analyses of how the mining industry uses legal frameworks like IPRA to suppress Indigenous dissent, see Asuncion et al., "Challenging the Binary of Home vs. Host State Governance"; Simbulan, "Indigenous Communities' Resistance to Corporate Mining in the Philippines."

37. For similar circumstances in Cambodia, see Milne, "Under the Leopard's Skin."

38. Montefrio, "State versus Indigenous Peoples' Rights."

39. Scott, *Weapons of the Weak.*

40. For more on why these strategies matter, see Rubis and Theriault, "Concealing Protocols."

41. The root of *keedatan* is *adat,* a term used in different parts of the Malay-speaking work most often in reference to customary law. Palawan use *adat* and its collective or plural

derivation *keedatan* to describe Palawan customary law and Palawan culture in a more general sense. When used in the singular, it refers to the personality or moral character of an individual. See Macdonald, *Uncultural Behavior.*

42. KSK stands for Kilusan Sagip Kalikasan (Nature Rescue Movement), PNNI for Palawan NGO Network, and ELAC for Environmental Legal Assistance Center.

43. I subsequently checked and photographed the notice in the municipal hall. It turned out to be a poster aiming to raise awareness of the Wildlife Act. It did not address Indigenous rights or land claims. Officials in the municipal DENR office referred me to their provincial office, although they said they thought "traditional" hunting practices were exempted from the Wildlife Act of 2001 (Republic Act 9147). I asked various members of the Mantalingahan management board about the legalities of hunting pig and other game. All of them said, in essence, that Palawan were legally permitted to hunt, as long as they did so for subsistence purposes only (i.e., no selling game) and used traditional equipment (i.e., no firearms or other modern tools). One official said they could hunt for ritual purposes and then imitated Palawan dancing. When I asked her which of their rituals involve pig hunting or pig meat, she referred vaguely to the ritual offering of pig meat.

44. *Meyaqat* and *menunga*—the terms Bordo used to describe Manila and Palawan, respectively—have both aesthetic and moral implications.

45. For a perceptive account of the aftermath of this period, see Abinales, "Asia's Last People's War."

46. I was not the only one who came away with this lesson. After Bordo finished, a couple of men who had been listening (whom I had not met before) made it a point to speak with me. They told me that Bordo was right about the rebels and the ancestral domain—that it was important to keep outsiders from taking their land and resources. They also wanted me to know that they did not agree with Bordo's implied support for a ban on hunting birds. Bordo had spoken against selling birds, but he had not defended hunting birds in the same manner as hunting pigs. The men were eager to ensure that I would record bird hunting as a "traditional" practice, alongside pig hunting.

47. Casumbal-Salazar, "The Indeterminacy of the Philippine Indigenous Subject"; Cooke and Johari, "Positioning of Murut and Bajau Identities"; Paredes, "Between Rights Protection and Development Aggression."

48. The NGO that recognized Bordo was NATRIPAL (United Tribes of Palawan), which has been very active in helping its member associations obtain ancestral domains, including the one that Bordo's association oversees. At the time of my research, Bordo considered himself and his association to be members of NATRIPAL, but key NATRIPAL personnel had distanced themselves from him.

49. Padwe, *Disturbed Forests, Fragmented Memories.*

50. Parnell, "Story-Telling and Social Change."

51. "Kabisayaan" is the collective form of the demonym "Bisaya," which denotes people from the Visayas region of the central Philippines. Despite denoting a particular ethnolinguistic region, "Kabisayaan" is the term the Palawan use to refer to all Christian Filipinos.

52. The precise identity of these powerful beings varied from one speaker to another. Some said that *empuq it nagbaal* (the creator) or *empuq it nagsalad* (the weaver) would punish Palawan for their transgressions. Others said they did not know or that it could be various deities, such as those that control *barat* (the southwest monsoon) or the wind.

53. Smith, "Weather from Incest"; Smith, *Mountains of Blame.*

54. In this respect, my findings parallel those of Smith, who argues that Palawan on the eastern side of the Mantalingahan range blame their own moral decline, particularly incest, for ecological disruption. Unlike Smith, I found a clear attribution of this moral decline to the influence of the Kabisayaan, their role in deforestation, and their efforts to ban swidden and other Palawan livelihood practices. Smith, *Mountains of Blame.*

55. Palawan frequently referred to fertilizer and pesticide as examples of the "medicine" (*ubat*) the Kabisayaan used to protect themselves from the consequences of their ethical faults. Some also referred to more mysterious forms of "magic" (*kependayan*) they suspected the Kabisayaan of having. For insight into Palawan cosmology and associated practices, see Macdonald, *Uncultural Behavior;* Revel, "Corps en jeu (je) ou la chasse généralisée."

56. See also Macdonald, *Uncultural Behavior;* Revel, *Fleurs de paroles.*

57. Doolittle, *Property and Politics in Sabah;* Perez, *Green Entanglements.*

58. Doane, *Stealing Shining Rivers;* Rubis and Theriault, "Concealing Protocols"; West, *Conservation Is Our Government Now.*

59. Casumbal-Salazar, "The Indeterminacy of the Philippine Indigenous Subject."

60. Forsyth and Walker, *Forest Guardians, Forest Destroyers;* see also Dove, "Indigenous People and Environmental Politics"; Theriault, "Unravelling the Strings Attached."

61. Bryant, "Politicized Moral Geographies."

62. Neimark et al., "Not Just Participation."

63. See Alatout, "Towards a Bio-Territorial Conception of Power."

64. Mathews, *Instituting Nature.*

65. Cepek, "Foucault in the Forest"; Li, *Land's End;* Padwe, *Disturbed Forests, Fragmented Memories.*

66. The concept of metis is from Scott, *Seeing like the State.* For an example of how Indigenous ecological epistemologies and related practices differ radically from those of settler-colonial bureaucracy in Canada, see Nadasdy, *Hunters and Bureaucrats.*

67. George, "Lyric, History, and Allegory."

Chapter 4. Forest Dreams, Conservation Fantasies

1. The title for this chapter was inspired by Langston, *Forest Dreams, Forest Nightmares.*

2. According to Charles Macdonald's Palawan-English-Tagalog dictionary, Palawan in other areas also use the words *penglek* and *bangungut* to refer to this kind of nightmare. See https://philippines.sil.org/resources/works_in_progress/palawan/dictionary.

3. My Palawan hosts described people, including other-than-human persons, as having multiple *kurudwa,* some associated with particular parts of the body, such as the head, heart, and feet. See also Macdonald, *Uncultural Behavior.*

4. Sobrevila, "The Role of Indigenous Peoples in Biodiversity Conservation."

5. Tsing, "Becoming a Tribal Elder and Other Green Development Fantasies."

6. "Ontology" refers to a person or group's theory of physical and metaphysical existence. Many readers will be familiar with the ontological theory that our material existence is composed of atomic and subatomic particles, such as neutrons, protons, electrons, quarks, bosons. Many will recognize the basic ontological principles that animals and plants are alive, but rocks and robots are not; that our waking experiences are real, while our dreamed ones are not; and that "forces of nature," such as the weather, are universal to all human societies, while supernatural or paranormal ones like ghosts are culturally specific. Ontological theories do not

operate in isolation. They are connected to related cosmological theories, which concern the nature of the cosmos or universe. Many readers will be familiar with the cosmology that considers Earth a planet in our solar system, with all that this outlook entails for understanding the origins of the universe and the place of our planet in it. Some may also be familiar with the proposition that we live in a pluriverse or multiverse made up of "parallel" or "interwoven" universes. Such propositions are not just fodder for academic debates but have inspired innumerable works of speculative fiction, visual art, and public theology. Even so, I would hazard to guess that a large majority of those reading this book go about their daily lives tacitly accepting that we live on a planet that orbits a sun as part of a solar system, galaxy, and universe, all exploded into existence by a "big bang" billions of years ago. Not everyone agrees with these ideas—hello, biblical literalists. Still, many societies today use them as the basis for mainstream educational curriculum, scientific research, and infrastructures as varied as power plants, hospitals, agriculture, and space flight. These ideas are, in fact, theories rather than uncontestable, God-given facts. They have emerged historically and will always reflect the societal contexts in which they are proposed, debated, and enacted. Because ontological and cosmological theories often entail and reinforce one another, I often refer to them together as onto-cosmological theories.

7. For discussions of how different Palawan communities understand and interact with these beings, see Dressler, Smith, and Montefrio, "Ungovernable?"; Macdonald, *Uncultural Behavior;* Montefrio, "Cooperation and Resistance"; Novellino, "Palawan Attitudes toward Illness"; Revel, "Kudaman"; Revel, "The 'Gifts of the Weaver.'"

8. See also Novellino, "Sacrificing People for the Trees."

9. The word "traditional" is problematic, to the say the least. I use it here to describe those beliefs and practices that Palawan people themselves presented as having existed since time immemorial. Every belief and practice has a history of emergence and change, even if that history is repressed or not recoverable. What "traditional" signifies is not a primordial, never-changing set of beliefs or practices but a historical horizon against which Palawan measure beliefs and practices they see as consistent with those of their ancestors and those with a more recent provenance.

10. I am indebted to Eve Tuck's discussion of "complex personhood," a concept she adapts from Avery Gordon. See Tuck, "Suspending Damage."

11. From Escobar, my use of "world making" seeks to convey the cosmological, ontological, and material dimensions of the practices in question. While I agree with Ramos's and Nadasdy's respective reminders that different societies do not somehow live in different "worlds," I take on Carrier and West's point that societies vary in terms of the world-making practices that shape their relations with themselves, others, and their surroundings. These are more than differences of culture—they are alternative ways of producing the world in relation with other beings, agents, and entities. Carrier and West, "Surrounding, Selves, and Others"; Escobar, "Thinking-Feeling with the Earth"; Nadasdy, "How Many Worlds Are There?"; Ramos, "The Politics of Perspectivism."

12. Revel presents accounts from the central highlands of Palawan that divide the cosmos into fifteen layers, seven each below and above that of the visible world. Based on his research in five geographically distinct Palawan locales, Macdonald emphasizes variation in the structure of the cosmos.

13. Macdonald, *Uncultural Behavior,* 103.

14. Although I heard varying opinions, some told me that owls like the one that attacked me are one of the forms taken by malevolent people of the forest (*taw't talun*).

15. Macdonald, *Uncultural Behavior.*

16. Macdonald, *Uncultural Behavior,* 97.

17. Although I did not document it, it is likely that Palawan experience something similar to the "moral anxiety" that Rane Willerslev observed among Siberian hunters, who treat all animals as having personhood. I did not spend enough time with Palawan who hunt regularly to speak to that question. Palawan are not animists per se, and it seems less important to them that hunted animals may be persons than that hunted animals are given to them by invisible persons. Revel describes Palawan ontology as *la chasse généralisée* or generalized hunt, in which humans are both hunter and hunted. Ultimately, this sense of a generalized hunt involving visible and invisible beings is what my analysis seeks to evoke.

18. Rappaport, *Pigs for the Ancestors.*

19. Nadasdy, "The Gift in the Animal."

20. Blaser, "Ontological Conflicts and the Stories of Peoples in Spite of Europe"; Cadena, *Earth Beings;* Cadena and Blaser, *A World of Many Worlds;* Povinelli, *Geontologies;* Viveiros de Castro, "Perspectival Anthropology and the Method of Controlled Equivocation."

21. Nadasdy, "The Gift in the Animal," 26.

22. Nadasdy, "The Gift in the Animal," 36.

23. Latour, *Reassembling the Social.*

24. Nadasdy, "How Many Worlds Are There?"; see also Barad, *Meeting the Universe Halfway;* Mol, *The Body Multiple.*

25. Theriault, "A Forest of Dreams."

26. Nadasdy, "How Many Worlds Are There?," 358; see also Bessire and Bond, "Ontological Anthropology and the Deferral of Critique"; Ramos, "The Politics of Perspectivism"; Todd, "An Indigenous Feminist's Take on the Ontological Turn."

27. Nadasdy, "How Many Worlds Are There?," 358

28. See Blaser, "Ontological Conflicts and the Stories of Peoples in Spite of Europe."

29. A *barangay* is the smallest administrative unit in the Philippines. Each province (*probinsiya* or *lalawigan*) is divided into municipalities (*munisipyo* or *bayan*) and/or cities (*siyudad* or *lungsod*), and each municipality and city is divided into *barangay,* for which ward or district is the closest US equivalent.

30. A vast majority of Mantalingahan is classified as "core zone," in which no human "disruption" is supposed to occur. Another 20.4 percent is classified as restricted, controlled, or traditional use zone. In chapter 1, I noted the inherent contradiction in the notion that so much of a "landscape" could be made off-limits to "human disruption."

31. Our conversation was in Palawan except for where I used Tagalog words in place of words I did not know.

32. Nadasdy, *Hunters and Bureaucrats;* Nadasdy, *Sovereignty's Entailments;* Rubis, "The Orang Utan Is Not an Indigenous Name"; Rubis and Theriault, "Concealing Protocols"; Scott, *Seeing like a State.*

33. See Campbell, *Conjuring Property;* Cronon, *Changes in the Land;* Li, "What Is Land?"; Verdery, *The Vanishing Hectare;* Wittekind and Faxon, "Networks of Speculation."

34. According to Macdonald, *lihyen* are often associated with a particular type of *taw't talun,* the Meliwanen, who are "bent on seducing normal people, causing their deaths . . . [by leading them] to be stricken by thunder or devoured by crocodiles" (Macdonald, *Uncultural Behavior,* 103).

35. A similar observation is made about Southeast Asia in Dove, Sajise, and Doolittle, *Beyond the Sacred Forest.*

36. Regarding Yukaghir shamanic practices, Willerslev (*Soul Hunters*, 139) has written, "if . . . Yukaghir shamanship is *not* a system of belief but merely a system of techniques for manipulating the environment, and that these techniques, rather than being attributes of shaman alone, are specialized forms of abilities that may be practiced by all members of society to varying degrees, then it follows that we cannot simply judge the legacy of Siberian shamanism by the presence or absence of shamans themselves."

37. Novellino, "Contrasting Landscapes, Conflicting Ontologies."

38. Wainwright and Bryan, "Cartography, Territory, Property," 156.

39. Wainwright and Bryan, "Cartography, Territory, Property," 170.

40. Wainwright and Bryan, "Cartography, Territory, Property."

41. Atleo, *Principles of Tsawalk*.

42. Cadena, "Indigenous Cosmopolitics in the Andes"; Cadena, *Earth Beings*. See also Blaser, "Ontological Conflicts and the Stories of Peoples in Spite of Europe."

43. Paredes, "Experimental Science for the 'Bananapocalypse,'" 23.

44. Lido told me this story several times, most recently in July 2012. This quotation combines two sentences from his recounting, repeated in Tagalog as he would have spoken to the settler: "May kapit bahay tayo dito" (We have a neighbor here) and "May tao dyan kahit 'di mo sila nakikita" (There are people [living] there even if you can't see them).

Chapter 5. Indigenous Rights in the Orbit of Capital

1. *Barangay* is the smallest administrative unit in the Philippines and translates roughly as village. In rural areas, *barangay* can cover significant territory, often including a main town site and numerous hamlets. Punta Baja is the municipal seat and most populous *barangay* in the municipality of Rizal. Rural municipalities in the Philippines are roughly equivalent to counties in the United States.

2. This is my translation. The original text, in Tagalog, was "Pagpapabatid.—Ito ang lupaing ninuno ng katutubong Pala'wan sa barangay Punta Baja, Rizal, Palawan.—Binabalaan na ang sinomang pumasok na walang pahintulot sa kinikilalang pinuno ng komunidad ay paparusahan ayon sa aming batas katutubo.—Mahigpit na ipinagbabawal ang pagbili ng lupa sa loob ng aming lupaing ninuno.—Ang anomang kasunduan na walang konsultasyon sa komunidad ay walang bisa."

3. In Tagalog, the plural first-person pronoun has inclusive and exclusive forms, depending on whether the speaker wishes to include their interlocutors as referents of "we" or "us." The third line of the placard contains the phrase "aming lupaing ninuno," which in effect means "our, not your, ancestral domain."

4. "Dati, yung mga Islam ang nag-organize sa amin. Ngayon, yung NCIP at mga NGO." NCIP refers to the National Commission on Indigenous Peoples.

5. Arquiza et al., "From Barter Trade to Brad Pitt's Bed."

6. This is based on a price of 28 Philippine pesos per kilogram, which was the current price paid to harvesters at the Amas cooperative at the time of writing (US$1 ~ PHP 48). For reasons explained later, the price at Amas is higher than the price paid by most other buyers in southern Palawan.

7. The Palawan people share their demonym with the name of Palawan Island. The demonym is Anglicized in various ways—Pala'wan, Palaqwan, Pinalawan, Palawano—to reflect variation among Palawan subgroups and distinguish the island from the people. I simply use

Palawan because it doesn't specify any specific subgroup. In Norli's community, the term is pronounced Pelawan.

8. For a discussion of this history, particularly as it pertains to Borneo, see Dove, *The Banana Tree at the Gate.*

9. Arquiza et al., "From Barter Trade to Brad Pitt's Bed"; Dressler, "Governed from above, below and Dammed in Between"; Eder, "Zoning Resources, Zoning People."

10. Arquiza et al., "From Barter Trade to Brad Pitt's Bed"; Razal et al., *Value Chain Study on Palawan Almaciga Resin.*

11. Although I saw many Palawan use small amounts of almaciga to get their fires started in the morning, most of those I consulted saw it primarily as a commodity to be collected and sold.

12. Arquiza et al., "From Barter Trade to Brad Pitt's Bed," 158.

13. See McDermott, "Boundaries and Pathways." During my fieldwork, I saw some potentially overtapped trees in lower-elevation almaciga stands but not among the trees higher up in the mountains.

14. Almaciga-producing agathis trees of the sort found in Palawan can grow up to sixty-five meters tall (Arquiza et al., "From Barter Trade to Brad Pitt's Bed"). They are coniferous evergreens but do not have needle-shaped leaves.

15. Fabro, "A Philippine Resin Trade Proves Sustainable for Forests."

16. In 2019, 740 metric tons of almaciga were collected for commercial purposes in the Philippines, all in Palawan; in 2021, the total was 414 metric tons. These numbers reflect only what was reported to the Department of Environment and Natural Resources and are likely lower than the actual amounts collected. Department of Environment and Natural Resources, "Philippine Forestry Statistics 2019"; Department of Environment and Natural Resources, "Philippine Forestry Statistics 2021"; Fabro, "A Philippine Resin Trade Proves Sustainable for Forests."

17. Tsing, "Contingent Commodities."

18. Tsing, "Contingent Commodities," 29.

19. This is a close paraphrase of observations an elderly Palawan couple shared with me in July 2011.

20. This advantage only holds when wage labor is occasional and almaciga collection trips yield at least fifteen kilos per day of collection. With yields and trip length absolutely limited by what a person can carry and how long they can stay away from home, even maximal almaciga collection would be less remunerative than steady wage employment over a significant stretch of time.

21. Macdonald, "Kinship and Fellowship among the Palawan."

22. Although this remained true in the far south of Palawan as recently as 2019, it was not necessarily the case in the north, where tappers of migrant and Indigenous ethnic backgrounds have caused widespread tree mortality by overtapping. See Palawan Center for Appropriate Rural Technology, "Constraints and Potentials for Livelihood in Selected Mt. Mantalingahan Communities."

23. Arquiza et al., "From Barter Trade to Brad Pitt's Bed."

24. Latour, *Reassembling the Social.*

25. Bordo died in 2017. I am forever grateful to him for his kindness during my research, even as I was living with his bitter rival.

26. The NGO was Haribon-Palawan. Also as a result of this incident, fourteen Haribon-Palawan personnel were detained and investigated for "subversion." Human Rights Watch, "The Philippines Human Rights and Forest Management in 1990s."

27. McDermott, "Boundaries and Pathways"; Pinto, "Contesting Frontier Lands in Palawan."

28. McDermott, "Boundaries and Pathways," 94–96.

29. McDermott, "Boundaries and Pathways," points out that NTFP markets in Southeast Asia have been controlled for centuries by regional traders who use middlemen and debt to control local populations of collectors. While she is right in this respect, it is important to keep in mind the extent to which more recent changes have undermined traditional subsistence practices and thus made local collectors like the Palawan increasingly dependent on selling forest products to meet their basic needs. This distinction is also acknowledged by Dove, *The Banana Tree at the Gate,* in his effort to show the ancientness of upland swiddeners' involvement in commodity markets as a supplement to their subsistence practices.

30. Although several different international funders were sponsoring ancestral domain delineation in Palawan (see chapter 3), the USAID-affiliated Biodiversity Conservation Network furnished the organizational model employed for the Ancestral Domain in Rizal and at numerous other sites where NATRIPAL had member organizations.

31. Pinto, "Contesting Frontier Lands in Palawan," 71.

32. Cuasay, "Indigenizing Law or Legalizing Governmentality?"; Dressler, "Green Governmentality and Swidden Decline."

33. Pinto, "Contesting Frontier Lands in Palawan," 73–74, 132.

34. The successor to Jimi's father, a Palawan man reportedly brought by the government from a different area, was not hostile to the Ancestral Domain, but he did not participate in it directly.

35. In recent years, the NCIP has moved away from the title of chieftain in favor of *panglima. Panglima* was itself an import from the Sulu sultanate, but it has since become an Indigenous term for experts in customary law, who are also variously referred to as *manunukum* and *memimitsara.* Whatever the title, the role of state-recognized leaders is largely that of a spokesperson and representative who attends meetings, signs documents, and organizes consultations. (I am using masculine pronouns because at least in Rizal, all of the chieftains are male.) When non-Palawan people need to obtain free and prior informed consent for a project in an ancestral domain or want to buy land from a Palawan person, they go to the NCIP-recognized chieftain or *panglima* for the area in question. Their jurisdiction extends over a particular territorial unit, within which they are supposed to organize a tribal council consisting of *panglima.* Often this unit corresponds with that of the *barangay,* with each *panglima* being drawn from a different *sitio* or village. According to the Indigenous Peoples' Rights Act and derivative administrative guidelines, the NCIP is supposed to recognize Indigenous leaders according to the customary laws and practices of the communities they represent. Recognized leaders are not, therefore, supposed to be given authority beyond what they would normally have under customary law. Any agreements they make with the government or others are supposed to be valid only insofar as they are made in accordance with customary decision-making procedures. The intention of IPRA, as with many multiculturalist policies of recognition, is to give legal recognition to a political arrangement that already exists in customary form. For the Palawan, this presents a real dilemma. Palawan did not traditionally have hereditary leaders with territorial jurisdiction or councils of elders constituted as such. Instead, they had networks of kin, among whom particular individuals achieved varying degrees of renown for their expertise in customary law, shamanic healing, or both. One might learn such skills from a parent or elder, but the notion of inherited authority was

fundamentally foreign to Palawan egalitarianism. There was no enduring corporate entity (such as a clan system) outside the nuclear household unit. Juridical authority involved persuasion and reconciliation, not punitive rulings.

36. In my experience, Palawan people tended to express matters of personal autonomy in idioms of desire and refusal, rather than those of freedom and oppression.

37. For similar findings in Kalimantan, see Tsing, *In the Realm of the Diamond Queen.*

38. Palawan refer to any Christian settler as a *Bisaya* (plural: *Kabisayaan*), the demonym for those from the Visayan Islands, regardless of where the settler in question might trace their origin. They also use it as a metonym for the Philippine state and society. See the introduction for a fuller definition of the term.

39. Foucault, *Security, Territory, Population,* 48–49.

40. Povinelli, *Economies of Abandonment.*

41. Pinto, "Contesting Frontier Lands in Palawan."

42. The right to tap particular clusters of agathis is passed down within families. This is not a property right but a usufruct right dependent on proper care of the trees. Because people sometimes move away from their ancestral areas and rights to trees are sometimes transferred, some Palawan adults living in almaciga-producing areas do not have any trees under their care.

43. For the highest-quality "tipak" class of almaciga, which comprises large chunks of milky white resin without debris, harvesters are paid P30/kg, and this is sold to the factory for P51/kg. Class A, which includes more fragmented pieces of high-quality tipak and minimal debris, is bought for P28 and sold for P46. Proceeds from these sales cover the cooperative's operating costs (weighing, bagging, record-keeping, permits, taxes, etc.). The factory provides shipping from Amas, and this cost is reflected in the price it pays.

44. The regional branch of the DENR issues permits for forest products, but permit applicants must first obtain clearances from the *barangay* and municipal councils as well as NCIP. The DENR's permits only last one year, and the process is notoriously slow and complicated, often requiring technical support from NGOs.

45. Dove, *The Banana Tree at the Gate.*

46. Dove, *The Banana Tree at the Gate,* 17.

47. See also Paredes, "More Indigenous than Others."

48. Povinelli, *Cunning of Recognition.*

49. Nadasdy, "Boundaries among Kin," 500. See also Coulthard, *Red Skin, White Masks.*

50. Simpson, *Mohawk Interruptus.*

51. Kirsch, "Juridification of Indigenous Politics."

Conclusion

1. See chapter 4 for a description of the *tabuqan.*

2. See chapter 3 for a definition of the *purok.*

3. As detailed earlier, my Palawan hosts referred to all Christian Filipino settlers as Kabisayaan (Visayans) regardless of their specific ethnic ancestry.

4. Singh, "It's Time to Rethink the Idea of the 'Indigenous.'" For a more in-depth argument with a similar conclusion, see Kuper, *The Invention of Primitive Society;* Kuper, "The Return of the Native."

5. Singh, "It's Time to Rethink the Idea of the 'Indigenous.'"

6. Singh, "It's Time to Rethink the Idea of the 'Indigenous.'"

7. Singh, "It's Time to Rethink the Idea of the 'Indigenous.'"

8. Arvin, "Analytics of Indigeneity"; Kauanui, "'A Structure, Not an Event'"; Krawec and Goring, "'Global Indigeneity'"; Yao, "Arctic and Asian Indigeneities."

9. Byrd, *The Transit of Empire.*

10. Goodale, "Dark Matter."

11. Byrd, *The Transit of Empire,* xxix–xxx.

12. Theriault et al., "Living Protocols."

13. See also Mitchell, *Revenant Ecologies.*

14. *Rurungan* roughly translates as community, in the sense of a cluster of related households that live in proximity, often due to a common elder or *pegibutan.*

Bibliography

Abinales, Patricio. *Making Mindanao: Cotabato and Davao in the Formation of the Philippine Nation-State.* Ateneo University Press, 2000.

Abinales, Patricio. "Asia's Last People's War: The Communist Insurgency in the Post-Marcos Philippines." In *The Politics of Death: Political Violence in Southeast Asia,* edited by A. Croissant, B. Martín, and S. Kneip, pp. 189–218. Lit, 2006.

Abinales, Patricio. "The U.S. Army as Occupying Force in Muslim Mindanao, 1899–1913." In *Colonial Crucible: Empire in the Making of the Modern American State,* edited by A. W. McCoy and F. A. Scarano, pp. 410–420. University of Wisconsin Press, 2009.

Agoncillo, Teodoro A. *The Revolt of the Masses. The Story of Bobifacio and the Katipunan.* University of the Philippines, 2002 [1956].

Aguilar, Filomeno V. *Clash of Spirits: The History of Power and Sugar Planter Hegemony on a Visayan Island.* University of Hawaiʻi Press, 1998.

Aguilar, Filomeno V. "The Triumph of Instrumental Citizenship? Migrations, Identities, and the Nation-State in Southeast Asia." *Asian Studies Review* 23, no. 3 (1999): 307–336.

Aguilar, Filomeno V. "What Made the Masses Revolutionary? Ignorance, Character, and Class in Teodoro Agoncillo's 'the Revolt of the Masses.'" *Philippine Studies: Historical and Ethnographic Viewpoints* 68, no. 2 (2020): 137–178.

Alatout, Samer. "Towards a Bio-Territorial Conception of Power: Territory, Population, and Environmental Narratives in Palestine and Israel." *Political Geography* 25, no. 6 (2006): 601–621.

ALDAW. Caption on "Palawan: Our Struggle for Nature and Culture." YouTube, July 25, 2012. http://www.youtube.com/watch?v=LA_3mE92RAE.

Alejandro Leal, Pablo. "Participation: The Ascendancy of a Buzzword in the Neo-Liberal Era." *Development in Practice* 17, nos. 4–5 (2007): 539–548.

Amoroso, Donna J., and Patricio N. Abinales. *State and Society in the Philippines.* Rowman & Littlefield, 2005.

Andaya, Barbara Watson, and Yoneo Ishii. "Religious Developments in Southeast Asia, c. 1500–1800." In *Cambridge History of Southeast Asia: Volume One, Part Two, from c. 1500–c. 1800,* edited by Nicholas Tarling, pp. 508–571. Cambridge University Press, 1999.

Anderson, Benedict. "Cacique Democracy in the Philippines: Origins and Dreams." *New Left Review* 169 (1988): 3–31.

Anderson, Warwick. *Colonial Pathologies: American Tropical Medicine, Race, and Hygiene in the Philippines*. Duke University Press, 2006.

Anthias, Penelope. "Indigenous Peoples and the New Extraction: From Territorial Rights to Hydrocarbon Citizenship in the Bolivian Chaco." *Latin American Perspectives* 45, no. 5 (2018): 136–153.

Aquino, Belinda A. "Rethinking Magellan and Rediscovering the Philippines." In *The Age of Discovery: Impact on Philippine Culture and Society*, edited by B. Aquino and D. T. Alegado, 2nd ed., pp. 2–5. University of Hawai'i Press, 1993.

Arquiza, Yasmin D., Cristina S. Guerrero, Augusto B. Gatmaytan, and Arlynn C. Aquino. "From Barter Trade to Brad Pitt's Bed: NTFPs and Ancestral Domains in the Philippines." In *Wild Product Governance: Finding Policies That Work*, edited by S. A. Laird, R. McLain, and R. P. Wynberg, pp. 155–182. Earthscan, 2010.

Arvin, Maile. "Analytics of Indigeneity." In *Native Studies Keywords*, edited by S. N. Teves, A. Smith, and M. Raheja, pp. 119–129. University of Arizona Press, 2015.

Asuncion, Angela M., John Edison T. Ubaldo, Dominique Caouette, Beverly Besmanos, and Nicolas D. Brunet. "Challenging the Binary of Home vs. Host State Governance: Canadian Transnational Mining Behavior and Local Communities in the Philippines Extractive Industry." *Extractive Industries and Society* 12 (2022): 101166.

Atleo, E. Richard Umeek. *Principles of Tsawalk: An Indigenous Approach to Global Crisis*. University of British Columbia Press, 2011.

Austin, Rebecca L., and James F. Eder. "Environmentalism, Development, and Participation on Palawan Island, Philippines." *Society & Natural Resources* 20, no. 4 (2007): 363–371.

Bankoff, Greg. "One Island Too Many: Reappraising the Extent of Deforestation in the Philippines prior to 1946." *Journal of Historical Geography* 33 (2007): 314–334.

Bankoff, Greg. "Conservation and Colonialism: Gifford Pinchot and the Birth of Tropical Forestry in the Philippines." In *Colonial Crucible: Empire in the Making of the Modern American State*, edited by A. W. McCoy and F. A. Scarano, pp. 479–488. University of Wisconsin Press, 2009.

Barad, Karen. *Meeting the Universe Halfway: Quantum Physics and the Entanglement of Matter and Meaning*. Duke University Press, 2007.

Barrera, Alfredo. *Soil Survey of Palawan Province*. Bureau of Printing, 1960.

Barrows, David P. *The Bureau of Non-Christian Tribes for the Philippine Islands: Circular of Information, Instructions for Field Workers*. Museum of Ethnology, Natural History, and Commerce, 1901.

Baviskar, Amita. *In the Belly of the River: Tribal Conflicts over Development in the Narmada Valley*. Oxford University Press, 2004.

Baviskar, Amita. "Indian Indigeneities: Adivasi Engagements with Hindu Nationalism in India." In *Indigenous Experience Today*, edited by Marisol de la Cadena, pp. 275–304. Routledge, 2007.

Beban, Alice, Sokbunthoeun So, and Kheang Un. "From Force to Legitimation: Rethinking Land Grabs in Cambodia." *Development and Change* 48, no. 3 (2017): 590–612.

Beban, Alice, and Courtney Work. "The Spirits Are Crying: Dispossessing Land and Possessing Bodies in Rural Cambodia." *Antipode* 46, no. 3 (2014): 593–610.

Bello, Walden. "How Neoliberalism Killed the Philippines' EDSA Republic." *Green Left Weekly*, June 24, 2016. https://www.greenleft.org.au/content/walden-bello-how-neoliberalism-killed-philippines-edsa-republic.

Bello, Walden. "The Subversion of the Philippines' Indigenous People's Rights Act." *Focus on the Global South* (blog), October 7, 2020. https://focusweb.org/the-subversion-of-the-philippines-indigenous-peoples-rights-act/.

Bellwood, Peter. "Southeast Asia before History." In *The Cambridge History of Southeast Asia: From Early Times to c. 1500,* vol. 1, edited by N. Tarling, pp. 55–136. Cambridge University Press, 1999.

Bender, Joshua. "The Father, the Son, and the Aswang: Uncolonial Ontologies in Philippine Literature." M.A. thesis, University of Washington, 2021. https://www.proquest.com/docview/2629315470/abstract/F8C17E27ECC74F4EPQ/1.

Benjamin, Geoffrey. "Process and Structure in Temiar Social Organization." In *Minority Cultures of Peninsular Malaysia: Survival of Indigenous Heritage,* edited by R. Razha and K. W. J. Begum, pp. 124–149. Academy of Social Sciences, 1993.

Berlant, Lauren. *Cruel Optimism.* Duke University Press, 2011.

Bessire, Lucas, and David Bond. "Ontological Anthropology and the Deferral of Critique." *American Ethnologist* 41, no. 3 (2014): 440–556. https://doi.org/10.1111/amet.12083.

Blanchetti-Revelli, Lanfranco. "Sea Harvesters, Traders, and Corporations: Local and Global Dynamics in the World Seaweed-Carrageenan Economy." PhD diss., Johns Hopkins University, 1995.

Blaser, Mario. "Ontological Conflicts and the Stories of Peoples in Spite of Europe: Toward a Conversation on Political Ontology." *Current Anthropology* 54, no. 5 (2013): 547–568.

Blaser, Mario, Harvey Feit, and Glenn McRae, eds. *In the Way of Development: Indigenous Peoples, Life Projects and Globalization.* Zed Books, 2004.

Bracking, Sarah. "Financialization and the Environmental Frontier." In *The Routledge International Handbook of Financialization,* edited by P. Mader, D. Mertens, and N. van der Zwan, pp. 213–223. Routledge, 2020.

Brewer, John. "Microhistory and the Histories of Everyday Life." *Cultural and Social History* 7, no. 1 (2010): 87–109.

Broad, Robin, and John Cavanagh. *Plundering Paradise: The Struggle for the Environment in the Philippines.* University of California Press, 1994.

Brown, Wendy. "Defending Society." In *Defending Society,* edited by E. Klinenberg, S. Marcus and C. Zaloom, pp. 225–232. Columbia University Press, 2019.

Bryant, Raymond L. "Politicized Moral Geographies: Debating Biodiversity Conservation and Ancestral Domain in the Philippines." *Political Geography* 19, no. 6 (2000): 673–705.

Bryant, Raymond L. "Non-Governmental Organizations and Governmentality: 'Consuming' Biodiversity and Indigenous People in the Philippines." *Political Studies* 50, no. 2 (2002): 268–292.

Bryant, Raymond L. *Nongovernmental Organizations in Environmental Struggles: Politics and the Making of Moral Capital in the Philippines.* Yale University Press, 2005.

Bulloch, Hannah. *In Pursuit of Progress: Narratives of Development on a Philippine Island.* University of Hawai'i Press, 2017.

Bureau of Forestry. *Annual Reports of the Director of Forestry of the Philippine Islands, 1913–1914.* Bureau of Printing, 1914.

Bureau of Forestry. *Annual Reports of the Director of Forestry of the Philippine Islands, 1915–1924.* Bureau of Printing, 1916.

Bureau of Forestry. *Annual Reports of the Director of Forestry of the Philippine Islands, 1915–1924.* Bureau of Printing, 1921.

Bureau of Forestry. *Annual Reports of the Director of Forestry of the Philippine Islands, 1915–1924.* Bureau of Printing, 1924.

Burow, Paul Berne, Samara Brock, and Michael R. Dove. "Unsettling the Land: Indigeneity, Ontology, and Hybridity in Settler Colonialism." *Environment and Society* 9 (2018): 57–74.

Büscher, Bram. "Derivative Nature: Interrogating the Value of Conservation in 'Boundless Southern Africa.'" *Third World Quarterly* 31, no. 2 (2010): 259–276.

Büscher, Bram, Wolfram Dressler, and Robert Fletcher, eds. *Nature Inc.: Environmental Conservation in the Neoliberal Age.* University of Arizona Press, 2014.

Byrd, Jodi A. *The Transit of Empire: Indigenous Critiques of Colonialism.* University of Minnesota Press, 2011.

Cadena, Marisol de la. "Indigenous Cosmopolitics in the Andes: Conceptual Reflections beyond 'Politics.'" *Cultural Anthropology* 25, no. 2 (2010): 334–370.

Cadena, Marisol de la. *Earth Beings: Ecologies of Practice across Andean Worlds.* Duke University Press, 2015.

Cadena, Marisol de la, and Mario Blaser, eds. *A World of Many Worlds.* Duke University Press, 2018.

Cagalanan, Dominique. "Governance Challenges in Community-Based Forest Management in the Philippines." *Society & Natural Resources* 28, no. 6 (2015): 609–624.

Camba, Alvin A. "From Colonialism to Neoliberalism: Critical Reflections on Philippine Mining in the 'Long Twentieth Century.'" *Extractive Industries and Society* 2, no. 2 (2015): 287–301.

Campbell, Jeremy M. *Conjuring Property: Speculation and Environmental Futures in the Brazilian Amazon.* University of Washington Press, 2015.

Candelaria, John L. "1521, Duterte, and the Politics of Commemoration in the Philippines." *Conflict, Justice, Decolonization* (blog), 2021. https://cjdproject.web.nycu.edu.tw/2021/08/20/1521-duterte-and-the-politics-of-commemoration-in-the-philippines/.

Carrier, James G., and Daniel Miller, eds. *Virtualism: A New Political Economy.* Berg, 1998.

Carrier, James G., and Paige West. "Surrounding, Selves, and Others: The Political Economy of Environment and Identity." *Landscape Research* 34, no. 2 (2009): 157–170.

Casumbal-Salazar, Melisa S. L. "The Indeterminacy of the Philippine Indigenous Subject." *Amerasia Journal* 41, no. 1 (2015): 74–94.

Cattelino, Jessica R. "The Double Bind of American Indian Need-Based Sovereignty." *Cultural Anthropology* 25, no. 2 (2010): 235–262.

Cepek, Michael L. "Foucault in the Forest: Questioning Environmentality in Amazonia." *American Ethnologist* 38, no. 3 (2011): 501–515.

Cepek, Michael L. *A Future for Amazonia: Randy Borman and Cofán Environmental Politics*. University of Texas Press, 2012.

Cepek, Michael L. "There Might Be Blood: Oil, Humility, and the Cosmopolitics of a Cofán Petro-Being." *American Ethnologist* 43, no. 4 (2016): 623–635.

Chao, Sophie. *In the Shadow of the Palms: More-than-Human Becomings in West Papua*. Duke University Press, 2022.

Charbonneau, Oliver. *Civilizational Imperatives: Americans, Moros, and the Colonial World*. Cornell University Press, 2020.

Chua, Liana, and Rusaslina Idrus. "Introduction: Unpacking Indigeneity in Southeast Asia." *Sojourn: Journal of Social Issues in Southeast Asia* 37, no. 1 (2022): 1–26.

Concepcion, Fray Juan de la. "General History of the Discalced Augustinian Fathers, Volume 5, Chapter 3, 1624." In *The Philippine Islands, 1493–1898*, vol. 21, edited by E. H. Blair and A. J. Robertson. A. H. Clark, 1904.

Cooke, Bill, and Uma Kothari, eds. *Participation: The New Tyranny?* Zed Books, 2001.

Cooke, Fadzilah Majid, and Sofia Johari. "Positioning of Murut and Bajau Identities in State Forest Reserves and Marine Parks in Sabah, East Malaysia." *Journal of Southeast Asian Studies* 50, no. 1 (2019): 129–149.

Coulthard, Glen S. *Red Skin, White Masks: Rejecting the Colonial Politics of Recognition*. University of Minnesota Press, 2014.

Cramb, R. A., Carol Colfer, Wolfram H. Dressler, Pinkaew Laungaramsri, Quang Le, Elok Mulyoutami, Nancy Peluso, and Reed Wadley. "Swidden Transformations and Rural Livelihoods in Southeast Asia." *Human Ecology* 37, no. 3 (2009): 323–346.

Cronon, William. *Changes in the Land: Indians, Colonists, and the Ecology of New England*. Hill and Wang, 1983.

Cuasay, Peter. "Indigenizing Law or Legalizing Governmentality? The Philippine Indigenous Peoples Rights Act and Postcolonial Legal Hybridity." In *Commonplaces and Comparisons*, edited by P. Cuasay and C. Vaddhanaphuti, pp. 54–78. Chiang Mai University Press, 2005.

Daytec-Yangot, Cheryl L. "Transcending Aboriginality and Minority: Indigeneity in Asia as a Construct of Structural Oppression under the Economic Globalization Regime." *Asian-Pacific Law & Policy Journal* 19, no. 2 (2018): 21–68.

Deloria, Philip J. *Indians in Unexpected Places*. University Press of Kansas, 2004.

Dentan, Robert K. *Overwhelming Terror: Love, Fear, Peace, and Violence among Semai of Malaysia*. Rowman & Littlefield, 2008.

Department of Environment and Natural Resources. "Philippine Forestry Statistics 2019." Republic of the Philippines, 2019.

Department of Environment and Natural Resources. "Philippine Forestry Statistics 2021." Republic of the Philippines, 2021.

Dietrich, Alexa S. "Coercive Harmony, Deep Capture and Environmental Justice in Puerto Rico." *Development and Change* 42, no. 6 (2011): 1441–1463.

Dizon, Mark. *Reciprocal Mobilities: Indigeneity and Imperialism in an Eighteenth-Century Philippine Borderland*. University of North Carolina Press, 2023.

Doane, Molly. *Stealing Shining Rivers: Agrarian Conflict, Market Logic, and Conservation in a Mexican Forest.* University of Arizona Press, 2012.

Doolittle, Amity A. *Property and Politics in Sabah, Malaysia: Native Struggles over Land Rights.* University of Washington Press, 2011.

Dove, Michael R. "Hybrid Histories and Indigenous Knowledge among Asian Rubber Smallholders." *International Social Science Journal* 54, no. 173 (2002): 349–359.

Dove, Michael R. "Indigenous People and Environmental Politics." *Annual Review of Anthropology* 35 (2006): 191–208. https://doi.org/10.1146/annurev.anthro.35.081705.123235.

Dove, Michael R. *The Banana Tree at the Gate: A History of Marginal Peoples and Global Markets in Borneo.* Yale University Press, 2011.

Dove, Michael R., Percy E. Sajise, and Amity Doolittle, eds. *Beyond the Sacred Forest: Complicating Conservation in Southeast Asia.* Duke University Press, 2011.

Dressler, Wolfram H. *Old Thoughts in New Ideas: State Conservation Measures, Development and Livelihood on Palawan Island.* Ateneo de Manila University Press, 2009.

Dressler, Wolfram H. "Green Governmentality and Swidden Decline on Palawan Island, the Philippines." *Transactions of the Institute of British Geographers* 39, no. 2 (2014): 250–264.

Dressler, Wolfram H. "Governed from above, below and Dammed in Between: The Biopolitics of (Un)making Life and Livelihood in the Philippine Uplands." *Political Geography* 73 (2019): 123–137.

Dressler, Wolfram H. *For the Sake of Forests and Gods: Governing Life and Livelihood in the Philippine Uplands.* Cornell University Press, 2025.

Dressler, Wolfram H., Jessica de Koning, Marvin Montefrio, and Jennifer Firn. "Land Sharing Not Sparing in the 'Green Economy': The Role of Livelihood Bricolage in Conservation and Development in the Philippines." *Geoforum* 76 (2016): 75–89.

Dressler, Wolfram H., and Eulalio R. Guieb. "Violent Enclosures, Violated Livelihoods: Environmental and Military Territoriality in a Philippine Frontier." *Journal of Peasant Studies* 42, no. 2 (2015): 323–345.

Dressler, Wolfram H., Melanie McDermott, Will Smith, and Juan Pulhin. "REDD Policy Impacts on Indigenous Property Rights Regimes on Palawan Island, the Philippines." *Human Ecology* 40, no. 5 (2012): 679–691. https://doi.org/10.1007/s10745-012-9527-y.

Dressler, Wolfram H., and Will Smith. "Blood, Timber and Plantations: The Violence of Enclosing Lives and Livelihoods in the Philippines." *Journal of Peasant Studies* 50, no. 6 (2023): 2406–2436.

Dressler, Wolfram H., Will Smith, and Marvin J. F. Montefrio. "Ungovernable? The Vital Natures of Swidden Assemblages in an Upland Frontier." *Journal of Rural Studies* 61 (2018): 343–354.

Duncan, Christopher R., ed. *Civilizing the Margins: Southeast Asian Government Policies for the Development of Minorities.* Cornell University Press, 2004.

Edelman, Marc, Carlos Oya, and Saturnino M. Borras. "Global Land Grabs: Historical Processes, Theoretical and Methodological Implications and Current Trajectories." *Third World Quarterly* 34, no. 9 (2013): 1517–1531.

Eder, James F. *On the Road to Tribal Extinction: Depopulation, Deculturation, and Adaptive Well-Being among the Batak of the Philippines*. New Day, 1987.

Eder, James F. "Deforestation and Detribalization in the Philippines: The Palawan Case." *Population & Environment* 12, no. 2 (1990): 99–115.

Eder, James F. *A Generation Later: Household Strategies and Economic Change in the Rural Philippines*. University of Hawai'i Press, 1999.

Eder, James F. "Coastal Resource Management and Social Differences in Philippine Fishing Communities." *Human Ecology* 33, no. 2 (2005): 147–169.

Eder, James F. *Migrants to the Coasts: Ethnicity, Community, and Resource Management in the Philippines*. Cengage Learning, 2008.

Eder, James F. "Muslim Palawan Diversity and Difference on the Periphery of Philippine Islam." *Philippine Studies* 58, no. 3 (2010): 407–420. https://doi.org/10.2307/42634641.

Eder, James F. "Zoning Resources, Zoning People: Ecogovernmentality and Non-Timber Forest Products Collection in the Philippines." Second Philippine Studies Conference of Japan, Tsukuba, 2010.

Eder, James F. "Converts to Islam and the Muslim Community in the Christian Philippines." *Contemporary Islam* 16, no. 1 (2022): 1–18.

Eder, J. F., and O. Evangelista, eds. *Palawan and Its Global Connections*. Ateneo de Manila University Press, 2014.

Eder, James F., and Janet O. Fernandez. "Introduction: Palawan, a Last Frontier." In *Palawan at the Crossroads: Development and the Environment on a Philippine Frontier*, edited by J. F. Eder and J. O. Fernandez, pp. 1–22. Ateneo de Manila University Press, 1996.

Eder, James F., and Thomas M. McKenna. "Minorities in the Philippines: Ancestral Lands and Autonomy in Theory and Practice." In *Civilizing the Margins: Southeast Asian Government Policies for the Development of Minorities*, edited by C. R. Duncan, pp. 56–85. Cornell University Press, 2004.

Erni, Christian. *The Concept of Indigenous Peoples in Asia: A Resource Book*. International Work Group for Indigenous Affairs, 2008.

Escobar, Arturo. "After Nature: Steps to an Antiessentialist Political Ecology." *Current Anthropology* 40, no. 1 (1999): 1–30.

Escobar, Arturo. *Territories of Difference: Place, Movements, Life*, Redes. Duke University Press, 2008.

Escobar, Arturo. "Thinking-Feeling with the Earth: Territorial Struggles and the Ontological Dimension of the Epistemologies of the South." *AIBR Revista de antropología iberoamericana* 11, no. 1 (2016): 11–32.

Escobar, Arturo. *Designs for the Pluriverse: Radical Interdependence, Autonomy, and the Making of Worlds*. Duke University Press, 2018.

Esquire Philippines. "Palawan Leads Deforestation in the Philippines and No One Knows about It." *Esquire Philippines* online, August 26, 2021. https://www.esquiremag.ph/politics/news/palawan-leads-deforestation-a00293-20210826-lfrm.

Estes, Nick. *Our History Is the Future: Standing Rock versus the Dakota Access Pipeline, and the Long Tradition of Indigenous Resistance*. Verso Books, 2019.

Fabinyi, Michael. *Fishing for Fairness: Poverty, Morality and Marine Resource Regulation in the Philippines*. Australian National University E-Press, 2011.

Fabro, Keith Anthony. "A Philippine Resin Trade Proves Sustainable for Forests, but Not Tappers." *Mongabay Environmental News,* November 30, 2022. https://news.mongabay.com/2022/11/a-philippine-resin-trade-proves-sustainable-for-forests-but-not-tappers/.

Fairhead, James, and Melissa Leach. *Misreading the African Landscape: Society and Ecology in a Forest-Savanna Mosaic.* Cambridge University Press, 1996.

Fay, Chip. *Counter-Insurgency and Tribal Peoples in the Philippines.* Survival International USA, 1987.

Finin, Gerard A. *The Making of the Igorot: Ramut Ti Panagkaykaysa Dagiti Taga Cordillera (Contours of Cordillera Consciousness).* Ateneo de Manila University Press, 2005.

Fletcher, Robert. *Failing Forward: The Rise and Fall of Neoliberal Conservation.* University of California Press, 2023.

Forsyth, Tim, and Andrew Walker. *Forest Guardians, Forest Destroyers: The Politics of Environmental Knowledge in Northern Thailand.* University of Washington Press, 2008.

Foster, John Bellamy. "The Financialization of Capitalism." *Monthly Review,* April 1, 2007. https://monthlyreview.org/2007/04/01/the-financialization-of-capitalism/.

Foucault, Michel. "Of Other Spaces." *Diacritics* 16, no. 1 (1986): 22–27.

Foucault, Michel. *Security, Territory, Population: Lectures at the Collège de France, 1977–78.* Edited by Michel Senellart. Palgrave Macmillan, 2009.

Fox, Jefferson, Yayoi Fujita, Dimbab Ngidang, Nancy Peluso, Lesley Potter, Niken Sakuntaladewi, Janet Sturgeon, and David Thomas. "Policies, Political-Economy, and Swidden in Southeast Asia." *Human Ecology* 37, no. 3 (2009): 305–322.

Fox, Robert B. *Religion and Society among the Tagbanuwa of Palawan Island, Philippines.* National Museum of the Philippines, 1982.

Franco, Jennifer C., and Saturnino M. Borras. "The Global Climate of Land Politics." *Globalizations* 18, no. 7 (2021): 1277–1297.

Gatmaytan, Augusto B. "A Critical Appraisal of the Social Forestry Program." *Philippine Natural Resources Law Journal* 2 (1989): 9–12.

Gatmaytan, Augusto B. "Advocacy as Translation: Notes on the Philippine Experience." In *Communities and Conservation: Histories and Politics of Community-Based Natural Resource Management,* edited by J. P. Brosius, A. L. Tsing, and Charles Zerner, pp. 459–476. AltaMira Press, 2005.

Gatmaytan, Augusto B. "Indigenous Autonomy amid Counter-Insurgency: Cultural Citizenship in a Philippine Frontier." PhD diss., London School of Economics and Political Science, 2013. https://etheses.lse.ac.uk/3246/.

Gatmaytan, Augusto B. "Living with the Promise of Violence: The State and Indigenous People in a Militarized Frontier." *Philippine Studies: Historical & Ethnographic Viewpoints* 66, no. 2 (2018): 219–244.

Geertz, Clifford. *The Interpretation of Cultures.* Basic Books, 1973.

George, Kenneth M. "Lyric, History, and Allegory, or the End of Headhunting Ritual in Upland Sulawesi." *American Ethnologist* 20, no. 4 (1993): 696–716.

Gibson, Thomas. *Sacrifice and Sharing in the Philippine Highlands.* Athlone Press, 1986.

Go, Julian. "The Provinciality of American Empire: 'Liberal Exceptionalism' and U.S. Colonial Rule, 1898–1912." *Comparative Studies in Society and History* 49, no. 1 (2007): 74–108.

Goldman, Michael. *Imperial Nature: The World Bank and Struggles for Social Justice in the Age of Globalization.* Yale University Press, 2005.

Goodale, Mark. "Dark Matter: Toward a Political Economy of Indigenous Rights and Aspirational Politics." *Critique of Anthropology* 36, no. 4 (2016): 439–457.

Gozum, Iya. "Dumagat-Remontados Begin 9-Day March to Protest Kaliwa Dam Construction." *RAPPLER* (blog), February 15, 2023. https://www.rappler.com/nation/dumagat-remontados-begin-march-protest-kaliwa-dam-construction/.

Griffin, Bion P. "National Policy on Minority Cultural Communities: The Philippine Case." *Southeast Asian Journal of Social Science* 16, no. 2 (1988): 5–16.

Haenn, Nora. "Nature Regimes in Southern Mexico: A History of Power and Environment." *Ethnology* 41, no. 1 (2002): 1–26.

Hagen, Renée V., and Tessa Minter. "Displacement in the Name of Development. How Indigenous Rights Legislation Fails to Protect Philippine Hunter-Gatherers." *Society & Natural Resources* 33, no. 1 (2020): 65–82.

Hall, Stuart. "The Meaning of New Times 1989." In *Selected Political Writings: The Great Moving Right Show and Other Essays,* edited by S. Davison, D. Featherstone, M. Rustin, and B. Schwarz, pp. 248–265. Duke University Press, 2017.

Hammond, Don. "Asia-Pacific Forestry Sector Outlook Study: Commentary on Forest Policy in the Asia-Pacific Region (A Review for Indonesia, Malaysia, New Zealand, Papua New Guinea, Philippines, Thailand and Western Samoa)." Working Paper Series of the Food and Agriculture Organization of the United Nations, 1997.

Harvey, David. *A Short History of Neoliberalism.* Oxford University Press, 2005.

Hawkins, Michael C. *Making Moros: Imperial Historicism and American Military Rule in the Philippines' Muslim South.* Cornell University Press, 2012.

Headland, Thomas N. *The Tasaday Controversy: Assessing the Evidence.* American Anthropological Association, 1992.

Hilhorst, Dorothea. *The Real World of NGOs: Discourse, Diversity and Development.* Ateneo de Manila University Press, 2003.

Hirtz, Frank. "It Takes Modern Means to Be Traditional: On Recognizing Indigenous Cultural Communities in the Philippines." *Development and Change* 34, no. 5 (2003): 887–914.

Hodgson, Dorothy L. *Being Maasai, Becoming Indigenous: Postcolonial Politics in a Neoliberal World.* Indiana University Press, 2011.

Hoganson, Kristin L., and Jay Sexton. "Introduction." In *Crossing Empires: Taking U.S. History into Transimperial Terrain,* edited by K. L. Hoganson and J. Sexton, pp. 1–22. Duke University Press, 2020.

Holden, William, Kathleen Nadeau, and R. Daniel Jacobson. "Exemplifying Accumulation by Dispossession: Mining and Indigenous Peoples in the Philippines." *Geografiska Annaler: Series B, Human Geography* 93, no. 2 (2011): 141–161.

Human Rights Watch. "The Philippines Human Rights and Forest Management in 1990s." *Human Rights Watch* 8, no. 3 (April 1996).

Hutterer, Karl L. "Prehistoric Trade and the Evolution of Philippine Societies: A Reconsideration." In *Economic Exchange and Social Interactions in Southeast Asia: Perspectives from Prehistory, History, and Ethnography,* edited by K. L. Hutterer, pp. 177–196. University of Michigan Center for South and Southeast Asian Studies, 1977.

Igoe, James. "Global Indigenism and Spaceship Earth: Convergence, Space, and Re-Entry Friction." *Globalizations* 2, no. 3 (2005): 377–390.

Igoe, James. "Becoming Indigenous Peoples: Difference, Inequality, and the Globalization of East African Identity Politics." *African Affairs* 105, no. 420 (2006): 399–420.

Igoe, James, Katja Neves, and Dan Brockington. "A Spectacular Eco-Tour around the Historic Bloc: Theorising the Convergence of Biodiversity Conservation and Capitalist Expansion." *Antipode* 42, no. 3 (2010): 486–512.

Ilagan, Karol. "7M Hectares of Philippine Land Are Forested—And That's Bad News." Pulitzer Center, 2021. https://pulitzercenter.org/stories/7m-hectares-philippine-land-are-forested-and-thats-bad-news.

Ilagan, Karol. "Palawan IPs Seek to Stop Consent Process for 2 Nickel Mines in Brooke's Point." *Philippine Center for Investigative Journalism* (blog), 2022. https://pcij.org/article/8903/palawan-ips-seek-to-stop-anomalous-consent-process-for-two-nickel-mines-in-brookes-point.

Immerwahr, Daniel. *How to Hide an Empire: A History of the Greater United States.* Picador, 2019.

Jacka, Jerry K. *Alchemy in the Rain Forest: Politics, Ecology, and Resilience in a New Guinea Mining Area.* Duke University Press, 2015.

Jackson, Michael. *Paths toward a Clearing: Radical Empiricism and Ethnographical Inquiry.* Indiana University Press, 1989.

Joaquin, Nick. "Lapu-Lapu and Humabon: The Filipino as Twins." *Philippine Quarterly of Culture and Society* 7, nos. 1/2 (1979): 51–58.

Jonsson, Hjorleifur. "Paths to Freedom: Political Prospecting in the Ethnographic Record." *Critique of Anthropology* 32, no. 2 (2012): 158–172.

Jordana y Morera, R. *Estudio forestal acerca de la India inglesa, Java y Filipinas.* Imprenta de Moreno y Rojas, 1891.

Junge, Benjamin. "NGOs as Shadow Pseudopublics: Grassroots Community Leaders' Perceptions of Change and Continuity in Porto Alegre, Brazil." *American Ethnologist* 39, no. 2 (2012): 407–424.

Kauanui, J. Kēhaulani. "'A Structure, Not an Event': Settler Colonialism and Enduring Indigeneity." *Lateral* 5, no. 1 (2016).

Kavanagh, Sarah Schneider. "Haunting Remains: Educating a New American Citizenry at Indian Hill Cemetery." In *Phantom Past, Indigenous Presence: Native Ghosts in North American Culture and History,* edited by C. E. Boyd and C.-P. Thrush, pp. 151–180. University of Nebraska Press, 2011.

Keating, Neal B. "Kuy Alterities: The Struggle to Conceptualise and Claim Indigenous Land Rights in Neoliberal Cambodia." *Asia Pacific Viewpoint* 54, no. 3 (2013): 309–322.

Kelly, Alice B. "Conservation Practice as Primitive Accumulation." *Journal of Peasant Studies* 38, no. 4 (2011): 683–701.

King, Tiffany Lethabo. "New World Grammars: The 'Unthought' Black Discourses of Conquest." *Theory & Event* 19, no. 4 (2016).

Kirsch, Scott. "Insular Territories: US Colonial Science, Geopolitics, and the (Re)mapping of the Philippines." *Geographical Journal* 182, no. 1 (2016): 2–14.

Kirsch, Stuart. *Reverse Anthropology: Indigenous Analysis of Social and Environmental Relations in New Guinea.* Stanford University Press, 2006.

Kirsch, Stuart. "Indigenous Movements and the Risks of Counterglobalization: Tracking the Campaign against Papua New Guinea's Ok Tedi Mine." *American Ethnologist* 34, no. 2 (2007): 303–321.

Kirsch, Stuart. "Juridification of Indigenous Politics." In *Law against the State: Ethnographic Forays into Law's Transformations,* edited by B. Donahoe, C. Strümpell, J. Eckert, and Z. Ö. Biner, pp. 23–43. Cambridge University Press, 2012.

Kirsch, Stuart. *Mining Capitalism: The Relationship between Corporations and Their Critics.* University of California Press, 2014.

Krawec, Patty, and Kerry Goring. "'Global Indigeneity' with Troy Storfjell and Joy Henderson." *Medicine for the Resistance* podcast, March 6, 2021. https://medicinefortheresistance.substack.com/p/global-indigeneity.

Kress, Jonathan H. "Contemporary and Prehistoric Subsistence Patterns on Palawan." In *Cultural-Ecological Perspectives on Southeast Asia,* edited by W. Wood, pp. 29–47. Ohio University Center for International Studies, 1977.

Kumar, Krishan. "Nation-States as Empires, Empires as Nation-States: Two Principles, One Practice?" *Theory and Society* 39, no. 2 (2010): 119–143.

Kummer, David M. "Measuring Forest Decline in the Philippines: An Exercise in Historiography." *Forest & Conservation History* 36, no. 4 (1992): 185–189.

Kummer, David M. "Deforestation in the Philippines, 1950–2000." In *Muddied Waters: Historical and Contemporary Perspectives on Management of Forests and Fisheries in Island Southeast Asia,* edited by P. Boomgaard, D. Henley, and M. Osseweijer, pp. 307–322. KITLV Press, 2005.

Kuper, Adam. *The Invention of Primitive Society: Transformations of an Illusion.* Routledge, 1988.

Kuper, Adam. "The Return of the Native." *Current Anthropology* 44, no. 3 (2003): 389–402.

Lacuna-Richman, Celeste. "Subsistence Strategies of an Indigenous Minority in the Philippines: Nonwood Forest Product Use by the Tagbanua of Narra, Palawan." *Economic Botany* 58, no. 2 (2004): 266–285.

Langston, Nancy. *Forest Dreams, Forest Nightmares: The Paradox of Old Growth in the Inland West.* University of Washington Press, 1995.

Lapniten, Karlston. "Collusion, Corruption Allegations Hound Dam Projects in Last Nature Frontier of the Cordillera." *Philippine Center for Investigative Journalism* (blog), 2022. https://pcij.org/article/9261/collusion-corruption-allegations-hound-dam-projects-in-last-nature-frontier-of-the-cordillera.

Larner, Wendy. "Neoliberalism: Policy, Ideology, Governmentality." *Studies in Political Economy* 63 (2000): 5–25.

Latour, Bruno. "Whose Cosmos, Which Cosmopolitics? Comments on the Peace Terms of Ulrich Beck." *Common Knowledge* 10, no. 3 (2004): 450–462.

Latour, Bruno. *Reassembling the Social: An Introduction to Actor-Network-Theory*. Oxford University Press, 2005.

Legazpi, Miguel de. "Letter to Felipe II, Cebu, 26 June 1568." In *The Philippine Islands, 1493–1803*, edited by E. H. Blair and A. J. Robertson, vol. 2, p. 242. A. H. Clark, 1903.

Li, Tania Murray. "Ethnic Cleansing, Recursive Knowledge, and the Dilemmas of Sedentarism." *International Social Science Journal* 54, no. 173 (2002): 361–371.

Li, Tania Murray. *The Will to Improve: Governmentality, Development, and the Practice of Politics*. Duke University Press, 2007.

Li, Tania Murray. "Indigeneity, Capitalism, and the Management of Dispossession." *Current Anthropology* 51, no. 3 (2010): 385–414.

Li, Tania Murray. *Land's End: Capitalist Relations on an Indigenous Frontier*. Duke University Press, 2014.

Li, Tania Murray. "What Is Land? Assembling a Resource for Global Investment." *Transactions of the Institute of British Geographers* 39, no. 4 (2014): 589–602.

Lightfoot, Sheryl. *Global Indigenous Politics: A Subtle Revolution*. Routledge, 2016.

Ludlow, Francis, Lauren Baker, Samara Brock, Chris Hebdon, and Michael R. Dove. "The Double Binds of Indigeneity and Indigenous Resistance." *Humanities* 5, no. 53 (2016): 1–19.

Lunstrum, Elizabeth. "Capitalism, Wealth, and Conservation in the Age of Security: The Vitalization of the State." *Annals of the American Association of Geographers* 108, no. 5 (2018): 1022–1037.

Lynch, Owen. "Native Title, Private Right and Tribal Land Law: An Introductory Survey." *Philippine Law Journal* 57 (1982): 268–305.

Lynch, Owen. "Concepts and Strategies for Promoting Legal Recognition of Community-Based Property Rights: Insights from the Philippines and Other Nations." In *Communities and Conservation: Histories and Politics of Community-Based Natural Resource Management*, edited by J. P. Brosius, A. L. Tsing, and C. Zerner, pp. 391–426. AltaMira Press, 2005.

Lynch, Owen. "Disenfranchisement qua Paternalism: The Non-Christian Fiefdom of the United States in the Philippine Islands." *AghamTao* 20 (2011): 1–48.

Macdonald, Charles J.-H. "Mythe de création Palawan. Analyse structurale d'un mythe et de ses rapports avec le chamanisme." *Archipel* 8, no. 1 (1974): 91–118.

Macdonald, Charles J.-H. *Une société simple: Parenté et résidence chez les Palawan (Philippines)*. Institut d'ethnologie, 1977.

Macdonald, Charles J.-H. "Bons et mauvais coups de tonnerre." *L'Homme* 28, nos. 106/107 (1988): 58–74.

Macdonald, Charles J.-H. *Uncultural Behavior: An Anthropological Investigation of Suicide in the Southern Philippines*. University of Hawai'i Press, 2007.

Macdonald, Charles J.-H. "Indigenous Peoples as Agents of Change and as Changing Agents." *Palawan State University Journal* 1, no. 1 (2008): 63–86.

Macdonald, Charles J.-H. "Kinship and Fellowship among the Palawan." In *Anarchic Solidarity*, edited by T. Gibson and K. Sillander, pp. 119–140. Yale University Press, 2011.

Maruyama, Junko. "From 'Displaced Peoples' to 'Indigenous Peoples': Experiences of The!Xun and Khwe San in South Africa." *African Study Monographs*, suppl. 54 (2018): 137–154.

Massé, Francis, and Elizabeth Lunstrum. "Accumulation by Securitization: Commercial Poaching, Neoliberal Conservation, and the Creation of New Wildlife Frontiers." *Geoforum* 69 (2016): 227–237.

Mathews, Andrew S. *Instituting Nature: Authority, Expertise, and Power in Mexican Forests*. MIT Press, 2011.

McCoy, Alfred W. *An Anarchy of Families: State and Family in the Philippines*. Ateneo de Manila University Press, 1993.

McCoy, Alfred W. *Policing America's Empire: The United States, the Philippines, and the Rise of the Surveillance State*. University of Wisconsin Press, 2009.

McDermott, Melanie Hughes. "Boundaries and Pathways: Indigenous Identity, Ancestral Domain, and Forest Use in Palawan, the Philippines." PhD diss., University of California, Berkeley, 2000.

McDermott, Melanie Hughes. "Invoking Community: Indigenous People and Ancestral Domain in Palawan, the Philippines." In *Communities and the Environment*, edited by A. Agrawal and C. C. Gibson, pp. 32–62. Rutgers University Press, 2001.

McMichael, Philip. "The Land Grab and Corporate Food Regime Restructuring." *Journal of Peasant Studies* 39, nos. 3–4 (2012): 681–701.

Melucci, Alberto. "The New Social Movements: A Theoretical Approach." *Social Science Information* 19, no. 2 (1980): 199–226.

Merlan, Francesca. "Indigeneity: Global and Local." *Current Anthropology* 50, no. 3 (2009): 303–334.

Milne, Sarah. "Under the Leopard's Skin: Land Commodification and the Dilemmas of Indigenous Communal Title in Upland Cambodia." *Asia Pacific Viewpoint* 54, no. 3 (2013): 323–339.

Milne, Sarah. *Corporate Nature: An Insider's Ethnography of Global Conservation*. University of Arizona Press, 2022.

Minter, Tessa. "The Agta of the Northern Sierra Madre: Livelihood Strategies and Resilience among Philippine Hunter-Gatherers." PhD diss., Leiden University, 2010.

Mitchell, Audra. *Revenant Ecologies: Defying the Violence of Extinction and Conservation*. University of Minnesota Press, 2024.

Mojares, Resil B. "Lapulapu in Folk Tradition." *Philippine Quarterly of Culture and Society* 7, nos. 1/2 (1979): 59–68.

Mol, Annemarie. *The Body Multiple: Ontology in Medical Practice*. Duke University Press, 2003.

Montefrio, Marvin Joseph F. "State versus Indigenous Peoples' Rights: Comparative Analysis of Stable System Parameters, Policy Constraints and the Process of Delegitimation." *Journal of Comparative Policy Analysis: Research and Practice* 16, no. 4 (2014): 335–355.

Montefrio, Marvin Joseph F. "Cooperation and Resistance: Negotiating Rubber in Upland Philippines." *Journal of Rural Studies* 46 (2016): 111–120.

Montefrio, Marvin Joseph F. "Land Control Dynamics and Social-Ecological Transformations in Upland Philippines." *Journal of Peasant Studies* 44, no. 4 (2017): 796–816.

Morgan, Rhiannon. *Transforming Law and Institution: Indigenous Peoples, the United Nations and Human Rights*. Routledge, 2016.

Morton, Micah F., and Ian G. Baird. "From Hill Tribes to Indigenous Peoples: The Localisation of a Global Movement in Thailand." *Journal of Southeast Asian Studies* 50, no. 1 (2019): 7–31.

Municipality of Rizal. "Greetings from the Mayor!" August 12, 2008. http://rizalpal.wordpress.com/2008/08/12/greetings-from-the-mayor/.

Nadasdy, Paul. *Hunters and Bureaucrats: Power, Knowledge, and Aboriginal-State Relations in the Southwest Yukon*. University of British Columbia Press, 2003.

Nadasdy, Paul. "The Gift in the Animal: The Ontology of Hunting and Human-Animal Sociality." *American Ethnologist* 34, no. 1 (2007): 25–43.

Nadasdy, Paul. "Boundaries among Kin: Sovereignty, the Modern Treaty Process, and the Rise of Ethno-Territorial Nationalism among Yukon First Nations." *Comparative Studies in Society and History* 54, no. 3 (2012): 499–532.

Nadasdy, Paul. *Sovereignty's Entailments: First Nation State Formation in the Yukon*. University of Toronto Press, 2017.

Nadasdy, Paul. "How Many Worlds Are There?" *American Ethnologist* 48, no. 4 (2021): 357–369.

Nader, Laura. "Controlling Process: Tracing the Dynamic Components of Power." *Current Anthropology* 38, no. 5 (1997): 711–737.

Neimark, Benjamin, Sango Mahanty, Wolfram H. Dressler, and Christina Hicks. "Not Just Participation: The Rise of the Eco-Precariat in the Green Economy." *Antipode* 52, no. 2 (2020): 496–521.

Niezen, Ronald. *The Origins of Indigenism: Human Rights and the Politics of Identity*. University of California Press, 2003.

Novellino, Dario. "Sacrificing People for the Trees: The Cultural Cost of Forest Conservation on Palawan Island (Philippines)." *Indigenous Affairs* 4 (1998): 4–14.

Novellino, Dario. "Palawan Attitudes toward Illness." *Philippine Studies* 49, no. 1 (2001): 78–93.

Novellino, Dario. "Contrasting Landscapes, Conflicting Ontologies: Assessing Environmental Conservation on Palawan Island, Philippines." In *Ethnographies of Conservation: Environmentalism and the Distribution of Privilege,* edited by D. G. Anderson and E. Berglunc, pp. 171–188. Berghahn, 2003.

Novellino, Dario. "'Talking about Kultura and Signing Contracts': The Bureaucratization of the Environment on Palawan Island (the Philippines)." In *Sustainability and Communities of Place,* edited by C. Maida, pp. 82–108. Berghahn, 2007.

Novellino, Dario. "From Local Struggles to Global Advocacy: Mining Expansion and Indigenous Peoples' Responses on the 'Last Frontier.'" In *Palawan and Its Global Connections,* edited by J. F. Eder and O. Evangelista, pp. 254–286. Ateneo de Manila University Press, 2014.

Novellino, Dario, and Wolfram H. Dressler. "The Role of 'Hybrid' NGOs in the Conservation and Development of Palawan Island, the Philippines." *Society & Natural Resources* 23, no. 2 (2009): 165–180.

Ocampo, Nilo S. *Katutubo, Muslim, Kristyano: Palawan, 1621–1901.* Salazar and Mendoza-Urban, 1985.

Ocampo, Nilo S. "A History of Palawan." In *Palawan at the Crossroads: Development and the Environment on a Philippine Frontier,* edited by J. F. Eder and J. O. Fernandez, pp. 22–37. Ateneo de Manila University Press, 1996.

Padwe, Jonathan. *Disturbed Forests, Fragmented Memories: Jarai and Other Lives in the Cambodian Highlands.* University of Washington Press, 2020.

Palawan Center for Appropriate Rural Technology. "Constraints and Potentials for Livelihood in Selected Mt. Mantalingahan Communities." Southern Palawan Planning Council, 2011.

Palawan Council for Sustainable Development. *State the Environment: 2009 Updates.* Palawan Council for Sustainable Development, 2010.

Paredes, Alyssa. "Experimental Science for the 'Bananapocalypse': Counter Politics in the Plantationocene." *Ethnos* 88, no. 4 (2023): 837–863.

Paredes, Oona. *A Mountain of Difference: The Lumad in Early Colonial Mindanao.* Cornell University Press, 2013.

Paredes, Oona. "Between Rights Protection and Development Aggression: Indigenous Peoples." In *Routledge Handbook of the Contemporary Philippines,* edited by M. R. Thompson and E. V. C. Batalla, pp. 341–351. Routledge, 2018.

Paredes, Oona. "Preserving 'Tradition': The Business of Indigeneity in the Modern Philippine Context." *Journal of Southeast Asian Studies* 50, no. 1 (2019): 86–106.

Paredes, Oona. "More Indigenous than Others: The Paradox of Indigeneity among the Higaunon Lumad." *Sojourn: Journal of Social Issues in Southeast Asia* 37, no. 1 (2022): 27–57.

Parnell, Terry. "Story-Telling and Social Change: A Case Study of the Prey Lang Community Network." In *Conservation and Development in Cambodia,* edited by S. Milne and S. Mahanty, pp. 258–278. Routledge, 2015.

Parreñas, Juno Salazar. "From Decolonial Indigenous Knowledges to Vernacular Ideas in Southeast Asia." *History and Theory* 59, no. 3 (2020): 413–420.

Peck, Jamie, and Adam Tickell. "Neoliberalizing Space." *Antipode* 34, no. 3 (2002): 380–404.

Peñalba, Maileenit A. "Indigenous Peoples versus the State: FPIC and Resource Extraction in the Cordillera Region, Philippines." *Public Policy Journal* 14 (2016).

Perez, Padmapani L. *Green Entanglements: Nature Conservation and Indigenous Peoples' Rights in Indonesia and the Philippines.* University of the Philippines Press, 2018.

Perez, Padmapani L. "Living with the Problem of National Parks: Indigenous Critique of Philippine Environmental Policy." *Thesis Eleven* 145, no. 1 (2018): 58–76.

Phelan, John Leddy. *The Hispanization of the Philippines: Spanish Aims and Filipino Responses, 1565–1700.* University of Wisconsin Press, 1959.

Philippine Commission. *Report of the Philippine Commission to the Secretary of War.* Government Printing Office, 1910.

Philippine Commission. *Report of the Philippine Commission to the Secretary of War.* Government Printing Office, 1912.

Philippine Commission. *Report to the President, Volume 1.* Government Printing Office, 1900.

Philippine Commission. *Report to the President, Volume 3.* Government Printing Office, 1900.

Pigafetta, Antonio. *The First Voyage around the World, 1519–1522: An Account of Magellan's Expedition.* Translated by Theodore J. Chachey. University of Toronto Press, 2007.

Pinto, Eufemia Felisa. "Contesting Frontier Lands in Palawan, Philippines: Strategies of Indigenous Peoples for Community Development and Ancestral Domain Management." M.A. thesis, Clark University, 2000.

Potter, Lesley. "Forests versus Agriculture: Colonial Forest Services, Environmental Ideals and the Regulation of Land-Use Change in Southeast Asia." In *The Political Ecology of Tropical Forests in Southeast Asia,* edited by T.-P. Lye, W. de Jong, and K. Abe, pp. 29–71. Kyoto University Press, 2003.

Povinelli, Elizabeth A. *The Cunning of Recognition: Indigenous Alterities and the Making of Australian Multiculturalism.* Duke University Press, 2002.

Povinelli, Elizabeth A. *Economies of Abandonment: Social Belonging and Endurance in Late Liberalism.* Duke University Press, 2011.

Povinelli, Elizabeth A. *Geontologies: A Requiem to Late Liberalism.* Duke University Press, 2016.

Prasse-Freeman, Elliott. "Necroeconomics: Dispossession, Extraction, and Indispensable/Expendable Laborers in Contemporary Myanmar." *Journal of Peasant Studies* 49, no. 7 (2022): 1466–1496.

Pulhin, Juan M., and Maricel A. Tapia. "Devolving Bundles of Rights or Bundles of Responsibilities? Impacts of Forest Tenure Reform in the Philippines." *Ecosystems and Development Journal* 5, no. 2 (2015): 41–48.

Putnam, Lara. "To Study the Fragments/Whole: Microhistory and the Atlantic World." *Journal of Social History* 39, no. 3 (2006): 615–630.

Quirante, Alonso. "Expedition to the Mines of the Igorotes, Alingayen, 5 June 1624." In *The Philippine Islands, 1493–1803,* edited by Emma H. Blair and A. J. Robertson, vol. 20, pp. 267–268. A. H. Clark, 1903.

Rafael, Vicente L. *Contracting Colonialism: Translation and Christian Conversion in Tagalog Society under Early Spanish Rule.* Ateneo de Manila University Press, 1988.

Ramos, Alcida Rita. "The Politics of Perspectivism." *Annual Review of Anthropology* 41, no. 1 (2012): 481–494.

Rappaport, Roy A. *Pigs for the Ancestors: Ritual in the Ecology of a New Guinea People.* Yale University Press, 1984.

Razal, Ramon, Aeron Maralit, Norlita Colili, Loreta Alsa, and Ruth Canlas. *Value Chain Study on Palawan Almaciga Resin.* Non-Timber Forest Products Task Force, 2013.

Reid, Ben. "Poverty Alleviation and Participatory Development in the Philippines." *Journal of Contemporary Asia* 35, no. 1 (2005): 29–52.

Republic of the Philippines. *Republic Act 1888: An Act to Effectuate in a More Rapid and Complete Manner the Economic, Social, Moral and Political and Advancement of the Non-Christian Filipinos*. 1957.

Republic of the Philippines. *Republic Act 7586: National Integrated Protected Areas System Act*. 1992.

Republic of the Philippines. *Republic Act 8371: The Indigenous Peoples' Rights Act*. 1997.

Republic of the Philippines. *Republic Act 11038: Expanded National Integrated Protected Areas System Act*. 2018.

Resurreccion, Bernadette P. "Gender, Identity and Agency in Philippine Upland Development." *Development and Change* 37, no. 2 (2006): 375–400.

Revel, Nicole. *Fleurs de paroles: Histoire naturelle Palawan*. Vols. 1–3. Peeters, SELAF, 1990.

Revel, Nicole. "Kudaman: An Oral Epic in the Palawan Highlands." *Oral Tradition* 11, no. 1 (1996): 108–132.

Revel, Nicole. "Corps en jeu (je) ou la chasse généralisée: Biocénose Palawan, Philippines." In *Le corps humain supplicé, possédé, cannibalisé*, edited by M. Goldelier and M. Panoff, pp. 71–86. Editions des Archives Contemporaines, 1998.

Revel, Nicole. "The 'Gifts of the Weaver' and Their Becoming at the Turn of the 21st Century." *AghamTao* 20 (2011): 49–67.

Rice, Mark. *Dean Worcester's Fantasy Islands: Photography, Film, and the Colonial Philippines*. University of Michigan Press, 2014.

Rico, Ruth Lusterio. "Civil Society Groups and the Legislative Process: The Enactment of the Indigenous Peoples' Rights Act." *Philippine Political Science Journal* 28, no. 51 (2007): 55–84.

Rigg, Jonathan, Albert Salamanca, and Eric C. Thompson. "The Puzzle of East and Southeast Asia's Persistent Smallholder." *Journal of Rural Studies* 43 (2016): 118–133.

Rocamora, Joel. "The Political Uses of PANAMIN." *Southeast Asia Chronicle* 67 (1979): 11–21.

Romanillos, Emmanuel L. "Augustinian Recollect Contributions to the Church History and Cultural Patrimony of Palawan." *Philippine Social Science Journal* 1, no. 1 (2018): 81–96.

Rosales, Antulio. "Radical Rentierism: Gold Mining, Cryptocurrency and Commodity Collateralization in Venezuela." *Review of International Political Economy* 26, no. 6 (2019): 1311–1332.

Rubis, June M. "The Orang Utan Is Not an Indigenous Name: Knowing and Naming the Maias as a Decolonizing Epistemology." *Cultural Studies* 34, no. 5 (2020): 811–830.

Rubis, June M., and Noah Theriault. "Concealing Protocols: Conservation, Indigenous Survivance, and the Dilemmas of Visibility." *Social & Cultural Geography* 21, no. 7 (2020): 962–984.

Salman, Michael. *The Embarrassment of Slavery: Controversies over Bondage and Nationalism in the American Colonial Philippines*. University of California Press, 2001.

Salman, Michael. "'The Prison that Makes Men Free': The Iwahig Penal Colony and the Simulacra of the American State in the Philippines." In *Colonial Crucible: Empire in the Making of the Modern American State*, edited by A. W. McCoy and F. A. Scarano, pp. 116–130. University of Wisconsin Press, 2009.

Sawyer, Suzana. *Crude Chronicles: Indigenous Politics, Multinational Oil, and Neoliberalism in Ecuador.* Duke University Press, 2004.

Schreer, Viola. "The Absent Agent: Orangutans, Communities, and Conservation in Indonesian Borneo." *Conservation and Society* 21, no. 1 (2023): 17–27.

Schurz, William Lytle. *The Manila Galleon*. E. P. Dutton, 1939.

Scott, James C. *Weapons of the Weak: Everyday Forms of Peasant Resistance.* Yale University Press, 1985.

Scott, James C. *Domination and the Arts of Resistance: Hidden Transcripts.* Yale University Press, 1990.

Scott, James C. *Seeing like a State: How Certain Schemes to Improve the Human Condition Have Failed.* Yale University Press, 1998.

Scott, James C. *The Art of Not Being Governed: An Anarchist History of Upland Southeast Asia.* Yale University Press, 2009.

Scott, William Henry. *Prehispanic Source Materials for the Study of Philippine History.* New Day, 1984.

Scott, William Henry. *Slavery in the Spanish Philippines.* De La Salle University Press, 1991.

Seki, Koki. "Green Neoliberalism, Ecogovernmentality, and Emergent Community: A Case of Coastal Resource Management in Palawan, the Philippines." *Philippine Studies* 57, no. 4 (2009): 543–578.

Seki, Koki, ed. *Ethnographies of Development and Globalization in the Philippines: Emergent Socialities and the Governing of Precarity.* Routledge, 2020.

Sellato, Bernard. *Nomads of the Borneo Rainforest: The Economics, Politics, and Ideology of Settling Down.* University of Hawaiʻi Press, 1994.

Shah, Alpa. *In the Shadows of the State: Indigenous Politics, Environmentalism, and Insurgency in Jharkhand, India.* Duke University Press, 2010.

Sidel, John Thayer. *Capital, Coercion, and Crime: Bossism in the Philippines.* Stanford University Press, 1999.

Simbulan, Roland G. "Indigenous Communities' Resistance to Corporate Mining in the Philippines." *Peace Review* 28, no. 1 (2016): 29–37.

Simon, Scott E. *Truly Human: Indigeneity and Indigenous Resurgence on Formosa.* University of Toronto Press, 2023.

Simpson, Audra. *Mohawk Interruptus: Political Life across the Borders of Settler States.* Duke University Press, 2014.

Singh, Manvir. "It's Time to Rethink the Idea of the 'Indigenous.'" *New Yorker*, February 20, 2023. https://www.newyorker.com/magazine/2023/02/27/its-time-to-rethink-the-idea-of-the-indigenous.

Smith, Neil. *The New Urban Frontier: Gentrification and the Revanchist City.* Routledge, 1996.

Smith, Will. "Weather from Incest: The Politics of Indigenous Climate Change Knowledge on Palawan Island, the Philippines." *Australian Journal of Anthropology* 29, no. 3 (2018): 265–281.

Smith, Will. *Mountains of Blame: Climate and Culpability in the Philippine Uplands.* University of Washington Press, 2021.

Smith, Will, and Wolfram H. Dressler. "Forged in Flames: Indigeneity, Forest Fire and Geographies of Blame in the Philippines." *Postcolonial Studies* 23, no. 4 (2020): 527–545.

Sobrevila, Claudia. "The Role of Indigenous Peoples in Biodiversity Conservation: The Natural but Often Forgotten Partners." World Bank Working Paper no. 44300, July 1, 2010. http://documents.worldbank.org/curated/en/995271468177530126/The-role-of-indigenous-peoples-in-biodiversity-conservation-the-natural-but-often-forgotten-partners.

Stengers, Isabelle. "The Cosmopolitical Proposal." In *In Making Things Public: Atmospheres of Democracy,* edited by B. Latour and P. Weibel, pp. 994–1003. MIT Press, 2005.

Stewart-Harawira, Makere. *The New Imperial Order: Indigenous Responses to Globalization.* Zed Books, 2005.

Survival International. "Philippine Mining Plans Blocked." Press release, August 17, 2010. http://www.survivalinternational.org/news/6377.

Tebtebba. "Indigenous Peoples and the Sustainable Development Goals." Indigenous Peoples' International Centre for Policy Research and Education, 2019.

Theriault, Noah. "The Micropolitics of Indigenous Environmental Movements in the Philippines." *Development and Change* 42, no. 6 (2011): 1417–1440.

Theriault, Noah. "Environmental Politics and the Burden of Authenticity." In *Palawan and Its Global Connections,* edited by J. F. Eder and O. Evangelista, pp. 347–370. Ateneo de Manila University Press, 2014.

Theriault, Noah. "A Forest of Dreams: Ontological Multiplicity and the Fantasies of Environmental Government in the Philippines." *Political Geography* 58 (2017): 114–127.

Theriault, Noah. "Unravelling the Strings Attached: Philippine Indigeneity in Law and Practice." *Journal of Southeast Asian Studies* 50, no. 1 (2019): 107–128.

Theriault, Noah, Timothy Leduc, Audra Mitchell, June M. Rubis, and Norma Jacobs Gaehowako. "Living Protocols: Remaking Worlds in the Face of Extinction." *Social & Cultural Geography* 21, no. 7 (2020): 893–908.

Thongchai, Winichakul. *Siam Mapped: A History of the Geo-Body of a Nation.* University of Hawai'i Press, 1994.

Todd, Zoe. "An Indigenous Feminist's Take on the Ontological Turn: 'Ontology' Is Just Another Word for Colonialism." *Journal of Historical Sociology* 29, no. 1 (2016): 4–22.

Tsing, Anna Lowenhaupt. *In the Realm of the Diamond Queen: Marginality in an Out-of-the-Way Place.* Princeton University Press, 1993.

Tsing, Anna Lowenhaupt. "Agrarian Allegory and Global Futures." In *Nature in the Global South,* edited by P. Greenough and A. L. Tsing, pp. 125–169. Duke University Press, 2003.

Tsing, Anna Lowenhaupt. "Natural Resources and Capitalist Frontiers." *Economic and Political Weekly* 38, no. 48 (2003): 5100–5106.

Tsing, Anna Lowenhaupt. "Becoming a Tribal Elder, and Other Green Development Fantasies." *In Transforming the Indonesian Uplands,* pp. 157–200. Routledge, 2005.

Tsing, Anna Lowenhaupt. *Friction: An Ethnography of Global Connection.* Princeton University Press, 2005.

Tsing, Anna Lowenhaupt. "How to Make Resources in Order to Destroy Them (and Then Save Them?) on the Salvage Frontier." In *Histories of the Future,* edited by S. Harding and D. Rosenberg, pp. 53–76. Duke University Press, 2005.

Tsing, Anna Lowenhaupt. "Contingent Commodities: Mobilizing Labor in and beyond Southeast Asian Forests." In *Taking Southeast Asia to Market: Commodities, Nature, and People in the Neoliberal Age,* edited by J. Nevins and N. L. Peluso, pp. 27–42. Cornell University Press, 2008.

Tuck, Eve. "Suspending Damage: A Letter to Communities." *Harvard Educational Review* 79, no. 3 (2009): 409–428.

Tucker, Richard P. *Insatiable Appetite: The United States and the Ecological Degradation of the Tropical World.* University of California Press, 2000.

Uddin, Nasir. "In Search of Self: Identity, Indigeneity, and Cultural Politics in Bangladesh." In *Indigeneity on the Move,* edited by N. Uddin, E. Gerharz, and P. Chakkarath, pp. 119–140. Berghahn Books, 2018.

Verdery, Katherine. *The Vanishing Hectare: Property and Value in Postsocialist Transylvania.* Cornell University Press, 2018.

Vidal y Soler, Sebastian. *Memoria sobre el ramo de montes en las islas Filipinas.* Aribau y Ca., 1874.

Viveiros de Castro, Eduardo. "Perspectival Anthropology and the Method of Controlled Equivocation." *Tipit'ı—Journal of the Society for the Anthropology of Lowland South America* 2, no. 1 (2004): 3–22.

Vizenor, Gerald. *Native Liberty: Natural Reason and Cultural Survivance.* University of Nebraska Press, 2009.

Wainwright, Joel, and Joe Bryan. "Cartography, Territory, Property: Postcolonial Reflections on Indigenous Counter-Mapping in Nicaragua and Belize." *Cultural Geographies* 16, no. 2 (2009): 153–178.

Warren, James F. *The Sulu Zone, 1768–1898: The Dynamics of External Trade, Slavery, and Ethnicity in the Transformation of a Southeast Asian Maritime State.* Singapore University Press, 1981.

Warren, James F. *Iranun and Balangingi: Globalization, Maritime Raiding, and the Birth of Ethnicity.* New Day, 2002.

Watson, Mark K. *Japan's Ainu Minority in Tokyo: Diasporic Indigeneity and Urban Politics.* Routledge, 2014.

Webb, Sarah. "Domestic 'Eco' Tourism and the Production of a Wondrous Nature in the Philippines." In *Green Asia: Ecocultures, Sustainable Lifestyles, and Ethical Consumption,* edited by T. Lewis, pp. 81–98. Routledge, 2016.

West, Harry G. *Kupilikula: Governance and the Invisible Realm in Mozambique.* University of Chicago Press, 2005.

West, Paige. *Conservation Is Our Government Now: The Politics of Ecology in Papua New Guinea.* Duke University Press, 2006.

White, Richard. *The Middle Ground: Indians, Empires, and Republics in the Great Lakes Region, 1650–1815.* Cambridge University Press, 1991.

Whitehead, John. "Notes on the Birds of Palawan." *Ibis* 32, no. 1 (1890): 38–61.

Whitehead, John. *Exploration of Mount Kinabalu, North Borneo*. Gurney and Jackson, 1893.

Whitman, Alden. "Lindbergh Traveling Widely as Conservationist." *New York Times*, June 23, 1969.

Willerslev, Rane. *Soul Hunters: Hunting, Animism, and Personhood among the Siberian Yukaghirs*. University of California Press, 2007.

Wittekind, Courtney T., and Hilary O. Faxon. "Networks of Speculation: Making Land Markets on Myanmar Facebook." *Antipode* 55, no. 2 (2023): 643–665.

Worcester, Dean C. *The Philippine Islands and Their People: A Record of Personal Observation and Experience, with a Short Summary of the More Important Facts in the History of the Archipelago*. Macmillan, 1899.

Worcester, Dean C. *The Philippines Past and Present, Vol. 2*. Mills & Boon, 1914.

Worcester, Dean C. "Philippine Forest Wealth." *American Forestry* 21, no. 1 (1915): 1–18.

World Wildlife Fund. "A Biodiversity Hotspot in the Philippines." 2010. http://worldwildlife.org/blogs/wwf-travel-blog/posts/a-biodiversity-hotspot-in-the-philippines.

World Wildlife Fund. "Palawan Moist Forests." 2013. http://wwf.panda.org/about_our_earth/ecoregions/palawan_moist_forests.cfm.

Yao, Xine. "Arctic and Asian Indigeneities, Asian/North American Settler/Colonialism: Animating Intimacies and Counter-Intimacies in *Avatar: The Last Airbender*." *Journal of Asian American Studies* 24, no. 3 (2021): 471–504.

Zakaria, Faizah. *The Camphor Tree and the Elephant: Religion and Ecological Change in Maritime Southeast Asia*. University of Washington Press, 2023.

Index

Page numbers in boldface type refer to illustrations.

actor-network theory, 117

adat: as ancestral ways, 45, 98, 111, 130; as customary law, 48, 99, 111; as personal conduct, 102; concept of, 98, 178n41

Agathis philippinensis: care for, 142–143, 186n42; ecology of, 137–138, 142, **143**, 184n14; logging of, 59, 100. *See also* almaciga

agency, 4–5, 15, 69, 112, 154, 160; of invisible beings, 15, 110, 132

agriculture, 33, 38–39, 46, **103**, 131; intensive, 60–61. *See also* plantations; swidden

Aguilar, Filomeno V., 15

ALDAW, 24, 167n8

almaciga: collection of, 137, **139**, 141, **151**, 186n42; commodification of, 47, **53**, 54, 61, 124, 138–155; debt and, 61, 76, 140; depletion of, 69, 76, 138; disputes over, 55, 101, 143–149; market control and, 140, 150–154; price of, 137, 141, 183n6, 186n43; production volume of, 138, 184n16; properties of, 141–143; regulation of, 67, 140, 145, 186n44; uses of, 61. See also *Agathis philippinensis;* Palawan Bagtik Association

Amas, **136**, 151–154

American colonization, 16, 35–42

ancestral domains: ancestral lands vs., 174n59; applications for, 7–8, 66–67; codification of, 64–65; conservation and, 73, 86, 89, 92–96, 120, 129; regulation of, 144–146. *See also* Certificate of Ancestral Domain Claim/Title; Indigenous Peoples Rights Act

animals, 21, 80–81, 100, 115, 124, **125**, 182n17. *See also* hunting; wildlife trafficking

anthropology, 39, 116

assimilation, 3, 39, 56, 86, 112, 154

Atleo, E. Richard (Umeek), 16, 131

Augustinian Recollects, 27, 29, 32

bangungut. See *deletdet*

Batak (people), 130

begtik. *See* almaciga

belyan, 48, 96, 102, 108, **125**, 160

biodiversity, 6, 68–70, 110, 121, 145. *See also* conservation

Blaser, Mario, 16

Bordo, 55, 73, 81, 99–105, 135, 143–149

Brooke's Point, 151–154

Brown, Wendy, 7

"bureaucratic Orientalism," 66

bureaucratization, 10, 67

Bureau of Forestry, 36–39, 170n72

Bureau of Non-Christian Tribes, 39, 56, 171n84

Cadena, Marisol de la, 16, 131

Campung Ulay (*barangay*), 49, 72

capitalism, 6–7, 14, 131, 140–141, 148–150, 153–154. *See also* conservation; development; liberalism

Cariño doctrine, 9, 87, 90

Cepek, Michael, 16

Certificate of Ancestral Domain Claim/Title, 8, 64–65, 73, 145, 174n57, 178n31–32
charcoal, 76, 120–123, **121**, 126, 148, 176n96
Charles II, King of Spain, 34
chieftains, 48, 54–55, 64, 135, 144–146
Chinese merchants, 29–30
civets, **80**
"coercive harmony," 94
colonialism, 24–27, 131, 154–155, 159. *See also* American colonization; Spanish colonization
community-based forest management, 68, 175n75
conservation: capitalism and, 6, 75; cosmology of, 110; dispossession and, 38, 75; enclosures, 3, 78, 82; financing of, 6, 69, 176n93; Indigenous rights and, 6–7, 66, 82, 86, 90–94, 119; Marcos regime and, 57; Palawan analyses of, 102–104; nongovernmental organizations and, 6, 44, 69, 151; policies for, 69–70, 74, 88–90, 176n85; primitivism and, 44; territorialization and, 126. *See also* ancestral domains; eco-indigenism; forestry; "harmonization"; Mt. Mantalingahan Protected Landscape; National Integrated Protected Areas System
conservation agreements, 73, 119
Conservation International, 73, 95, 118, 176n92
Constitution of 1987, 63
copal. *See* almaciga
cosmology, 110, 180n6. *See also* ontology; Palawan (people)
Coulthard, Glen, 17
customary law. See *adat*

"dark matter," 7, 159
datu, 10, 29–30, 34, 40, 61–62
debt, 61, 76, 129, 136, 140, 153
decline: narratives of, 104, 112, 180f54
deforestation, 33, 61, 68, **76**, 102, **103**, 137, 177n98
deletdet, 108, 117, 180n2
Department Administrative Order 2, 64, 144
Department of Environment and Natural Resources, 64–72, 79, 89–93, 99–101, 145–147, 175n76, 176n92, 178n27, 179n43, 186n44
development: Indigenous analyses of, 14, 17; international agencies, 6, 58, 71, 73; Marcos era, 56–58; post-Marcos, 78
"disenchantment," 15
dispossession, 8–9, 35, 58–61, 75, 112, 137, 153. *See also* capitalism; conservation; mining
divination, 103, 110, 127, **128**, 130
diwata, 113, 124. *See also* Palawan (people)
Dove, Michael, 13, 154, 184n8, 185n29
dreams, 108–110, 127, 132. See also *deletdet*
Dressler, Wolfram, 181n7
"dual economy," 154
Duterte, Rodrigo, 68, 167n3, 176n85

eco-governmentality, 89–90, 145
eco-indigenism, 7, 66. *See also* conservation
Eder, James F., 42, 64, 174n42
empuq, 46, 113–115, 125, 179n52. *See also* Palawan (people)
Environmental Critical Areas Network, 71, **119**, 178n27
Environmental Legal Assistance Center, 99, 179n42
environmental narratives: definition of, 25–26, 82–84, 177n3; in practice, 88–96; nationalist, 86–87; Palawan engagements with, 96–105; rights-based, 87–88
Escobar, Arturo, 181n11
ethnography, 12, 16, 116, 160–161
European Union, 73, 176n89, 178n27

Fabinyi, Michael, 26
financialization, 6
forest products: ancestral domains and, 8; historical trade of, 13, 27–34, 40, 61; Palawan reliance on, 46–47, 50–52; regulation of, 40, 67, 72, 124, 135, 140. *See also* almaciga; ancestral domains; conservation; forestry; honey; rattan

forestry, 57–58, 68, 70, 170n72. *See also* Bureau of Forestry; conservation
Forestry Code of 1975, 88, 93
Foucault, Michel, 26, 149
Fox, Robert, 61
free and prior informed consent: codification of, 66, 175n64; conservation and, 93–94; politics of 6, 9, 148, 185n35
freedom, 13, 143–150, 186n36
frontier narratives, 23–27, 34, 43, 45, 56, 78

gender, 107, 142
Goodale, Mark, 7, 159

Haribon Foundation, 69, 176n89, 184n26
"harmonization," 73, 86, 90–98, 105–106
highland peoples of Southeast Asia, 13–14, 17, 154
Hilhorst, Dorothea, 63
honey, 113, **123**, 124, 141–142. *See also* forest products
hunting, 46–47, 91, 99, 114–115, 179n43, 179n46, 182n17

Igorot peoples, 35, 63
indeterminacy, 16, 117, 127. *See also* ontology
indigeneity: as political identity, 10, 163n4; authenticity and, 66, 121, 148; codification of, 10, 63–67, 159, 163n8; conservation and, 70–77; co-optation of, 7, 158–160; in Asia, 16–18; marginalization and, 17, 65, 158; Palawan concepts of, 1–5, 99, 103–106, 122, 132, 148–149; paradox of, 2–5, 10–12, 101. *See also* "dark matter"; eco-indigenism; Indigenous Peoples Rights Act
Indigenous Peoples Rights Act, 7–9, 65–70, 88–90, 94, 99, 148–150, 178n31, 178n36, 185n35. *See also* National Commission on Indigenous People
Inspección General de Montes, 33–34
Integrated Social Forestry Program, 58, 175n75
interpersonal analysis, 12–14, 160–161
invisible beings. See *taw't talun*
Isu, 55, **125**, 127, 160–161

Jackson, Michael, 17, 116
Jiha, 54, 80–81
Jimi: as chieftain, 81, 84–85, 97–98, 111–112; as elder, 107–108, 111–112; as entrepreneur, 148–149; as farmer, 127–128; dispute with Bordo, 101–102, 146–150; introduction of, 10–12, 54–56
Jonsson, Hjorleiffur, 13

Kabisayaan, 22, 43, 62, 102–104, 149, 156, 179n51, 180n54–55
kaingin. *See* swidden
keedatan et keguranggurangan, 45, 98, 130. See also *adat*
kependayan, 22, 104, 108, 114–115, 172n20, 180n55
knowledge: environmental narratives and, 25, 89, 106; Indigenous, 69, 102, 109, 118, 150; interpersonal, 12, 157
Kummer, David, 177n98

land classification/zoning, 39–40, 63–75, **74**, 86–89, 110, **119**, 129, 178n27. *See also* ancestral domain; conservation; forestry; National Integrated Protected Areas System
land rights, 2, 35, 63, 87–90, 137, 154. *See also* ancestral domains; Indigenous Peoples Rights Act
land use, 36, 110, 115, 118, 126–130
Lapu-Lapu, 21–22, 42–43, 114, 167n5
Latour, Bruno, 16, 117
Legazpi, Miguel de, 33
Li, Tania Murray, 14, 163n6, 164n20
"liberal exceptionalism," 7, 23–26, 168n11
liberalism, 90, 149. *See also* neoliberalism
lihyen, 97, 127–130, 182n34
Lindbergh, Charles, 44–45
logging, 36–37, 57–62, 68, 137, 141, 170n80, 175n75. *See also* deforestation; forestry
Lynch, Owen, 35, 86

Macdonald, Charles, 30–31, 46–47, 62, 112–115, 142, 167n4, 180n55, 180n3, 181n12, 182n34
Magellan, Ferdinand, 21–22, 42–43, 114, 167n3, 167n5, 169n43
magic. See *kependayan*
Malambunga River/watershed, **4**, **49**–50, 58–62, 84, **136**, **143**, 151–154, 172n20
Manila, 32–34, 100, 179n44
Manila copal. *See* almaciga
Mantalingahan. *See* MMPL
Marcos, Ferdinand, 56–61, 68, 100
marginality, 12, 97, 101
marginalization, 13, 17, 65, 78, 82–83, 106. *See also* highland peoples of Southeast Asia; indigeneity; Palawan (people)
McDermott, Melanie Hughes, 8, 145
migration, 22, 40–42, 60–61, 75, 132
Mindanao, 42, 131
mining, 9, 24, 64, **74**, 78, 84–96, 176n85, 178n36
Mining Act of 1995, 64, 78, 175n78
missionaries, 52–53. *See also* Augustinian Recollects
modernization, 15
"more than research," 161
Mt. Mantalingahan, 28
Mt. Mantalingahan Protected Landscape, 73–75, **74**, 79, 89–96, 109–111, 118–**119**, 176n85, 176n92–93, 182n30, 178n13
multiculturalism, 5–7, 90

Nadasdy, Paul, 16, 116–117, 154, 180n66
Nader, Laura, 94
National Commission on Indigenous Peoples, 8–9, 65–67, 81, 93–96, 146–149, 185n35, 186n44
National Integrated Protected Areas System, 69–70, 73–74, 87–94, 176n85
national parks, 40, 57, 69
NATRIPAL, 72–73, 144–146, 150–151, 179n48, 185n30
neoliberalism, 5–7, 69, 148–150
nongovernmental organizations, 64, 69–73, 94–95, 99, 135, 176n81, 176n89, 186n44
Non-Timber Forest Products Exchange Program, 150–153
non-timber forest products. *See* forest products
Novellino, Dario, 130

Ocampo, Nilo, 27, 168n15
offerings, 103, 112–113, **126**, 128–129, 179n43
Office of Southern Cultural Communities, 64, 144, 146
oil palm, **76**
"ontological split," 90
ontology: definition of, 180n6; dilemmas of, 109–110; dreams and, 120–122; politics of, 15–17, 118–120; theories of, 112, 116–117. *See also* cosmology; indeterminacy; world-making practices
oral history, 21–22
Oto, 120–122
owls, 108

Padwe, Jonathan, 12
Palawan Bagtik Association, 145
Palawan Council for Sustainable Development, 71, 99, 118
Palawan Island: American period, 35–42; as "last frontier," 23–27; geography of, 3–**4**, 27–28; Marcos period, 57–62; post-Marcos, 70–78; Spanish period, 31–35; Sulu Zone, 28–31
Palawan (people): cosmology, 46, 108, 112, 167n4; egalitarianism, 13, 46, 48; health and illness, 102, 113, 115; kinship, 46–47, 107; livelihood, 46–47; morality, 100–106, 113, 122, 171n100, 178n41, 180n54; ontology, 97, 112–115, 127–130; oral traditions, 112; rituals, 46, 113, 125, 167n4
Palawan Tropical Forest Protection Program, 73, 150
Palaya, 1–2, 10, 54, 79–81, 97, 107–108, 163n3
PANAMIN, 57, 60, 144, 173n26, 173n29
panglima, 48, 172n15, 185n35. *See also* Palawan (people)

Paredes, Alyssa, 131
Paredes, Oona, 16, 168n10
Penimusan, 10, 48, 62, 172n13
people of the forest. *See* taw't talun
performance, 48, 83, 96–98, 105, 157
personhood, 115, 147, 181n10, 182n17
Philip II, King of Spain, 33, 35, 169n48
Philippine-American War, 36
Philippine Commission, 36–41, 169n53
Philippine Revolution, 35
Pigafetta, Antonio, 31
Pinchot, Gifford, 170n72
plantations, 3, 15, 53, 75–**76**, 131, 154
"pluriversal politics," 131
political ecology, 15, 25
positionality: of author, 2, 54–56, 101, 160–161
Povinelli, Elizabeth, 16, 154
Presidential Decree 705, 58
property, 86–87, 126, 186n42
Puerto Princesa City, 30, 34
Punta Baja (*barangay*), 49, 72, 133, 144–146, 183n1

"radical empiricism," 116–117
Ransang (*barangay*), 50, 60, 172n20
rattan, 29, 52, 61, 69, 76, 124, 138, 141
rebels, 59–60, 100, 105, 141, 179n46
refusal, 17, 83, 146, 154
regalian doctrine, 9, 35, 63, 86–90
reservations, 39, 60
Revel, Nicole, 112–113, 167n4, 180n55, 182n17
Rizal (municipality), 23, 75, 86, 135, 144–145, 174n39
roads, 50–53, 75
Rubis, June, 178n40

Scott, James, 13, 85, 98, 180n66
shifting agriculture. *See* swidden
sibilais, 11–12, 17–18, 51–58, 158–161, 163n5
Simpson, Audra, 17, 154
Singh, Manvir, 158–159
slavery, 34–35
Smith, Neil, 26
Smith, Will, 17, 171n100, 180n54
social history, 15
sorcery. See *kependayan*
Southern Palawan Planning Council, 73, 79, 92
Spanish-American War, 35
Spanish colonization, 31–35. *See also* Augustinian Recollects; Inspección General de Montes
spirit beings. See *empuq; taw't talun*
Stengers, Isabelle, 16
Strategic Environmental Plan, 71
subsistence ethic, 93, 123, 129, 179n43
Sulu Sultanate, 29, 62, 172n15
Sulu Zone, 28–31, 169n34
Supreme Court of the Philippines, 9, 88, 90, 148
Supreme Court of the United States, 87
Survival International, 9–10
"survivance," 17
swidden: *lihyen* and, 97, 127–130; ontology of, 113, 115; practice of, 46–47, 51–52, 61, 74; suppression of, 33, 37–39, 81–82, 99–104, 119; *taw't talun* and, 115; tradition and, 112. See also *agriculture*

Tagbanua, 35, 37, 39–41, 61
Tasaday, 57
Tausug, 29, 169n51
taw't talun: agency of, 110, 120, 127–128, 132; dreams and, 109, 127–128; offerings to, 115, 125, 128; ontology of 112–114; Palawan relations with, 103. *See also* Palawan (people)
Tenga't Gebaq, 3–4, 11–12, 49–56, 58–60, 74–76, 84–**85**, **103**, 109, 156
territorialization, 126
Torrens system, 40, 87
"transit of empire," 159–160
tree planting, 84–**85**, 96–98
tribal councils, 64, 72, 140–147, 185n35
Tsing, Anna Lowenhaupt, 3–4, 109, 140, 186n37

uma. See swidden
UNESCO, 3, 70
ungsud. See offerings

United Nations, 2, 63, 138
usufruct rights, 40, 186n42

Vidal y Soler, Sebastian, 33
Viveiros de Castro, Eduardo, 16
Vizenor, Gerald, 17

Warren, James, 169n34
Whitehead, John, 30–31
wildlife trafficking, 24, 80, 100
Worcester, Dean, 37, 169n38, 170n74
world-making practices, 15–16, 111–117, 126–132, 181n11
World War II, 60, 173n22
World Wildlife Fund, 44, 69

Zomia, 13

About the Author

Noah Theriault is Associate Professor of Anthropology in the Department of History at Carnegie Mellon University. In addition to his long-term research on indigeneity and development in Palawan, he recently began investigating Manila's infamous mobility crisis. His publications have appeared in a variety of venues, including *Political Geography, Southeast Asian Studies,* and *Edge Effects.* Theriault earned a doctorate from the University of Wisconsin, Madison, and completed his undergraduate studies at Arizona State University.